McGRAW-HILL

SCIENCE

Macmillan/McGraw-Hill Edition

Richard Moyer • Lucy Daniel • Jay Hackett
H. Prentice Baptiste • Pamela Stryker • JoAnne Vasquez

NATIONAL GEOGRAPHIC SOCIETY

On the Cover:
The Siberian, or Amur, tiger lives primarily in the forests of eastern Russia. Some are also found in China and northern North Korea. Only about 400 of these beautiful animals still exist in the wild. About 500 captive Siberian tigers are in wildlife conservation programs. The survival of Siberian tigers in the wild depends on preserving their habitat and protecting them from poachers.

Macmillan McGraw-Hill
New York Farmington

Program Authors

Dr. Lucy H. Daniel
Teacher, Consultant
Rutherford County Schools, North Carolina

Dr. Jay Hackett
Professor Emeritus of Earth Sciences
University of Northern Colorado

Dr. Richard H. Moyer
Professor of Science Education
University of Michigan-Dearborn

Dr. H. Prentice Baptiste
Professor of Science and Multicultural Education
New Mexico State University
Las Cruces, New Mexico

Pamela Stryker, M.Ed.
Elementary Educator and Science Consultant
Eanes Independent School District
Austin, Texas

Dr. JoAnne Vasquez
Elementary Science Education Consultant
Mesa Public Schools, Arizona
NSTA Past President

NATIONAL GEOGRAPHIC SOCIETY

Washington, D.C.

The features in this textbook entitled "Invitation to Science," "Amazing Stories," and "People in Science," as well as the unit openers, were developed in collaboration with the National Geographic Society's School Publishing Division.

RFB&D
learning through listening

Students with print disabilities may be eligible to obtain an accessible, audio version of the pupil edition of this textbook. Please call Recording for the Blind & Dyslexic at 1-800-221-4792 for complete information.

Macmillan/McGraw-Hill
A Division of The McGraw-Hill Companies

Published by Macmillan/McGraw-Hill, of McGraw-Hill Education, a division of The McGraw-Hill Companies, Inc., Two Penn Plaza, New York, New York 10121.

Printed in the United States of America

ISBN 0-02-280073-5 / 5

5 6 7 8 9 071 07

Teacher Reviewers

Peoria, IL
Rolling Acres Middle School
Gail Truho

Rockford, IL
Rockford Public Schools
Dr. Sharon Wynstra
Science Coordinator

Newark, NJ
Alexander Street School
Cheryl Simeonidis

Albuquerque, NM
Jackie Costales
Science Coordinator, Montgomery Complex

Poughkeepsie, NY
St. Peter's School
Monica Crolius

Columbus, OH
St. Mary's School
Linda Cotter
Joby Easley

Keizer, OR
Cummings Elementary
Deanna Havel

McMinnville, OR
McMinnville School District
Kristin Ward

Salem, OR
Fruitland Elementary
Mike Knudson

Four Corners Elementary
Bethany Ayers
Sivhong Hanson
Cheryl Kirkelie
Julie Wells

Salem-Keizer Public Schools
Rachael Harms
Sue Smith,
Science Specialist

Yoshikai Elementary
Joyce Davenport

Norristown, PA
St. Teresa of Avila
Fran Fiordimondo

Pittsburgh, PA
Chartiers Valley Intermediate School
Rosemary Hutter

Memphis, TN
Memphis City Schools
Quincy Hathorn
District Science Facilitator

Life Science

Consultants

Dr. Carol Baskin
University of Kentucky
Lexington, KY

Dr. Joe W. Crim
University of Georgia
Athens, GA

Dr. Marie DiBerardino
Allegheny University of Health Sciences
Philadelphia, PA

Dr. R. E. Duhrkopf
Baylor University
Waco, TX

Dr. Dennis L. Nelson
Montana State University
Bozeman, MT

Dr. Fred Sack
Ohio State University
Columbus, OH

Dr. Martin VanDyke
Denver, CO

Dr. E. Peter Volpe
Mercer University
Macon, GA

Earth Science

Consultants

Dr. Clarke Alexander
Skidaway Institute of Oceanography
Savannah, GA

Dr. Suellen Cabe
Pembroke State University
Pembroke, NC

Dr. Thomas A. Davies
Texas A & M University
College Station, TX

Dr. Ed Geary
Geological Society of America
Boulder, CO

Dr. David C. Kopaska-Merkel
Geological Survey of Alabama
Tuscaloosa, AL

Physical Science

Consultants

Dr. Bonnie Buratti
Jet Propulsion Lab
Pasadena, CA

Dr. Shawn Carlson
Society of Amateur Scientists
San Diego, CA

Dr. Karen Kwitter
Williams College
Williamstown, MA

Dr. Steven Souza
Williamstown, MA

Dr. Joseph P. Straley
University of Kentucky
Lexington, KY

Dr. Thomas Troland
University of Kentucky
Lexington, KY

Dr. Josephine Davis Wallace
University of North Carolina
Charlotte, NC

Consultant for Primary Grades

Donna Harrell Lubcker
East Texas Baptist University
Marshall, TX

Teacher Panelists

Newark, NJ
First Avenue School
Jorge Alameda
Concetta Cioci
Neva Galasso
Bernadette Kazanjian-reviewer
Toby Marks
Janet Mayer-reviewer
Maria Tutela

Brooklyn, NY
P.S. 31
Janet Mantel
Paige McGlone
Madeline Pappas
Maria Puma-reviewer
P.S. 217
Rosemary Ahern
Charles Brown
Claudia Deeb-reviewer
Wendy Lerner
P.S. 225
Christine Calafiore
Annette Fisher-reviewer
P.S. 250
Melissa Kane
P.S. 277
Erica Cohen
Helena Conti
Anne Marie Corrado
Deborah Scott-DiClemente
Jeanne Fish
Diane Fromhartz
Tricia Hinz
Lisa Iside
Susan Malament
Joyce Menkes-reviewer
Elaine Noto
Jean Pennacchio
Jeffrey Hampton
Mwaka Yavana

Elmont, NY
Covert Avenue School
Arlene Connelly

Mt. Vernon, NY
Holmes School
Jennifer Cavallaro
Lou Ciofi
George DiFiore
Brenda Durante
Jennifer Hawkins-reviewer
Michelle Mazzotta
Catherine Moringiello
Mary Jane Oria-reviewer
Lucille Pierotti
Pia Vicario-reviewer

Ozone Park, NY
St. Elizabeth School
Joanne Cocchiola-reviewer
Helen DiPietra-reviewer
Barbara Kingston
Madeline Visco

St. Albans, NY
Orvia Williams

UNIT E

Physical Science

Properties of Matter and Energy PAGE E1

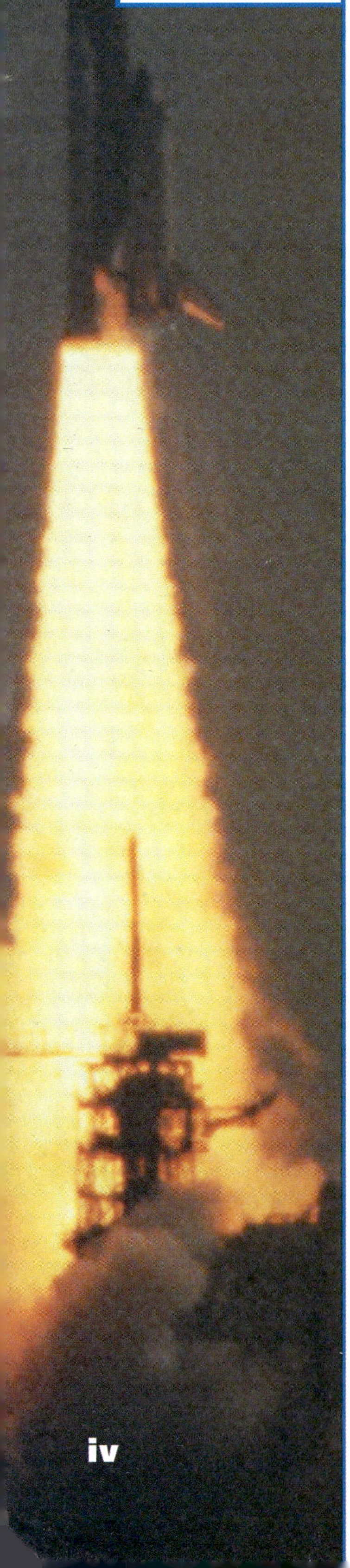

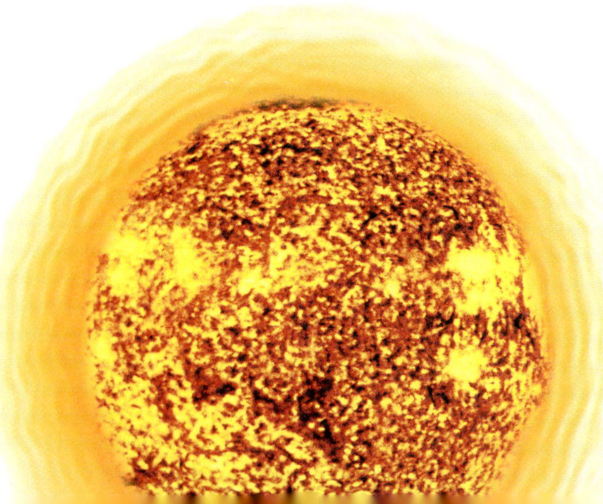

Reading In SCIENCE

As you study science, you will learn many new words. You will read about many new ideas. Read these pages. They will help you understand this book.

1. The **Vocabulary** list has all the new words you will learn in the lesson. The page numbers tell you where the words are taught.

2. The name tells you what the lesson is about.

3. **Get Ready** uses the picture on the page to help you start thinking about the lesson.

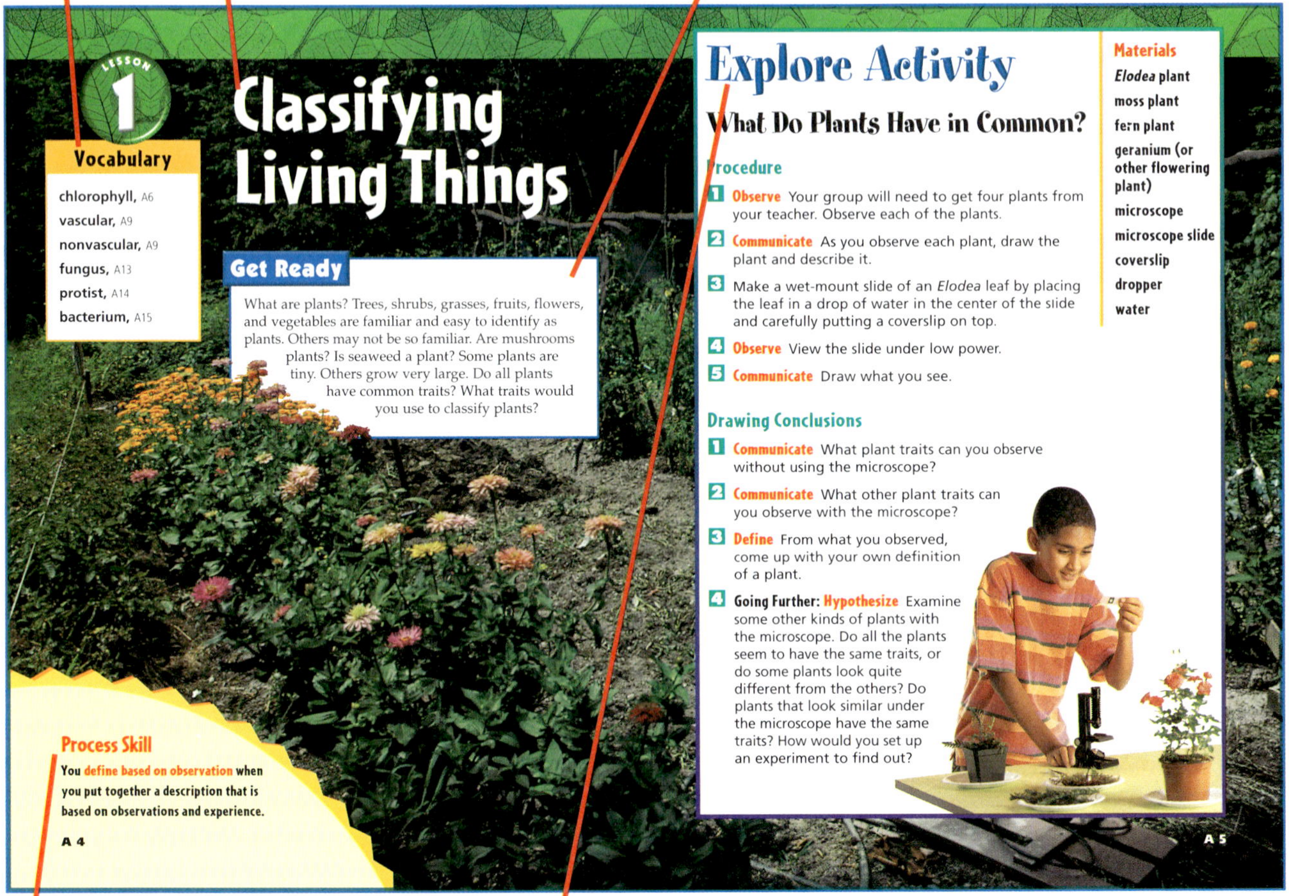

4. This **Process Skill** is used in the Explore Activity.

5. The **Explore Activity** is a hands-on way to learn about the lesson.

As you read a lesson, follow these three steps. They will help you to understand what you are reading.

1. This box contains the **Main Idea** of the lesson. Keep the main idea of the lesson in mind as you read.

2. Before Reading Read the large red question before you read the page. Try to answer this question from what you already know.

3. During Reading Look for new **Vocabulary** words in yellow. Look at the pictures. They will help you understand what you are reading.

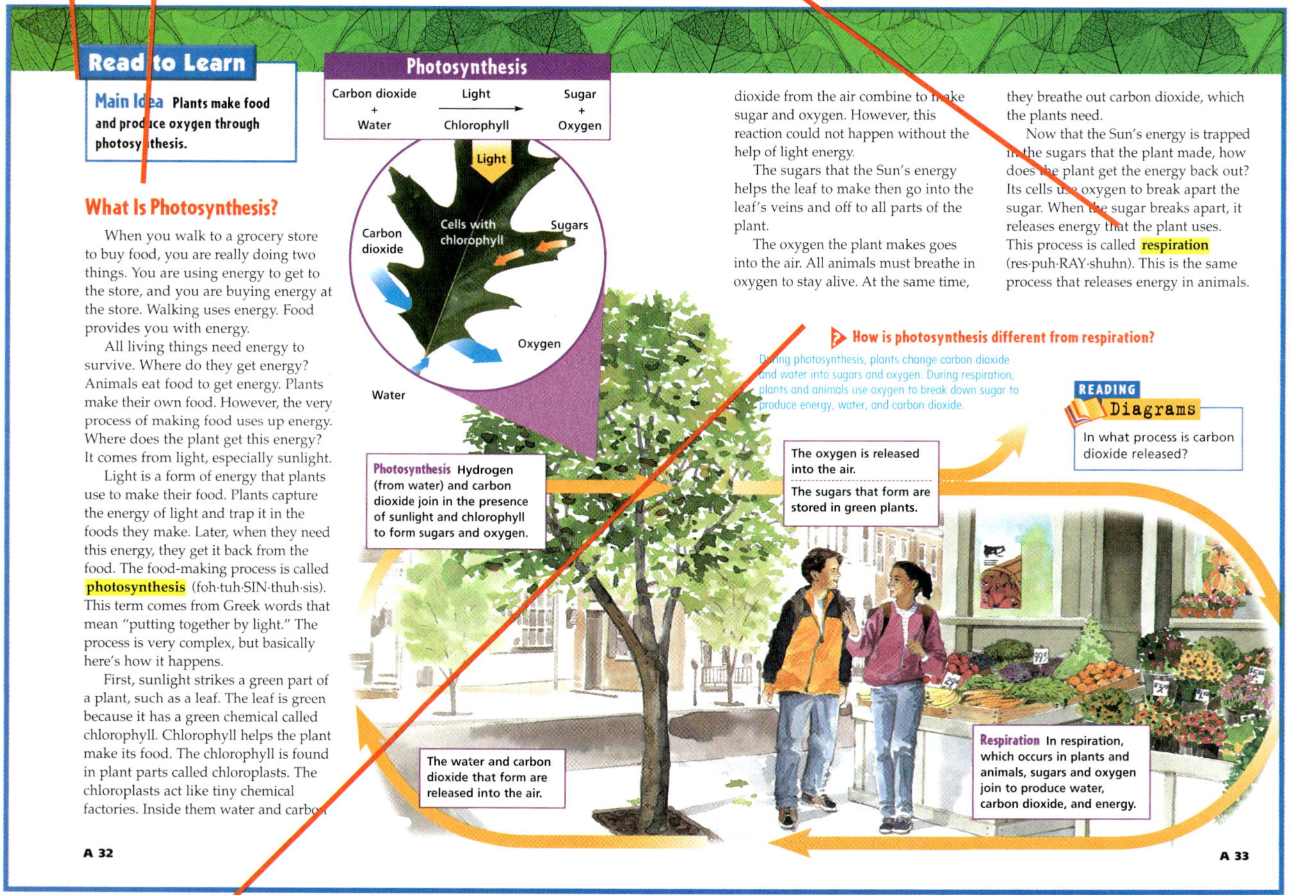

Read to Learn

Main Idea Plants make food and produce oxygen through photosynthesis.

What Is Photosynthesis?

When you walk to a grocery store to buy food, you are really doing two things. You are using energy to get to the store, and you are buying energy at the store. Walking uses energy. Food provides you with energy.

All living things need energy to survive. Where do they get energy? Animals eat food to get energy. Plants make their own food. However, the very process of making food uses up energy. Where does the plant get this energy? It comes from light, especially sunlight.

Light is a form of energy that plants use to make their food. Plants capture the energy of light and trap it in the foods they make. Later, when they need this energy, they get it back from the food. The food-making process is called **photosynthesis** (foh·tuh·SIN·thuh·sis). This term comes from Greek words that mean "putting together by light." The process is very complex, but basically here's how it happens.

First, sunlight strikes a green part of a plant, such as a leaf. The leaf is green because it has a green chemical called chlorophyll. Chlorophyll helps the plant make its food. The chlorophyll is found in plant parts called chloroplasts. The chloroplasts act like tiny chemical factories. Inside them water and carbon dioxide from the air combine to make sugar and oxygen. However, this reaction could not happen without the help of light energy.

The sugars that the Sun's energy helps the leaf to make then go into the leaf's veins and off to all parts of the plant.

The oxygen the plant makes goes into the air. All animals must breathe in oxygen to stay alive. At the same time, they breathe out carbon dioxide, which the plants need.

Now that the Sun's energy is trapped in the sugars that the plant made, how does the plant get the energy back out? Its cells use oxygen to break apart the sugar. When the sugar breaks apart, it releases energy that the plant uses. This process is called **respiration** (res·puh·RAY·shuhn). This is the same process that releases energy in animals.

Photosynthesis Hydrogen (from water) and carbon dioxide join in the presence of sunlight and chlorophyll to form sugars and oxygen.

Respiration In respiration, which occurs in plants and animals, sugars and oxygen join to produce water, carbon dioxide, and energy.

How is photosynthesis different from respiration?

During photosynthesis, plants change carbon dioxide and water into sugars and oxygen. During respiration, plants and animals use oxygen to break down sugar to produce energy, water, and carbon dioxide.

READING Diagrams

In what process is carbon dioxide released?

A 32 A 33

4. After Reading This arrow points to a question. It will help you check that you understand what you have read. Try to answer the question before you go to the next large red question.

Physical Science

UNIT E

Properties of Matter and Energy

NATIONAL GEOGRAPHIC

NATIONAL GEOGRAPHIC

Properties of Matter and Energy

LOOK!

With a mighty roar, the space shuttle blasts off. What kind of energy powers the space shuttle's engines?

CHAPTER

10

Properties and Structure of Matter

Did You Ever Wonder?

How can potters use their talent and creativity to turn clay and water into beautiful vases? When wet, clay has certain physical properties that allow potters to shape it into different forms. What happens to the clay when the vases are dried in a hot kiln, or oven?

LESSON 1

Physical Properties

Vocabulary

matter, E6
mass, E6
volume, E6
weight, E7
density, E8
conduct, E14
insulate, E14

Get Ready

When you say something is "bigger" than something else, what does "bigger" mean? What is bigger than a hot air balloon? What is smaller?

If the balloon is empty and folded up, are the same things bigger or smaller?

Bigger or smaller. More or less. In what ways can things be "more" or "less" than other things? Are there different ways something can be "more" than other things?

Process Skill

You experiment when you perform a test to support or disprove a hypothesis.

Explore Activity

Which Is More?

Procedure: Design Your Own

1 **Observe** Look at the golf ball (or wooden block) and blown-up balloon. Which is "more"? Think of how one object could be "more":

- more when you use a balance
- more when you put it in water and see how much the water level goes up, and so on

Record your observations.

2 Use the equipment to verify one way that one object is more than another. Decide which of the two objects is "more" and which one is "less."

3 Repeat your measurements to verify your answer.

4 Now use different equipment to compare the two objects. Is the same object still "more"? Explain.

5 Repeat your measurements to verify your answer.

Drawing Conclusions

1 **Communicate** Identify the equipment you used. Report your results.

2 For each test, which object was more? In what way was it more than the other object?

3 **Going Further: Experiment** What if you were given a large box of puffed oats and a small box of oatmeal? Which do you think would be more? Design an experiment to test your hypothesis. Tell what equipment you would use.

Materials

- golf ball or wooden block
- blown-up balloon
- equal-pan balance
- ruler
- string
- box, such as a shoe box
- pail of water

Read to Learn

Main Idea **Matter is anything that has mass and occupies space.**

What Is Matter?

All of the gases, liquids, and solids in the world around you—the air you breathe, the water you drink, and the chair you sit on—are made of **matter**. Testing to see whether a golf ball or a balloon is "more" measures *properties* of the matter in these objects.

A golf ball has more **mass** because it tips the balance more. However, a balloon has more **volume** because it fills up a greater amount of space.

Mass is a measure of the amount of matter in an object. The photo shows how a balance is used to measure mass. Mass is often measured in kilograms.

Volume describes how much space a sample of matter takes up. Volumes are often measured in milliliters (mL). As the photo shows, the volume of a liquid may be measured using a graduated cylinder, a beaker, or a measuring cup. The volume of a solid may be measured by multiplying its height times its length times its width. Solids don't always have regular shapes, however. We can also measure the volume of a solid by seeing how much water it displaces from a container. A solid with a volume of 1 cm^3 will make the water rise 1 mL, for example. A volume of 1 cm^3 equals 1 mL.

Matter is defined using the properties of mass and volume. Matter is anything that has mass and takes up space.

Measuring Mass and Volume

We determine the mass of an object by comparing it with known masses. The mass of this block is 25 g.

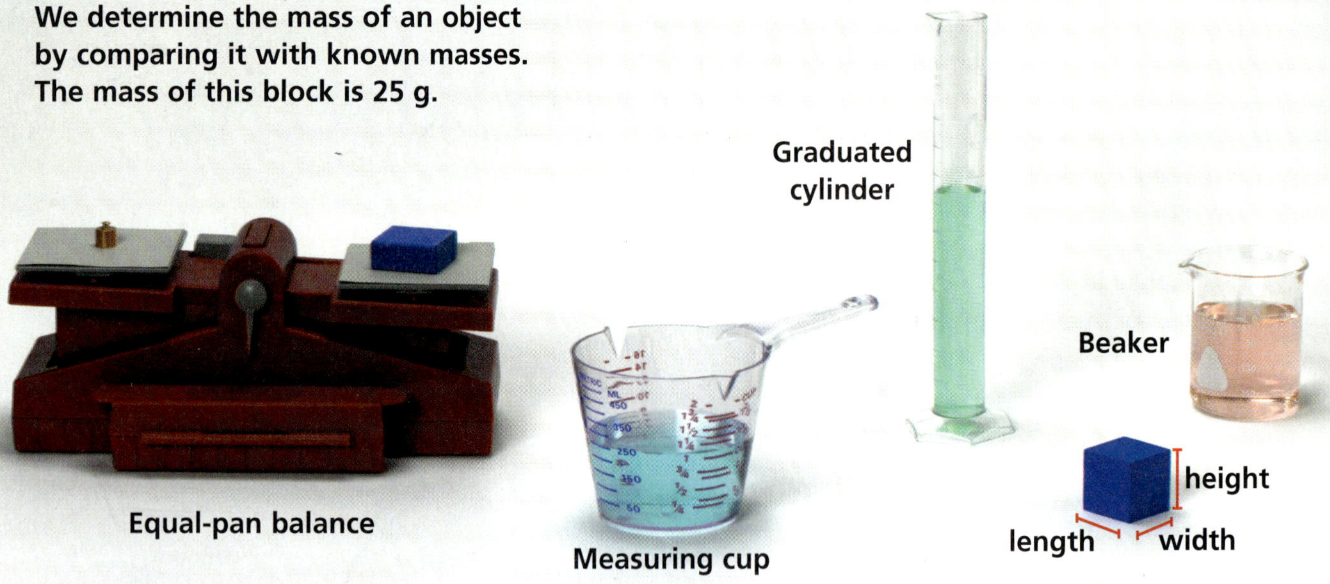

Weight

What if you find the mass of a certain book to be 1 kilogram? You might be tempted to say, "This book weighs 1 kilogram." However, this is incorrect. The book's **weight** is actually the force of gravity between Earth and the book. The book's mass, on the other hand, is a measure of the amount of matter in the book compared with known masses.

As you know, we can use kilograms to measure an object's mass. However, to measure weight, we must use a quantity that describes the force of gravity between two masses. Scientists prefer to use a quantity called the *newton* (N) to measure force. One newton is the same as 0.22 pound. (One pound is 4.45 newtons.) Newtons and pounds both describe the amount of pull or push a force produces. In this case the force is the pull of gravity.

An object's weight depends on its location in the universe. If you were to travel to the Moon, for example, you would have less weight. The Moon has less mass than Earth, so the force of gravity between your body and the Moon would be less. However, your mass would remain unchanged, as shown in the diagram.

What are two properties of matter?

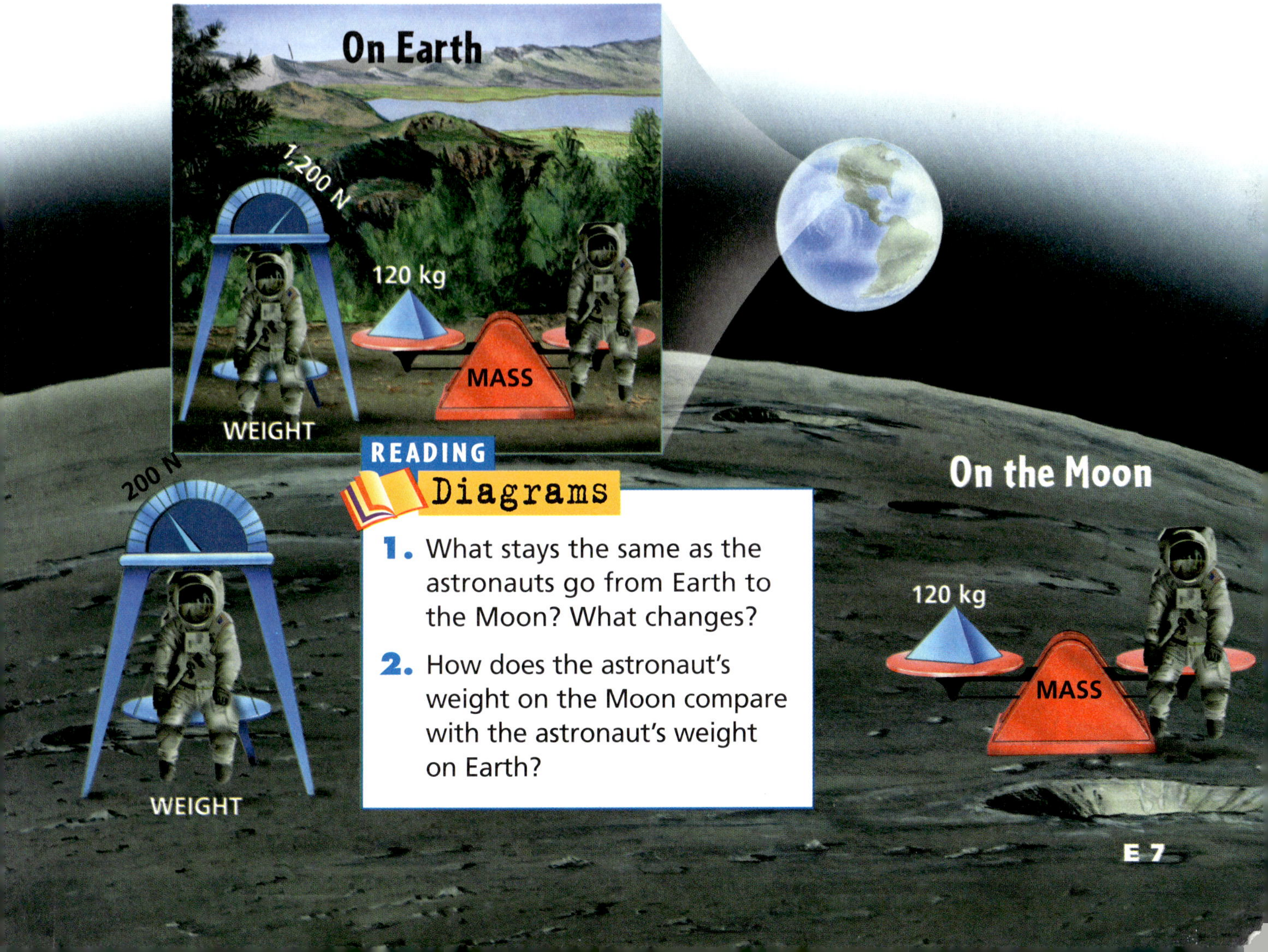

READING Diagrams

1. What stays the same as the astronauts go from Earth to the Moon? What changes?
2. How does the astronaut's weight on the Moon compare with the astronaut's weight on Earth?

What Is Density?

As you learned on page E6, mass and volume are two properties of matter. Can we use these properties to tell us more about matter? How can these two measurements tell us something new?

If we divide the mass of a sample by its volume, we get a new measurement of matter. This property is called **density**. The density of an object tells us how massive something is for its size. It compares an object's mass with its volume.

Let's look at an example. If 2 mL of water has a mass of 2 g, then 2 g divided by 2 mL equals 1 g per mL. The density is 1 g per mL. If we combined that water sample with another 2 mL sample, we would have 4 mL and 4 g of water. The density would still be 1 g per mL.

As long as conditions such as temperature do not change, the density of a substance does not change. The size of the sample does not matter. Density can be used to help identify materials because of this. If you had a piece of metal with a density of 11.3 g per mL, it would probably be lead. A similar-looking piece with a density of 2.7 g per mL, however, would probably be aluminum. Each material has its own density.

How can density be measured?

Calculating Density

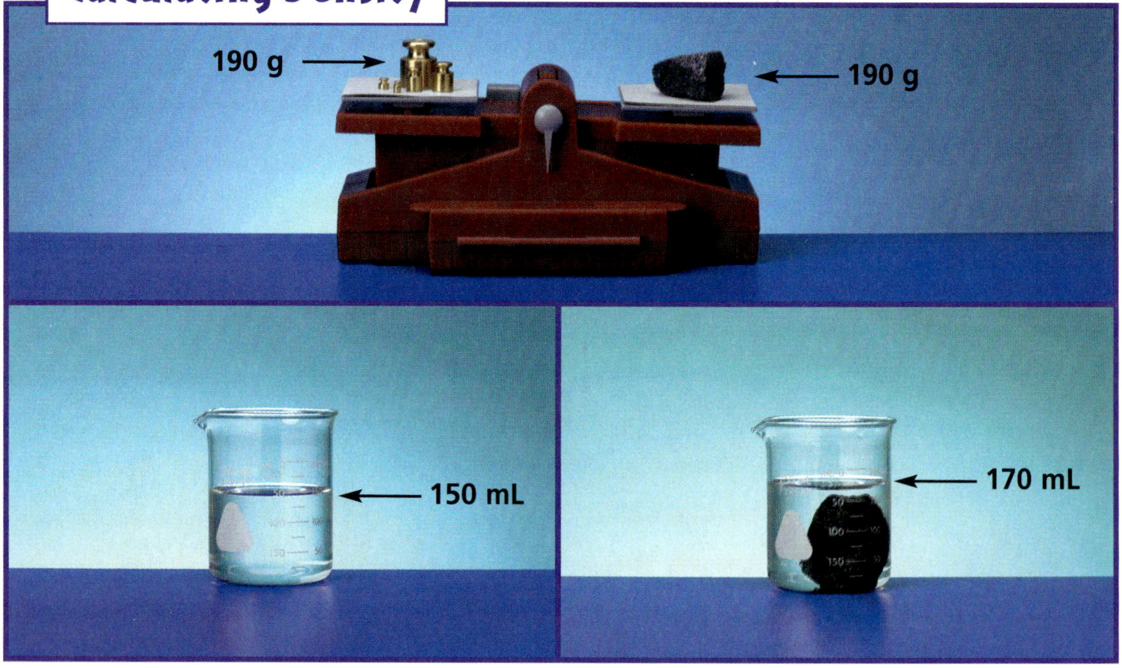

An object's density is calculated by dividing its mass by its volume. The mass of this rock is 190 g. Its volume can be determined by calculating how much water it displaces from the beaker. If you subtract the volume of the water from the volume of the water plus the rock, you get the volume of the rock. (170 mL – 150 mL = 20 mL). The volume of this rock is 20 mL. The density of this rock is: 190 g ÷ 20 mL = 9.5 g per mL.

Process Skill BUILDER

SKILL Make a Model

How Metal Boats Float

Think about objects that have more matter packed into the space they take up than water does. Will such objects sink or float in water? You have probably seen how a metal object like a nail or a spoon sinks in water. However, huge ships made of similar metal float even when they carry large cargoes. How is this possible? In this activity you will make a model of a metal boat. Scientists use models to help them understand properties of matter. Working with a model makes experimenting easier. Experiment to see how boats are designed so that they can carry heavy cargo.

Materials

- aluminum foil
- large paper clips
- pan of water

Procedure

1. **Make a Model** Make a boat out of a 10-cm by 10-cm (4-in. by 4-in.) piece of aluminum foil. Then float it on water.
2. **Predict** Write down what you think will happen when you place more and more matter in the empty space of the boat. What steps should you follow to test your prediction? Be sure to use only the materials listed above.
3. **Experiment** Carry out your procedure, keeping a written record of what you observe.

Drawing Conclusions

1. **Communicate** How well did your results agree with your prediction?
2. Compare your model with those of your classmates. Which boat held the most clips? Why?
3. **Make a Model** The aluminum foil boat is a model of a steel ship. Use the way your boat floats to explain how a steel ship floats. Why was using a model of a large ship helpful?
4. **Communicate** What changed as more and more matter was added to the empty space of the boat? What happened as a result of this change?

How Dense Are Solids, Liquids, and Gases?

Imagine cutting a piece of aluminum foil into smaller and smaller pieces until the pieces are tinier than specks of dust. All matter—solids, liquids, and gases—is made of similar tiny particles. An object's mass is related to the number and type of particles it has.

Density describes how tightly these particles are packed together. A high density means that many particles are packed tightly into a given space. A low density means that only a few particles fill the same amount of space.

The particles of a solid tend to be packed very tightly together. They don't have a lot of room to move around. However, the particles of a gas usually spread out. In general, matter in the solid state is more dense than in the liquid state. Likewise, matter in the liquid state tends to be more dense than in the gaseous state.

READING Main Idea
How do the densities of solids, liquids, and gases compare?

Water is special! Solid water, ice, is less dense than liquid water. The particles in ice are more spread out than the particles in liquid water.

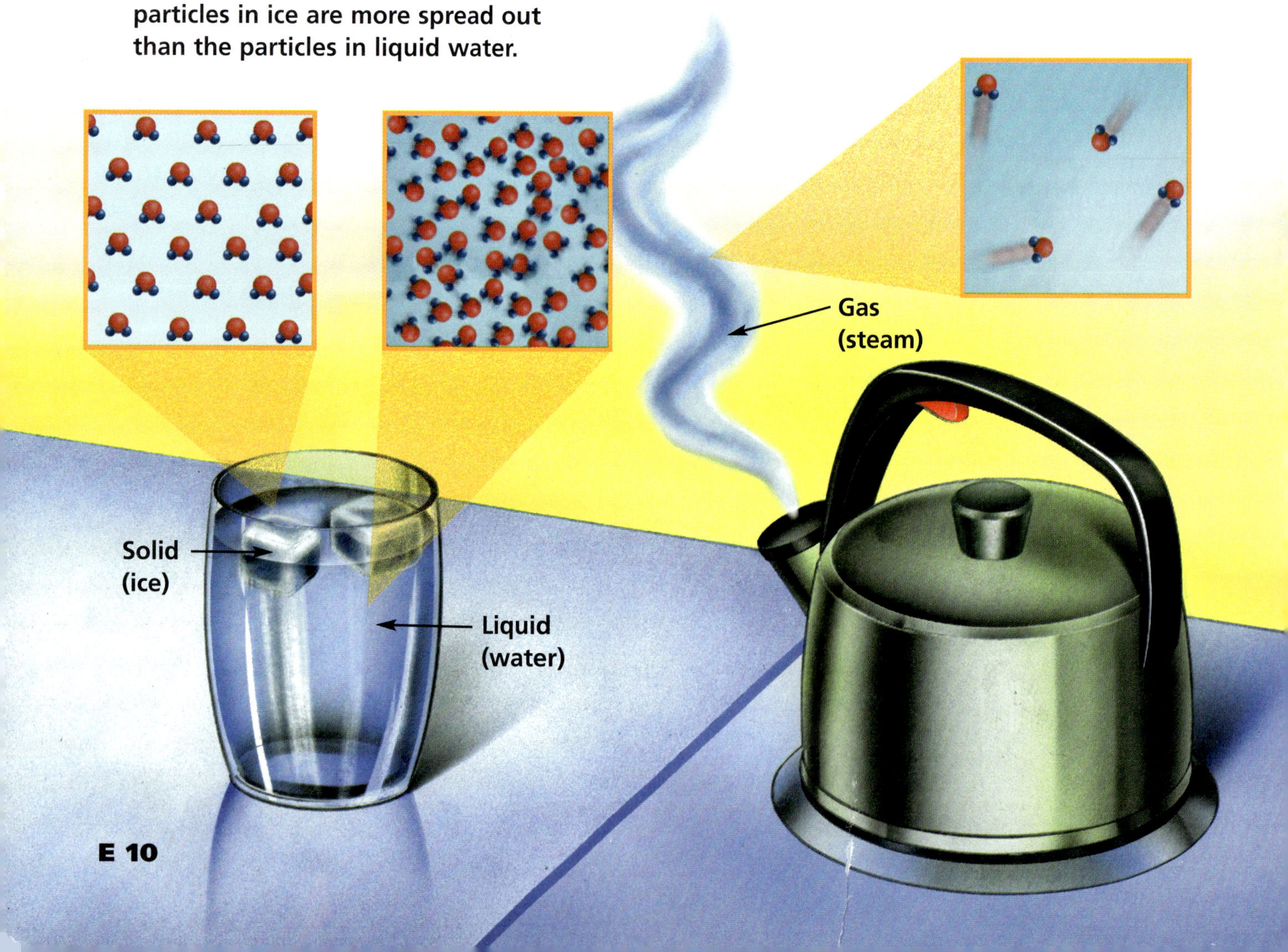

Densities of Common Substances

State	Substance		Density (g/cm^3)
Solid	 Aluminum	 Gold	Aluminum, 2.7 Gold, 18.9
Liquid	 Water	 Mercury	Water, 1.0 Mercury, 13.5
Gas	Helium 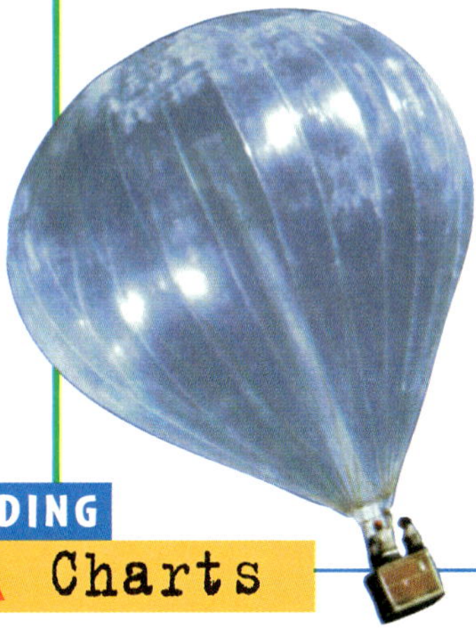	 Air	Helium, 0.00018 Air at sea level, 0.0012

READING Charts

1. Which is denser—aluminum or gold? Mercury or gold?
2. Organize the substances in the chart from the least dense to the most dense. Make a bar graph with the densities of these substances.

How Does Density Make Things Sink or Float?

Have you ever observed a beach ball floating in a pool? Have you ever dropped your towel in the water, only to see it sink to the bottom? What makes some things float, while others sink?

Density determines an object's ability to sink or float. An object floats in a liquid when its density is less than the liquid's density. A beach ball is filled with air. Air is less dense than water, so the beach ball floats. We describe an object's ability to float as its *buoyancy* (BOY·uhn·see).

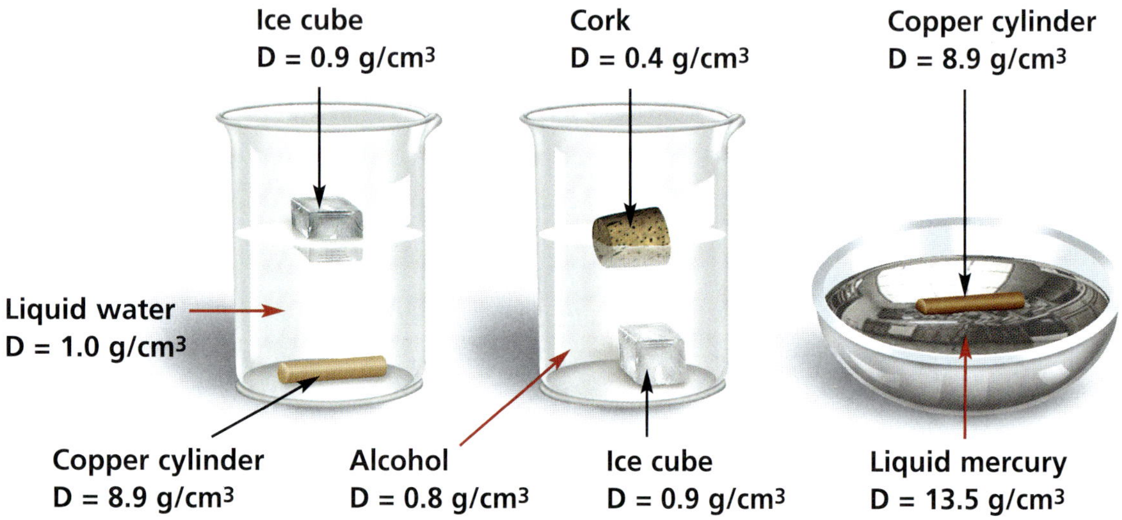

Why does ice float in water? Why does it sink in alcohol? The copper cylinder floats in mercury but sinks in water. Do you think it will sink or float in alcohol?

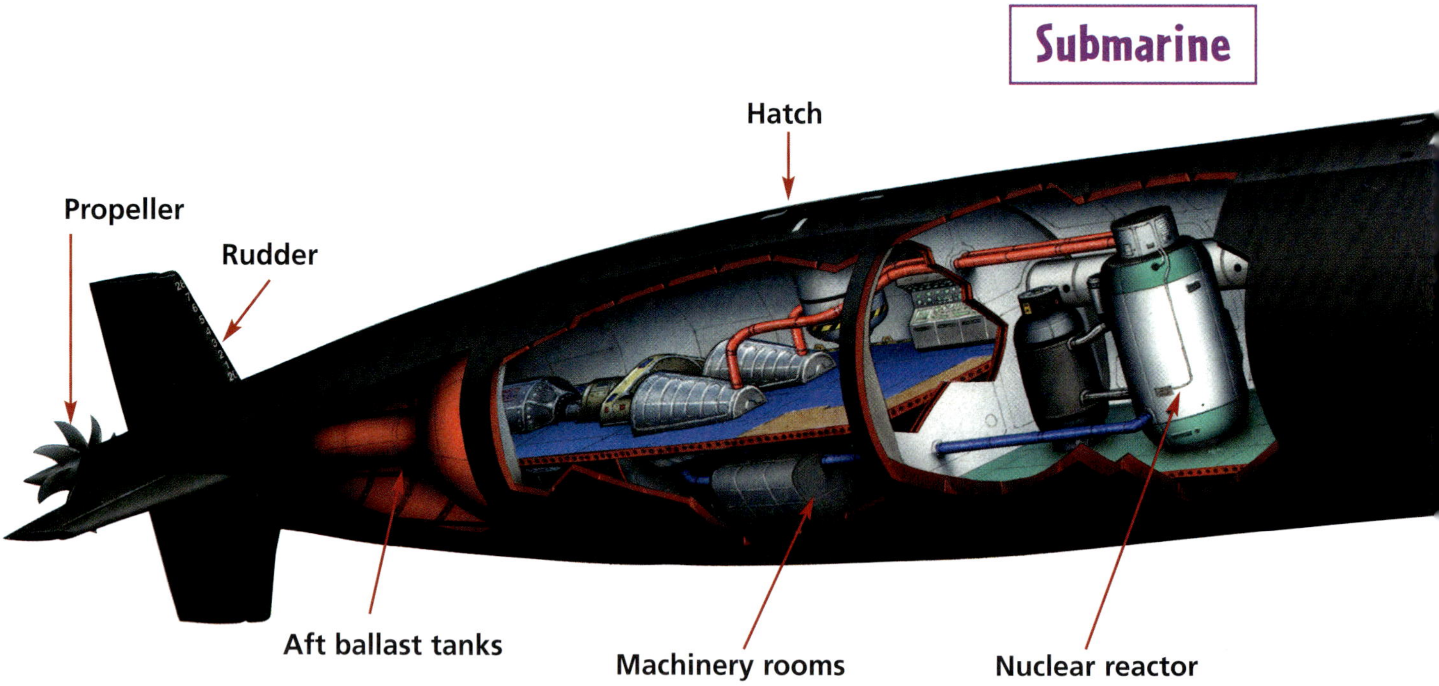

Helium balloons can float, too. However, they float in air instead of water. Helium is less dense than air, so helium balloons rise into the sky.

As you know, not all objects float. An object sinks in a liquid when it is more dense than the liquid. The copper cylinder shown in the diagram sinks in water. The ice cube sinks in alcohol.

It's easy to float in Utah's Great Salt Lake. That's because salt water is denser than fresh water. The lake has six billion tons of salt! Swimmers float higher in the lake than in ocean water.

How does density determine an object's ability to float in water?

Sailors pump seawater into ballast tanks on a submarine to bring its average density close to the density of the surrounding water. This makes the sub have little tendency to rise or sink.

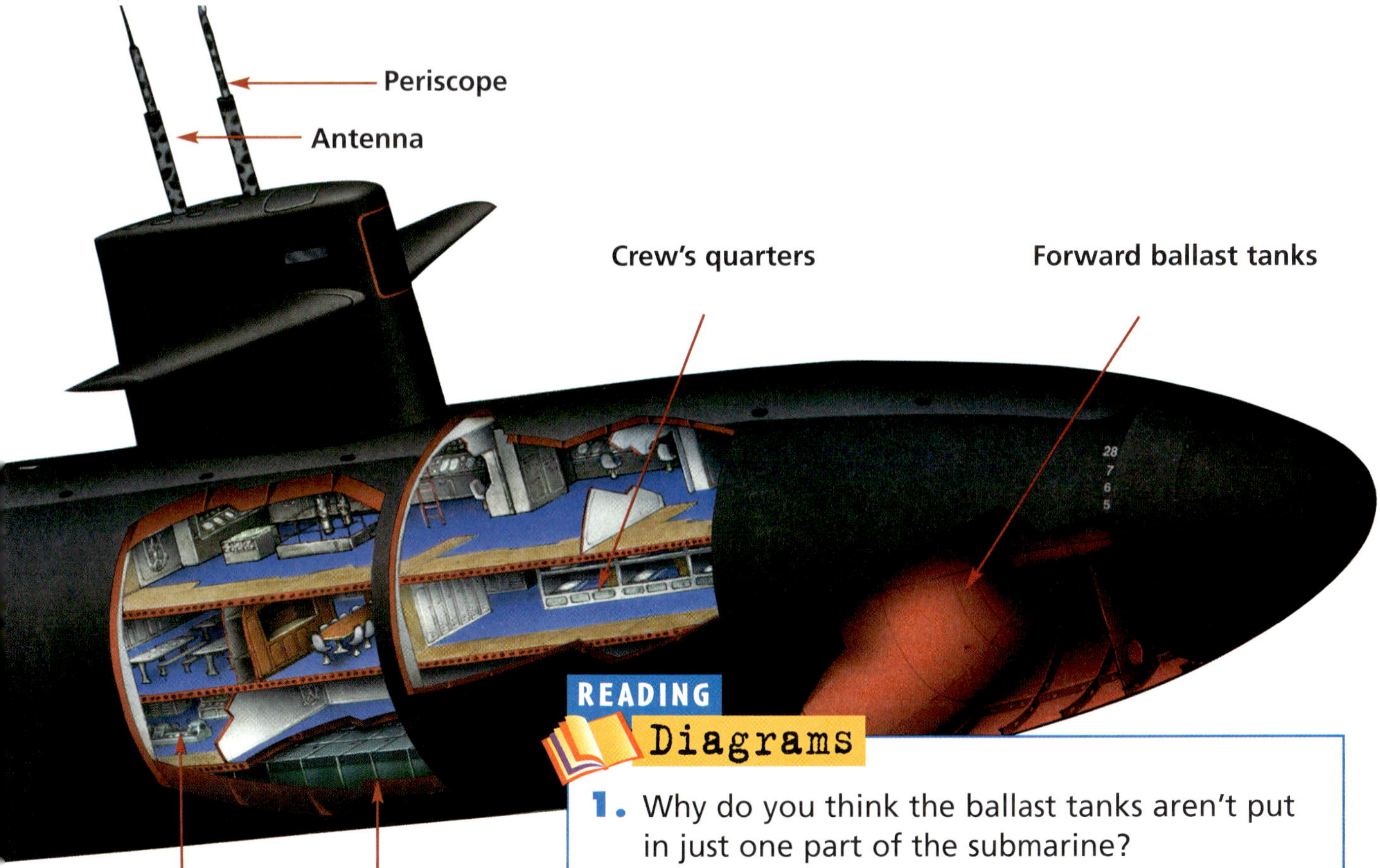

READING Diagrams

1. Why do you think the ballast tanks aren't put in just one part of the submarine?
2. What would adding more water to the ballast tanks do? What would letting water out of the ballast tanks do?

Which material in this pan is a conductor? Which is an insulator?

What Are Conductors and Insulators?

Matter has many important properties besides density. For example, some materials **conduct** energy very well. These materials allow energy to flow through them easily. However, other materials **insulate** against the passage of energy. They do not readily permit energy to flow. Look carefully at the photographs to learn about materials that conduct or insulate.

Cooking pots and pans are made of metal because metal conducts heat well. However, they should have wooden or ceramic handles. Such handles insulate against heat so you don't get burned when you touch the handles.

Metals like the copper in the wire are also good conductors of electricity. The electricity flows from the battery to the light bulb through the wire, producing light and heat. The plastic that coats the wire is an insulator. Anyone who touches the plastic coating will not be shocked, because the electricity cannot pass through it.

Sound booths are made of materials that insulate the room from outside noise. This property is important for musicians who are recording a new CD.

The walls of this room are made of a material that insulates sound. Why might this property be useful?

The wire is a good conductor of electricity. The plastic that coats the wire is an insulator. Why must electrical wire be insulated?

What do *insulate* and *conduct* mean?

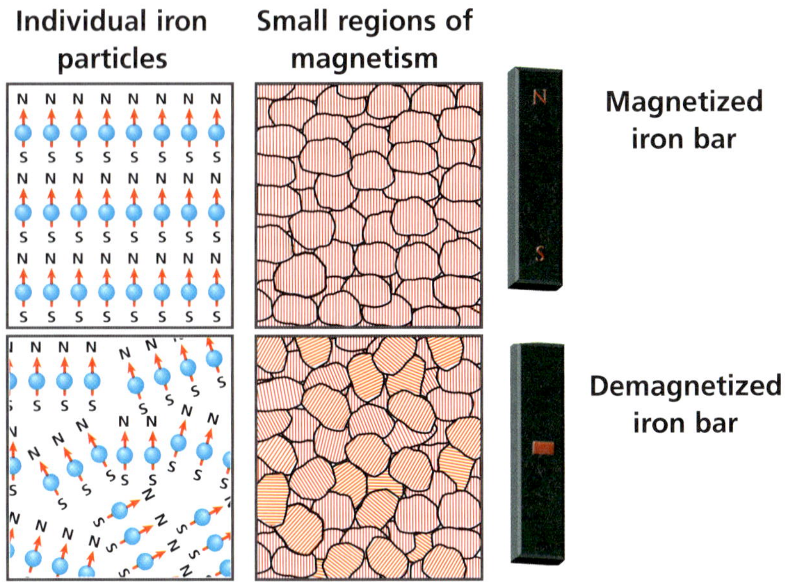

When iron particles in small areas of the metal line up, a permanent magnet is formed.

What makes a material magnetic?

What Is Magnetism?

Certain objects push or pull on each other because they are *magnetic*. Magnetism is another property of some kinds of matter. A magnet has a north pole and a south pole. North poles and south poles of magnets attract, but two poles that are alike repel. Magnets can also attract certain materials that are made of a metal like iron.

Like density, magnetism results from the combined effect of the properties of tiny particles. In iron, for example, each tiny particle of iron is itself a magnet.

Look at the diagram above. Each particle has a north and a south pole. When the particles line up, the material is magnetic. When the particles do not line up pole to pole, however, the material is not magnetic.

Earth acts like a huge magnet. A compass uses this property of matter to help you find your way home.

How Do We Use Properties of Matter?

Engineers and scientists use properties of matter when they design and build new things.

Aerogels are new materials with very low density and relatively great strength. They are made of tiny pockets of air surrounded by thin walls of silica. Silica is the same material found in sand and in window glass.

Aerogels are very good insulators of heat. Insulated windows containing aerogel would be from 10 to 20 times better at holding in heat than ordinary glass windows.

Scientists have discovered that some materials become perfect conductors of electricity when they are very cold. The photo shows a ceramic, glasslike material that conducts perfectly when cooled to –196°C (–320.8°F).

This white aerogel has such a low density that it can float on top of soap bubbles.

How are properties of matter used?

A magnetic cube floats above a disk made of a "superconducting" ceramic material. This effect can lift trains above the rails so that they can travel faster.

Lesson Review

Why It Matters

You use many different properties of matter every day. Matter that conducts electricity lets you use a reading lamp at night or listen to your favorite CDs. Density allows you to float in a boat on a lake or float through the sky in a hot air balloon. Magnets help you find your way home with a compass.

Think and Write

1. List four properties of matter.
2. If a rock were taken from Earth to the Moon, how would its mass and weight be affected?
3. What if you had paper clips, rubber bands, wood chips, straight pins, strips of aluminum foil, and glass beads? Using a property of matter you've learned, classify these objects. Show your results in a table.
4. **Make a Model** How does the density of warm water compare with the density of cold water? How would you design a model to test your ideas?
5. **Critical Thinking** Think of the properties of matter you use every day. In what ways are they important to you?

L·I·N·K·S

WRITING LINK

Write a paragraph. Tell about a typical day from the time you wake up until the time you go to sleep. What properties of matter do you rely on to get to school, do your homework, and play with your friends?

MATH LINK

Calculate density. Find some small objects around your classroom or house—a seashell, a rock, or even a piece of fruit. Measure its mass and its volume. Use its mass and volume to find its density.

LITERATURE LINK

Read *Moon Landing That Never Was* to learn about the spacecraft *Apollo 13*. Try the activities at the end of the book.

TECHNOLOGY LINK

At the Computer Visit **www.mhscience02.com** for more links.

Animals: Icy Survival

Imagine a world where water's like most other substances—it becomes denser as it freezes. Ice, now heavier than water, sinks to the bottoms of ponds. The water quickly freezes from the bottom up into solid blocks of ice. Fish in the ponds freeze, too. That's the end of most freshwater fish.

In summer the ice near the top of the ponds melts, but not the ice at the bottom. That ice never melts. Each summer things get worse. Before long there's no liquid water left on Earth!

Luckily that scenario is science fiction, but real water is stranger than science fiction! Why doesn't it become denser when it turns solid? The answer lies in what happens when water molecules get cold enough to freeze.

As you know, water molecules are made of two hydrogen atoms and one oxygen atom. When water freezes, the molecules are kept farther apart than they are in liquid water.

Ice is only nine-tenths as dense as

liquid water, so when water freezes, it expands. A given volume of ice weighs less than the same volume of water. That's why ice floats in your lemonade!

Ice forms a protective covering for ponds. Under the ice the water stays liquid, allowing plants and animals to survive the winter. Because ice floats, oceans have icebergs. They can mean trouble for ships, because most of an iceberg is underwater. Look at the ice cube in your next drink. How much of it is under the surface?

What Did I Learn?

1. Water is different from other substances because

A it is less dense as a solid than as a liquid
B it is more dense as a solid than as a liquid
C its molecules are packed more tightly as a solid
D none of the above

2. Ice helps plants and animals in ponds survive by

F preserving their habitat
G providing more molecules of water
H keeping the temperature low
J forming a protective covering

AT THE COMPUTER

Visit www.mhscience02.com to learn more about survival in cold.

LESSON 2

Elements and Compounds

Vocabulary

- **element,** E22
- **compound,** E24
- **atom,** E26
- **proton,** E27
- **neutron,** E27
- **electron,** E27
- **nucleus,** E27
- **molecule,** E30

Get Ready

How is Jupiter like Earth? How are they alike on the outside?

Both planets have atmospheres. What are the atmospheres made of? Are they similar? What are the planets made of "beneath" the atmospheres?

Here's a similar question. What is matter made of? If you cannot "look inside" something—a planet or a piece of matter—how can scientists tell what a planet or any piece of matter is made of?

Process Skill

You communicate when you share information.

Explore Activity

How Do We Know What's "Inside" Matter?

Materials

3 identical, sealed, opaque boxes

Procedure

1. **Observe** Examine the three boxes, but do not open them. You can lift them, shake them, listen to the noises they make, feel the way their contents shift as you move them, and so on. Record your observations.
2. **Infer** Try to determine what is in each box.

Drawing Conclusions

1. **Communicate** Describe what you think is in each box.
2. How did you make your decision?
3. Do these boxes have anything in common? In what ways are they similar? In what ways are they different?
4. **Going Further: Experiment** What if you have a can of peanuts and a can of stewed tomatoes? The cans look the same except for the labels. Now what if your baby brother takes the labels off? You want the peanuts, but you don't want to open the tomatoes by mistake. What experiments can you do to find out what is inside—before you open the cans?

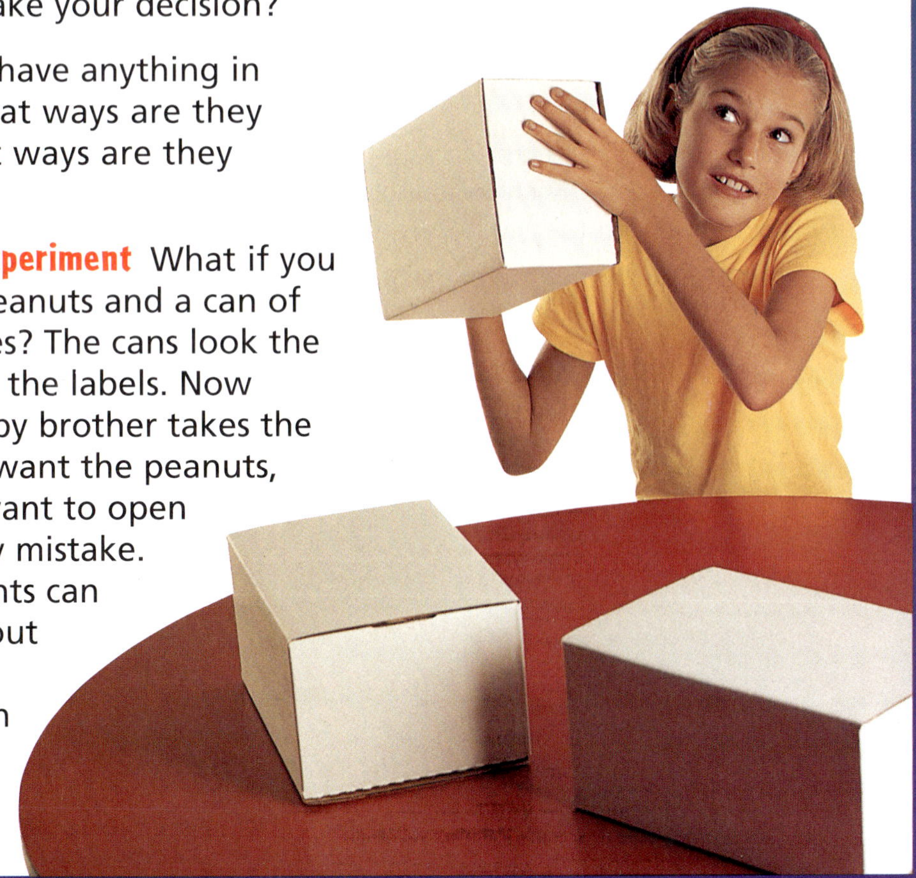

Read to Learn

Main Idea All matter is made of elements.

What Is Matter Made Of?

In studying matter scientists face a challenge. The basic particles that make up matter are too small to be seen directly. In the past the tests scientists performed on matter gave only hints about how matter is put together. That's because particles of matter cannot be observed.

People have experimented with matter for thousands of years. In ancient times the goal was often a practical product like a colorful dye, a metal sword, or a plow. In recent centuries matter has also been studied with carefully planned scientific experiments.

The ancient Greek philosopher Aristotle believed that all matter was composed of four elements—earth, air, fire, and water. However, during the last three centuries, scientists have identified the true chemical **elements**. These substances are the basic building blocks of all matter. One of the most interesting elements is shown in the photograph at the bottom of the page. It expands very evenly when warmed and makes a good liquid for thermometers. What is it?

This bronze coin was made about 2,500 years ago. Bronze is made by mixing the metals copper and tin.

The element mercury is also known as liquid silver. It is beautiful but highly poisonous. Mercury is often used in thermometers. Why?

The Elements

Elements are pure substances that cannot be broken down into any simpler substances. You are probably familiar with many of them. Several are shown in the photographs. How many do you recognize?

Many elements have been known since ancient times but were not truly recognized as elements until the last few centuries. Other elements were found for the first time only recently. For example, germanium was not discovered until 1885. Also, some elements are not even found in nature. They have been made by scientists in nuclear reactors and huge machines called particle accelerators. Even though there are many different elements, living organisms and most materials are made up of just a few elements.

Each element is given a special symbol of one or two letters. The first letter is always a capital. The second letter is never a capital. Sometimes the letters match the English name, such as Ni for nickel or Zn for zinc. In other cases the symbol comes from an ancient name. Gold, for instance, is given the symbol Au from its Latin name, *aurum*.

Gold
Au

Aluminum
Al

Carbon
C

Sulfur
S

Copper
Cu

Oxygen
O

A few elements are pictured here. How many other elements can you name?

READING **Main Idea**
What are the building blocks of matter?

What Are Compounds?

Imagine looking at pure water through a microscope. It would look the same everywhere. Water has this appearance because it is a single substance. However, the photograph below shows how passing electricity through water breaks it apart into two elements, hydrogen and oxygen. If water is a single substance, how could it contain the elements hydrogen and oxygen?

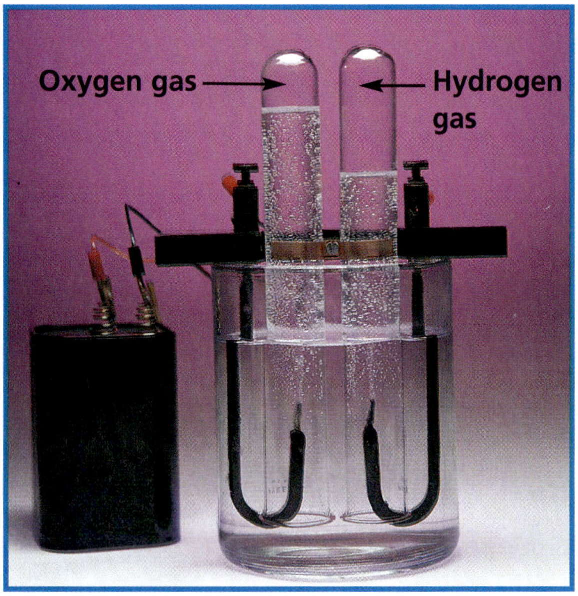

Water is made of hydrogen and oxygen, as this experiment shows.

Actually, the hydrogen and oxygen in water are chemically combined. This makes them act like a single substance. Any substance that is formed by the chemical combination of two or more elements is called a **compound**.

All compounds are single substances that can only be broken apart into simpler substances by chemical reactions. Compounds have different properties than the elements that make them up, as the lower photographs show.

How is a compound different from an element?

The compound sodium chloride is a solid at room temperature. We use it on our foods to give them more flavor. It belongs to a group of compounds called salts. Salts are always made up of a metal and a nonmetal.

Sodium and chlorine combine to make sodium chloride. Sodium is a soft, reactive metal that can explode on contact with water. Chlorine is a very poisonous gas.

Sodium

+

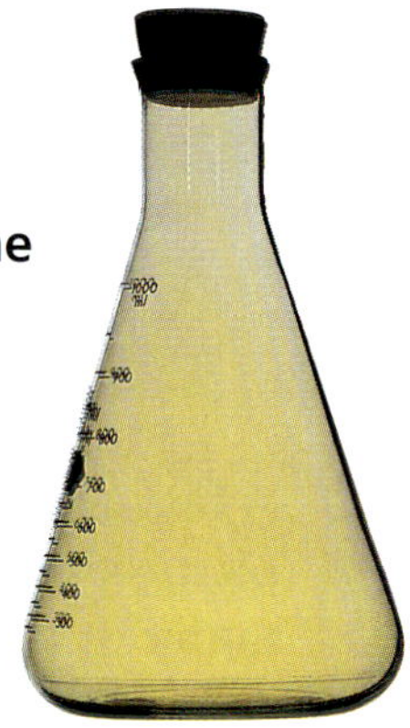

Chlorine

=

Sodium chloride (table salt)

1 When sulfuric acid is added to sugar, it breaks the compound apart into its elements.

2 The gas you observe is oxygen and hydrogen.

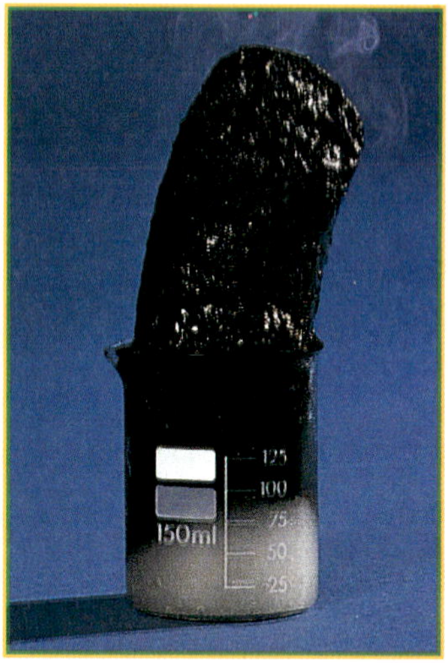

3 The black solid left behind is carbon.

How Do You Write a Compound's Name?

As you know, each element has a one or two letter symbol. Scientists also write symbols for compounds, which are called *chemical formulas*. A compound's chemical formula contains the symbols for the elements that make it up.

The formula also contains numbers below the element symbols called *subscripts*. The table shows chemical formulas for some familiar compounds.

The subscripts in a chemical formula tell us the number of particles that combine in a compound. For example, water is made up of two elements—hydrogen and oxygen. For every oxygen particle, there are two hydrogen particles. The formula for water is written H_2O.

Table sugar is made up of the elements carbon, hydrogen, and oxygen.

Common Compounds

Compound	Chemical Formula
Water	H_2O
Carbon dioxide	CO_2
Baking soda	$NaHCO_3$
Table salt	NaCl
Table sugar	$C_{12}H_{22}O_{11}$
Glucose (a sugar)	$C_6H_{12}O_6$

For every 12 carbon particles, there are 22 hydrogen particles and 11 oxygen particles. We write $C_{12}H_{22}O_{11}$ for table sugar's chemical formula.

The photo shows what happens to table sugar when it is treated with strong sulfuric acid. **(Warning: Sulfuric acid is a dangerous substance.)** The acid takes out all the hydrogen and oxygen, leaving a black mass, carbon.

What is a chemical formula?

What Are Elements Made Of?

In 1803 an English scientist named John Dalton stated an important theory: Matter is made up of tiny particles that cannot be cut apart into smaller pieces. Today we call Dalton's tiny particles **atoms**.

According to Dalton, the atoms of one element were all alike. Each element was made up of one kind of atom. However, the atoms of one element were different from the atoms of any other element. While many parts of Dalton's theory have been improved since 1803, the basic idea of atoms is correct. An atom is the smallest unit of an element that retains the properties of the element.

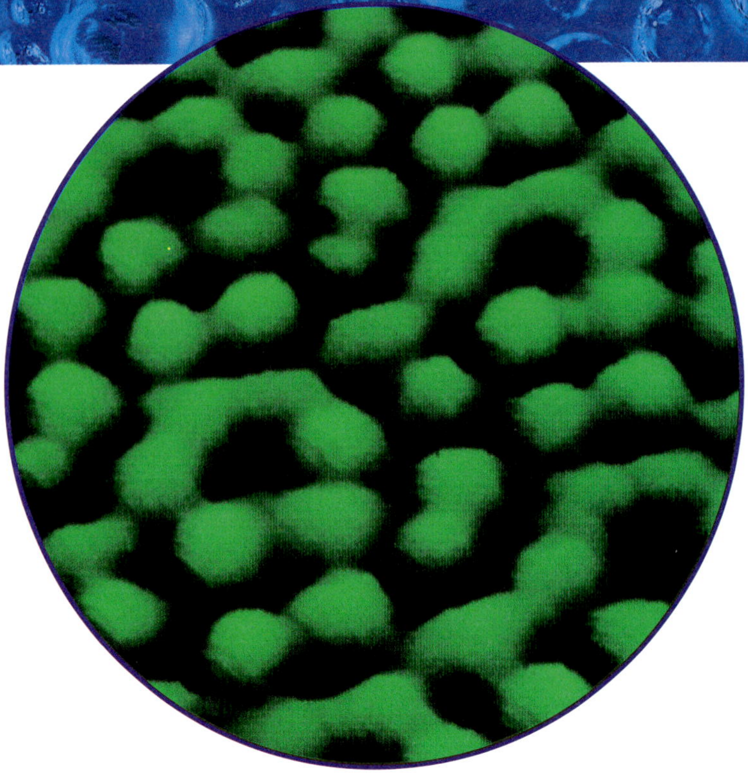

Individual carbon atoms

Dalton drew the symbols above for atoms. He believed that each element's atoms weighed a different amount from the atoms of other elements.

Many experiments since Dalton's day have shown us what atoms are like. Atoms are so small that we cannot see them directly, even through a microscope. Scientists have had to observe atoms indirectly. A special microscope called a *scanning tunneling microscope* uses a very sharp needle that can trace the bumps in a surface made by individual atoms. The photograph above shows some of what such special microscopes can "see."

Images made by these microscopes show that atoms are discrete and often occur in well-ordered arrays. For example, the carbon atoms in the photo are arranged in rings of six atoms each.

What is an atom?

What Is Inside Atoms?

John Dalton imagined that atoms were like tiny steel marbles—solid and unbreakable. However, we now know that atoms are made of still smaller particles. Atoms are far from being solid—they are mostly empty space!

Atoms contain three kinds of particles called **protons** (PROH·tahnz), **neutrons** (NEW·trahnz), and **electrons** (i·LEK·trahnz). The protons and neutrons are located in a tiny, very dense body in the atom's center, called the atomic **nucleus** (NEW·klee·uhs). The electrons are in the space outside the nucleus.

Protons and neutrons have nearly the same mass, but electrons are about 2,000 times less massive than protons and neutrons.

Protons carry one unit of positive electric charge, while electrons carry one unit of negative electric charge.

Neutrons have no electric charge. All atoms have equal numbers of electrons and protons, so they have no overall electric charge.

The number of protons in an atom determines what element it is. For example, any atom with six protons is a carbon atom. Any atom with eight protons is an oxygen atom.

Look carefully at the diagrams on this page to see how atoms are put together.

What are the three particles that make up an atom?

Atoms are made of protons, neutrons, and electrons. The number of protons an atom has determines what element it is.

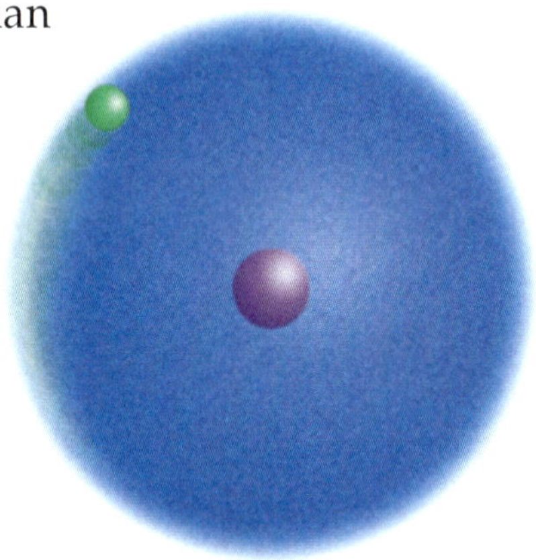

Hydrogen

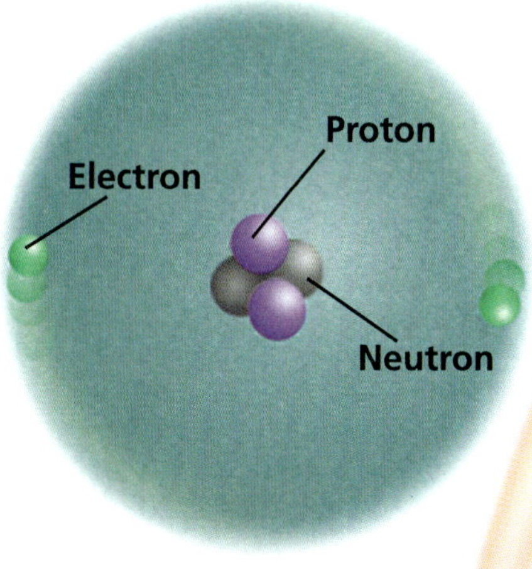

Helium

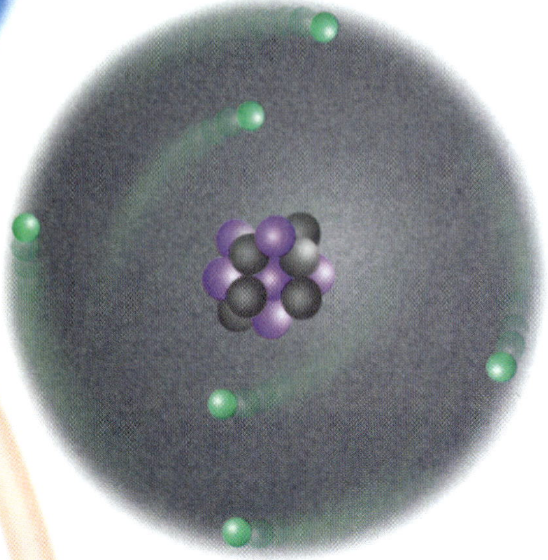

Carbon

What Properties Do Elements Have?

We now know of 112 elements. These substances have many different properties. There are patterns in the properties of the elements. Study the photographs on this page to learn about properties that can demonstrate these patterns.

Chemical Reactivity

Some elements take part in chemical reactions much more easily than others. The magnesium reacts rapidly with the acid, but the copper hardly reacts at all. Reactive elements, like magnesium, are usually combined with other elements when found in nature.

Metal Versus Nonmetal

About three-fourths of the elements are metallic, like copper, gold, silver, aluminum, iron, and nickel. Metals conduct electricity and heat well. Metals are also shiny when freshly polished, and many can be worked into thin sheets or different shapes. In contrast nonmetals, like iodine, phosphorus, and carbon, are often poor conductors of heat and electricity. They are not reflective like metals.

States at Room Temperature

The elements shown are all at room temperature, about 22°C (71.6°F). Copper, aluminum, and iodine are solids at 22°C. Bromine, though, is a liquid at 22°C. Neon is a gas at 22°C.

How can elements be classified?

Property: Chemical Reactivity

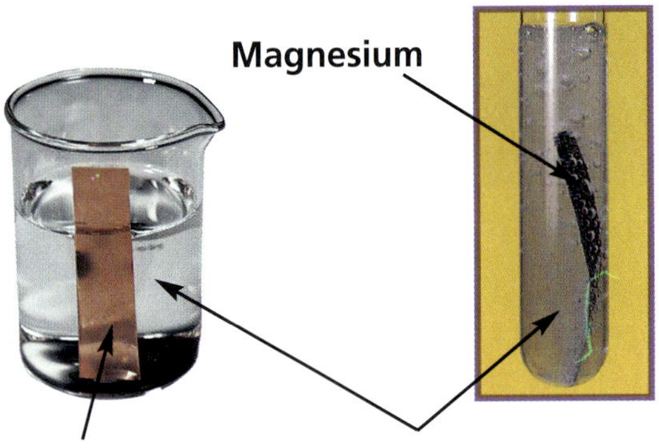

Magnesium takes part in chemical reactions much more easily than copper. Here the magnesium reacts rapidly with the acid. The copper hardly reacts at all.

Property: Metal Versus Nonmetal

Metals

Goldleaf

Aluminum

Copper

Nonmetals

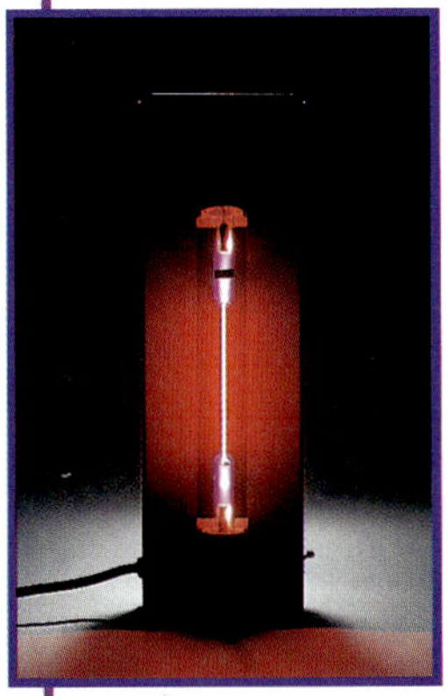

Neon

Bromine

Iodine

Metals, like copper, gold, silver, aluminum, iron, and nickel, are good conductors of heat and electricity. Nonmetals are often poor conductors of heat and electricity.

How Can the Elements Be Grouped?

In 1869 a Russian scientist named Dmitry Mendeleyev found that the properties of the elements went through repeating cycles. Mendeleyev created a table of elements based on these cycles. Each group in his table contains elements with similar chemical properties. For example, one group contains lithium (Li), sodium (Na), potassium (K), rubidium (Rb), and cesium (Cs). All of these elements combine with chlorine in the same way. The formulas for their chlorine compounds are LiCl, NaCl, KCl, RbCl, and CsCl.

We call Mendeleyev's table the periodic table after the "periodic" changes he found in the elements' properties.

The metals lie on the left, and the nonmetals lie mainly on the right, with elements called metalloids in between.

Most of the elements are solids at room temperature, and all metals are solids except mercury.

The most reactive metals are at the left, and the most reactive nonmetals are in the second column from the right.

What is the periodic table? How is it organized?

READING Charts

1. Is sodium a metal or a nonmetal? Is chlorine a metal or a nonmetal?
2. Which elements are liquid at 20°C?

The Modern Periodic Table

The number in each box is the number of protons an atom of that element has.

Metallic Properties: Li Metal; B Metalloid; C Nonmetal

Phase at 20°C: C Solid; Br Liquid; H Gas

H 1																	He 2
Li 3	Be 4											B 5	C 6	N 7	O 8	F 9	Ne 10
Na 11	Mg 12											Al 13	Si 14	P 15	S 16	Cl 17	Ar 18
K 19	Ca 20	Sc 21	Ti 22	V 23	Cr 24	Mn 25	Fe 26	Co 27	Ni 28	Cu 29	Zn 30	Ga 31	Ge 32	As 33	Se 34	Br 35	Kr 36
Rb 37	Sr 38	Y 39	Zr 40	Nb 41	Mo 42	Tc 43	Ru 44	Rh 45	Pd 46	Ag 47	Cd 48	In 49	Sn 50	Sb 51	Te 52	I 53	Xe 54
Cs 55	Ba 56	Lu 71	Hf 72	Ta 73	W 74	Re 75	Os 76	Ir 77	Pt 78	Au 79	Hg 80	Tl 81	Pb 82	Bi 83	Po 84	At 85	Rn 86
Fr 87	Ra 88	Lr 103	Rf 104	Db 105	Sg 106	Bh 107	Hs 108	Mt 109	110	111	112		114		116		118

La 57	Ce 58	Pr 59	Nd 60	Pm 61	Sm 62	Eu 63	Gd 64	Tb 65	Dy 66	Ho 67	Er 68	Tm 69	Yb 70
Ac 89	Th 90	Pa 91	U 92	Np 93	Pu 94	Am 95	Cm 96	Bk 97	Cf 98	Es 99	Fm 100	Md 101	No 102

Elements

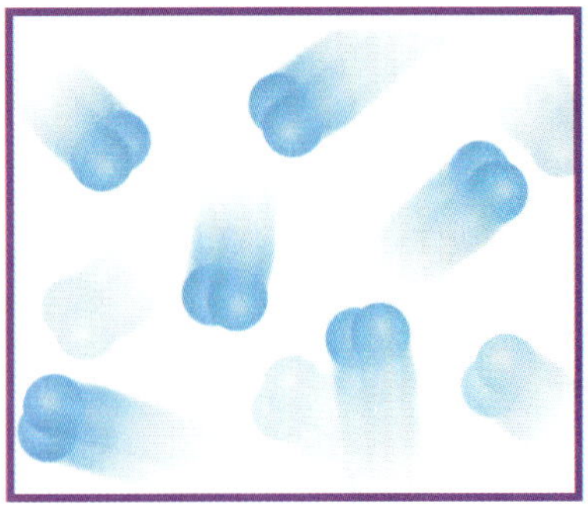

Nitrogen
N_2

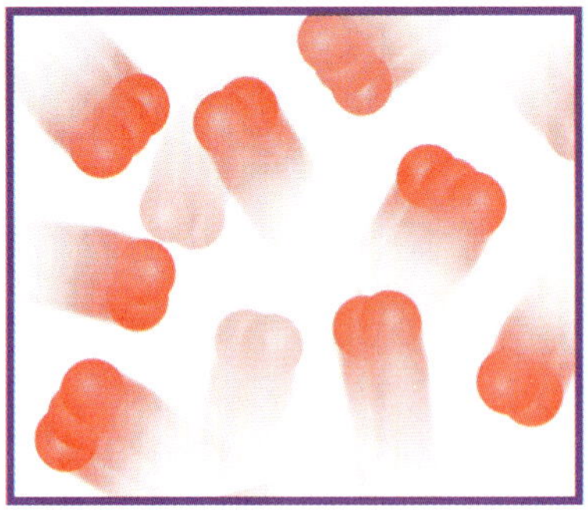

Oxygen
O_2 and O_3

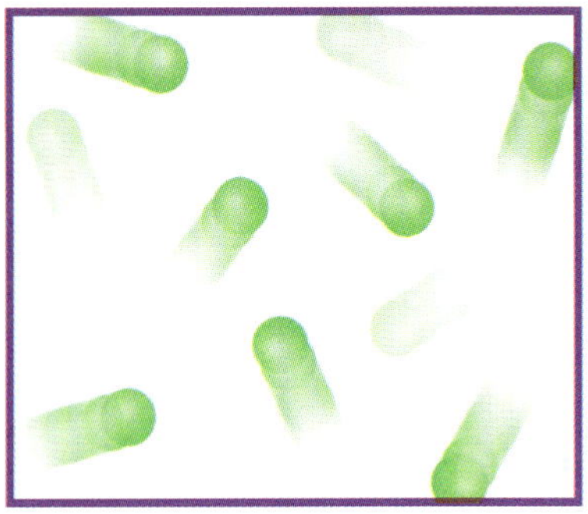

Neon
Ne

Compounds

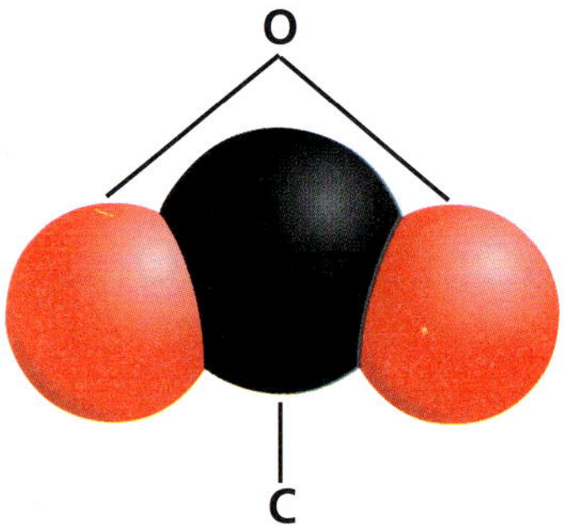

Carbon dioxide
CO_2

Water
H_2O

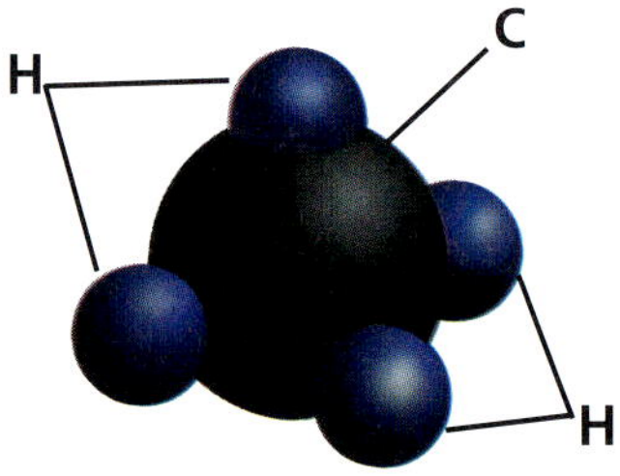

Methane
CH_4
(natural gas)

What Are Molecules?

Some elements, such as neon, are made up of single atoms that do not attach to any other atoms. Other elements have atoms that attach to one or more additional atoms. Particles that contain more than one atom joined together are called **molecules**.

Nitrogen is an example of an element that is made up of molecules. Its molecules are made up of two nitrogen atoms. Some elements even exist in more than one form, such as oxygen. Oxygen is usually made up of two-atom molecules, much like nitrogen, but oxygen can also exist as three-atom molecules. The three-atom form of oxygen is known as ozone. The three-atom ozone has properties different from the two-atom oxygen.

Molecules of elements always contain only one kind of atom. Compounds are made up of molecules that have different kinds of atoms joined together, as the lower diagram shows.

Note how the chemical formulas in both diagrams tell you the number of atoms in the molecules.

When a compound forms from elements, changes occur in the way that atoms are linked together. This causes the compound to have properties different from the elements. For example, water is a liquid, yet it is formed from two gases, hydrogen and oxygen. The diagram shows why water has properties different from hydrogen and oxygen gas—the atoms are linked in a new way when water forms.

What is the difference between a molecule of oxygen and a molecule of methane?

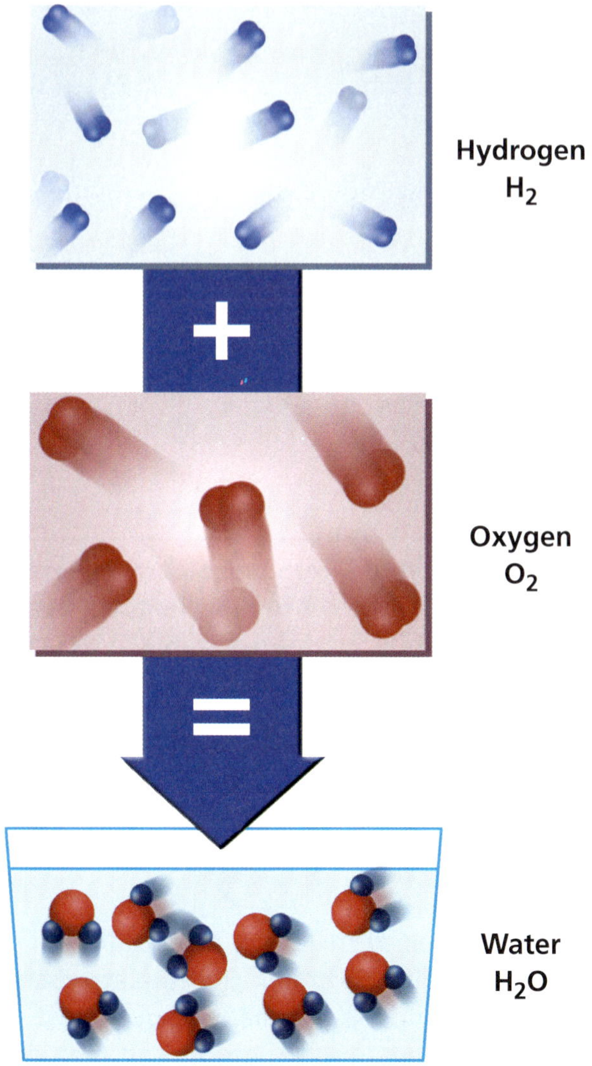

Hydrogen plus oxygen makes water.

FOR SCHOOL OR HOME

Modeling Molecules

1. Using small marshmallows for hydrogen atoms and large marshmallows for oxygen atoms, make two H_2 molecules and one O_2 molecule. Join the atoms with toothpicks.
2. **Use Numbers** Count the number of atoms of each type you have in your molecules. Record these numbers. Take this many more marshmallows and make as many water molecules as you can, using toothpicks to join the atoms.
3. **Observe** How many water molecules did you make?
4. **Infer** Why would real water molecules have properties different from real hydrogen and oxygen molecules?

How Do We Use Compounds?

By studying matter scientists have learned how to prepare compounds that are very useful. Many things are made from the atoms of just a small number of elements. The photographs on this page show several compounds that we depend on a great deal in modern life.

Take petroleum, for example. Petroleum is a complex mixture of *hydrocarbons*—compounds made of hydrogen and carbon atoms. Gasoline comes from petroleum. Its molecules usually have from 5 to 12 carbon atoms in chains. Gasoline gives off a lot of energy when it is burned, so we use it as a fuel in cars.

Many kinds of plastics are also made from hydrocarbons in petroleum or natural gas.

What are some useful compounds?

The bottle is made of polyethylene, a flexible plastic made from hydrocarbons.

Compounds from petroleum are used to make the rubber in this tire's tread. The rubber is treated to make it hard and durable.

This pan is coated with Teflon, a special polymer made of carbon and fluorine atoms. Teflon is very slippery and makes a good, tough, nonstick coating. Teflon doesn't melt at high temperatures as many other plastics do.

Lesson Review

Why It Matters

Imagine what the world would be like if there were no compounds. There wouldn't be any plants. There wouldn't be any water or food or animals or things people build. In fact, there wouldn't be any people either.

New compounds are discovered in nature every day. Scientists also develop new compounds in labs. Many compounds are used to help make life better.

Visit **www.mhscience02.com** to do a research project on the uses of new compounds.

Think and Write

1. Why must some element symbols have two letters instead of just one?
2. A beryllium atom is made of four protons, five neutrons, and four electrons. Draw a model of this type of atom.
3. Give an example of a compound whose properties are much different from the elements it is made of. Describe how it is different.
4. Why do scientists use models to study atoms and molecules?
5. **Critical Thinking** Are all molecules compounds? Explain.

L·I·N·K·S

SOCIAL STUDIES LINK

Write a biography. John Dalton was the scientist who defined atoms. Learn more about his life by doing research. Use the Internet or an encyclopedia.

HEALTH LINK

Research calcium. Calcium is an important element. You need to have calcium-rich foods in your diet. Why does your body need calcium? What foods are a good source of calcium?

ART LINK

Make a model. What is your favorite element? Helium? Oxygen? Copper or iron? Draw a picture or make a model of this element. Include its protons, electrons, and neutrons.

TECHNOLOGY LINK

At the Computer Visit **www.mhscience02.com** for more links.

LESSON 3

Solids, Liquids, and Gases

Vocabulary

state of matter, E36
melting point, E37
boiling point, E37
freezing point, E37

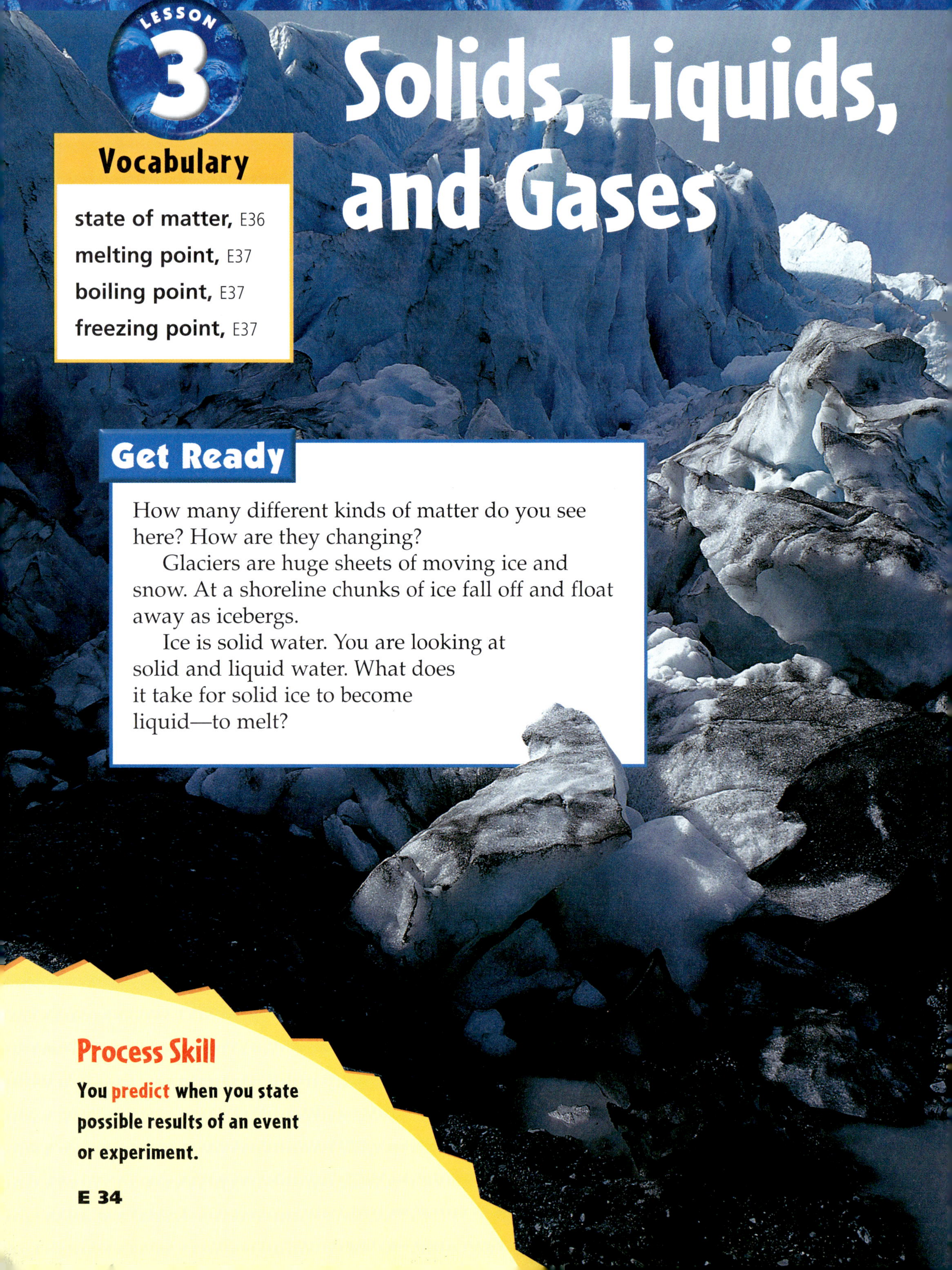

Get Ready

How many different kinds of matter do you see here? How are they changing?

Glaciers are huge sheets of moving ice and snow. At a shoreline chunks of ice fall off and float away as icebergs.

Ice is solid water. You are looking at solid and liquid water. What does it take for solid ice to become liquid—to melt?

Process Skill

You predict when you state possible results of an event or experiment.

Explore Activity

What Happens When Ice Melts?

Procedure

1. **Measure** Put ice cubes in the cup. Add 50 mL of water to the cup. Swirl the ice-and-water mixture together for 15 seconds.
2. **Measure** Place the thermometer in the cup. Wait 15 seconds. Then read the temperature. Record your observation.
3. **Measure** Put the cup under a heat source (lamp or sunlight). Take temperature readings every 3 minutes as the ice melts.
4. **Measure** After all the ice has melted, continue taking temperature readings every 3 minutes for another 15 minutes.

Drawing Conclusions

1. **Observe** What happened to the temperature as the ice melted?
2. **Hypothesize** Why do you think you got the results described in question 1?
3. **Going Further: Predict** What do you think would happen if you didn't add any water to the ice? What do you think would happen if you added more water to the ice? Design an experiment to test each of your predictions. What do you think happens as you freeze water? How would you design an experiment to test your prediction?

Materials

- ice cubes
- water
- graduated cylinder
- plastic or paper cup
- thermometer
- heat source (lamp or sunlight)
- watch or clock

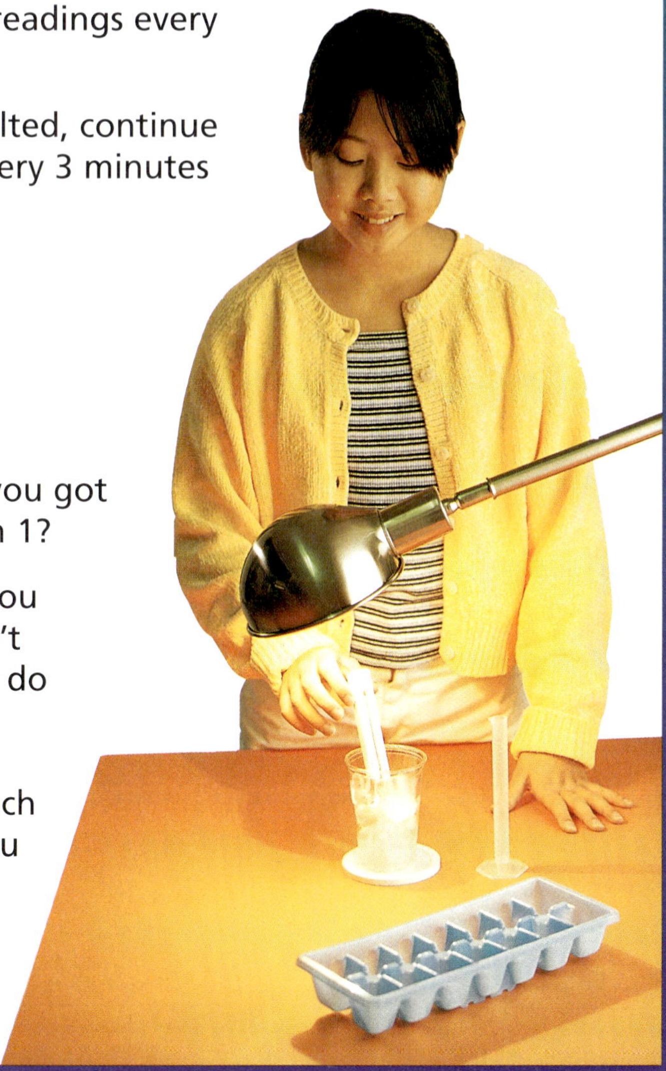

Read to Learn

Main Idea **Matter exists as a solid, a liquid, or a gas.**

What Are the States of Matter?

Water turns from a solid to a liquid when it absorbs enough heat. If even more heat is supplied, the water will turn to a gas called steam. Most substances exist in one of three **states of matter**—*solid, liquid, or gas.* Adding or removing heat can make substances change from one state to another.

When a change of state occurs, the identity of the substance remains the same. However, the substance gains new properties because the molecules are arranged in a different way.

The molecules of any substance are attracted to each other. The attraction is just a weaker form of the force that links the atoms in each of the molecules. When the molecules are arranged in organized positions, a solid results.

When heat is absorbed by a solid, the molecules vibrate faster and faster. At some point the molecules separate from one another. This causes the solid to become a liquid. When even more

Change of State

As heat is absorbed, molecules move faster and become less organized.

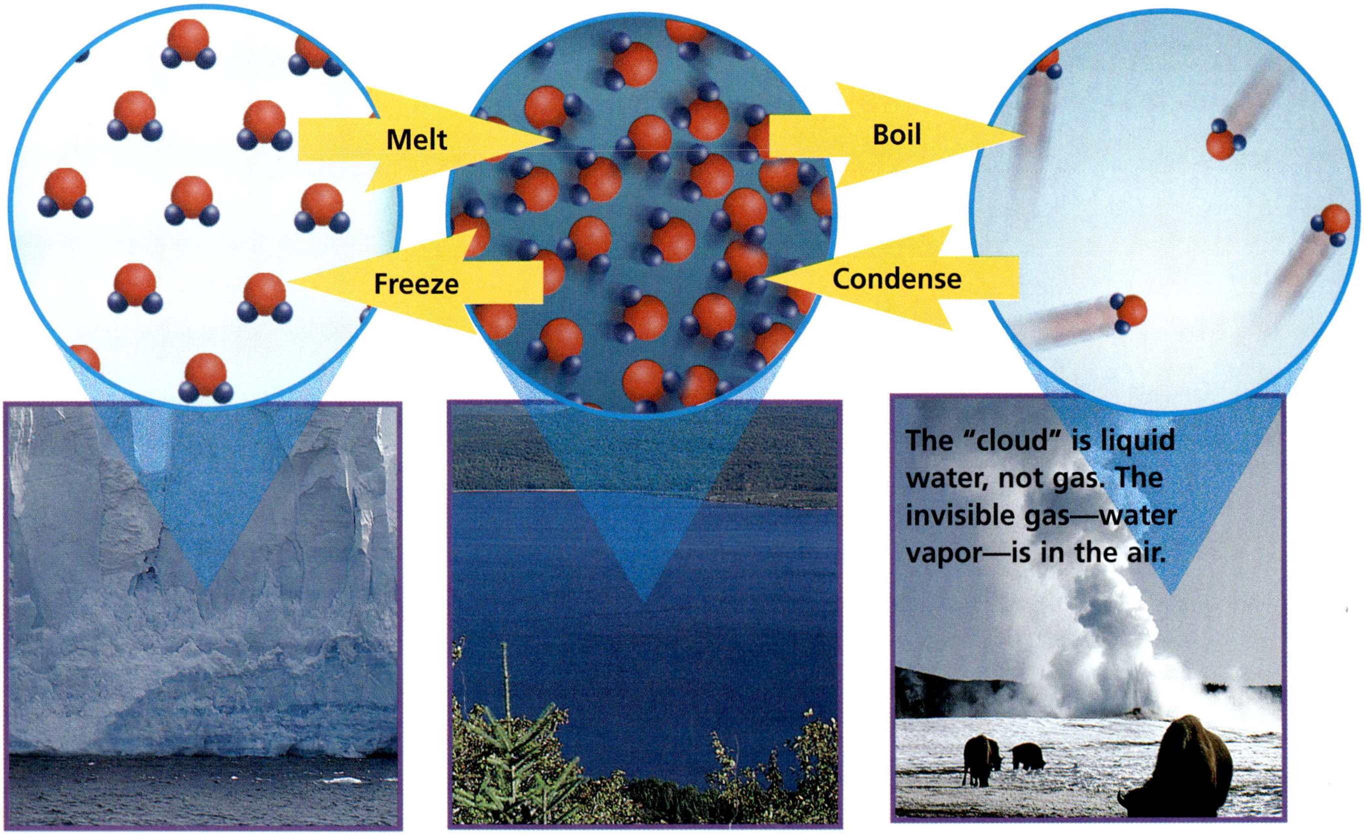

Solid

Liquid

Gas

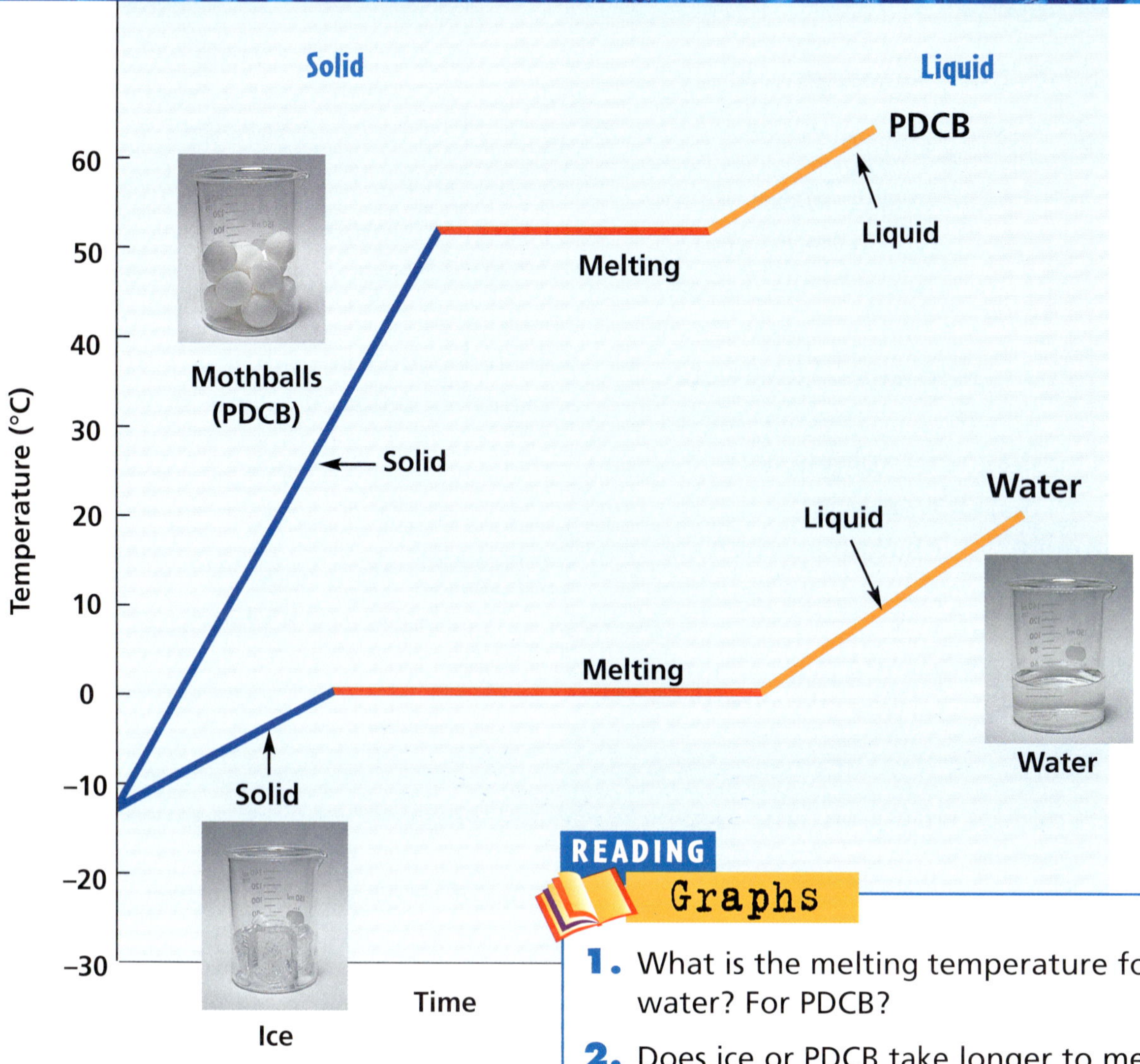

Melting of PDCB and water

READING Graphs

1. What is the melting temperature for water? For PDCB?
2. Does ice or PDCB take longer to melt? Explain how you got your answer.

heat is absorbed, the molecules move faster and form a gas.

The graph shows how the temperatures of two different compounds change as they are being heated. As you can see, these substances melt at different temperatures. In fact, each different pure substance has its own particular **melting point**. Each different substance also has its own boiling temperature, called the **boiling point**.

While a substance is melting or boiling, its temperature stays the same. It warms up only before or after the change of state.

What happens when heat is removed from the substance? It *condenses*—turns from a gas to a liquid—at the boiling temperature. It freezes—turns from a liquid to a solid—at the melting temperature. For this reason the melting point is also known as the **freezing point**.

What are melting and boiling points?

How Can Matter Change to a Gas?

You have probably seen water boiling on the stove. You have probably also observed that water evaporates out of wet clothes. When a liquid evaporates, it gradually changes to a gas. However, when a liquid boils, it changes to a gas rapidly. The diagram explains how boiling and evaporation occur.

Remember what happens when ice melts? The temperature of the melting ice does not change until all the ice has turned to water. Then the water begins to get warmer. In the same way, a substance remains at the same temperature while it boils. This happens because all the heat energy goes into turning the liquid into steam. Once all the liquid becomes steam, the temperature also goes up. The graph on page E39 shows the boiling points of common substances. Note how each substance has a different boiling point.

READING Main Idea
How is evaporation different from boiling?

Evaporation and Boiling

1. A few molecules escape into the air, causing evaporation at room temperature.

2. When the liquid is heated, more molecules escape. The liquid evaporates faster.

3. As more heat is absorbed over time, the liquid reaches its boiling temperature. Boiling begins at the boiling point.

READING Tables

1. Is butane a liquid or a gas at 10°C?
2. Which boils at a lower temperature, rubbing alcohol or oxygen?
3. Which state of matter is lead at 80°C?

Solid and Liquid Ranges of Common Substances (in degrees Celsius)

Name	Formula	Melting Point	Boiling Point
Oxygen	O_2	–218°	–183°
Nitrogen	N_2	–210°	–196°
Butane	C_4H_{10}	–138°	–0.5°
Rubbing alcohol	C_3H_8O	–90°	82.4°
Water	H_2O	0°	100°
Mercury	Hg	–39°	357°
Lead	Pb	327°	1,740°

The table lists the melting points and boiling points of some common substances.

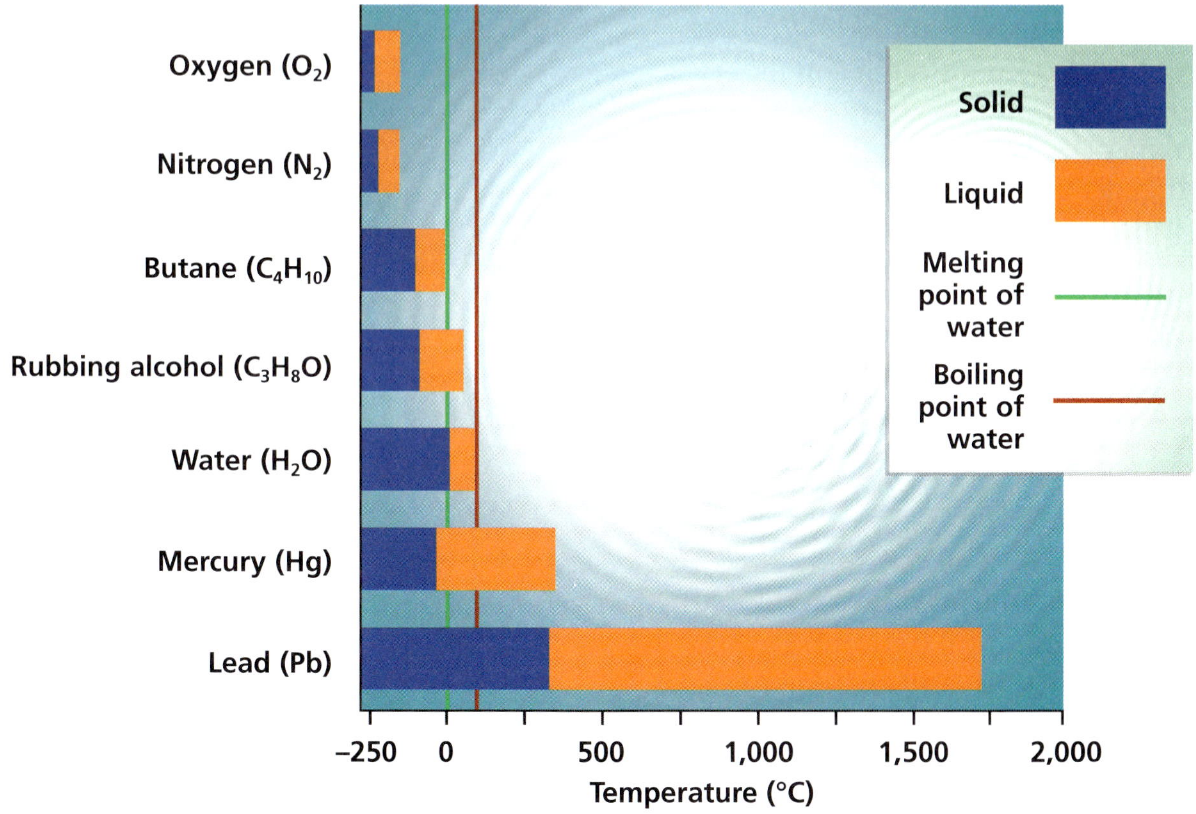

Use this graph to compare the melting points of the substances listed in the table.

What Are the Properties of Solids, Liquids, and Gases?

The aluminum cube in the first photo is a typical solid. It shows that solids retain their shape. Solids have the same volume no matter what container they are placed in. Also, solids cannot be poured, so they are not fluid.

Many solids form crystals, as in the second photograph. A gemlike crystal of alum is shown. The shape of such crystals results from the way the particles are arranged. The particles link together in an organized pattern.

Liquids have different properties from solids. Compare the first and third photographs. In the third photograph, the same volume of a colored liquid has been placed in two different containers. This shows that liquids, unlike solids, take on the shape of their containers. However, liquids do have a definite volume—they settle to the bottom of their containers. Also, as you know from pouring water, liquids are fluid.

Gases do not have a fixed volume of their own. The volume of a gas is determined by its container. The last photograph shows a yellowish gas in a tube separated from a second tube by a glass plate. When the plate is removed, the gas expands to fill both tubes. Gases always fill the full volume of their containers. Also, gases are fluid—they can be pumped through pipelines just like liquids.

Solids keep their shape.

Many solids form crystals.

Liquids take the shape of their containers.

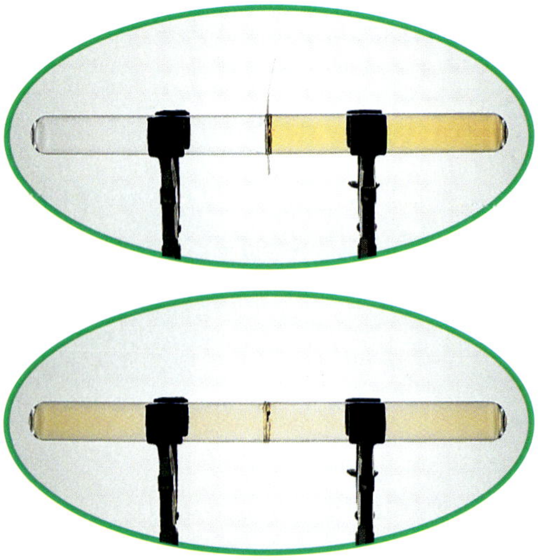

Gases fill the volume of their containers.

Expansion and Contraction

When the temperature of a material increases, its particles move faster. On average these particles tend to spread out more. This causes materials to *expand*—spread out—as they get hotter. The opposite happens when the temperature of a material decreases. Cool materials tend to *contract*—shrink. The material's particles tend to slow down and stay closer together. Gases expand or contract the most with changing temperature, but liquids and solids are also affected by temperature.

You have probably observed expansion and contraction in your everyday life. This property of matter makes bicycle tires and basketballs flat on cold days and your classroom door stick and be difficult to open on hot days. Can you think of other examples?

How are solids, liquids, and gases different?

FOR SCHOOL OR HOME

Collapsing Bottles

1. **Predict** How does heat affect an empty plastic bottle? What do you think will happen to the bottle when it is warmed? What do you think will happen to it when it is cooled? Record your predictions.
2. With the cap off, hold the bottle for a minute or two in a pail of hot tap water. Then screw the cap on tightly while the bottle is still sitting in the hot water.
3. **Experiment** Now hold the bottle in a pail of ice water for a few minutes.
4. **Communicate** Record your observations.
5. **Infer** Write out an explanation of why the bottle changed as it did. Be sure to use the idea of how molecules move at different temperatures.

How Can Expansion and Contraction Be Used?

You have probably had your temperature taken with a thermometer. Thermometers have liquid mercury or colored alcohol in a bulb connected to a very thin tube. The liquid expands or contracts with changes in temperature and moves up or down in the tube. The position of the liquid in the tube gives the temperature.

In the cylinders of a car's engine, burning fuel produces hot, expanding gases. The expanded gas pushes on the pistons in the cylinders. The pistons in turn provide the power that drives the car forward.

The solid materials that make up a bridge or sidewalk expand when warmed. If the sections are assembled tightly on a normal day, they will expand against each other on very hot days. This expansion can cause cracks to form. To guard against this problem, engineers leave some space between the sections and fill it with a flexible material. Look for these "expansion joints" in the photograph above.

Expansion joints keep roads and bridges from cracking on hot days when the road expands.

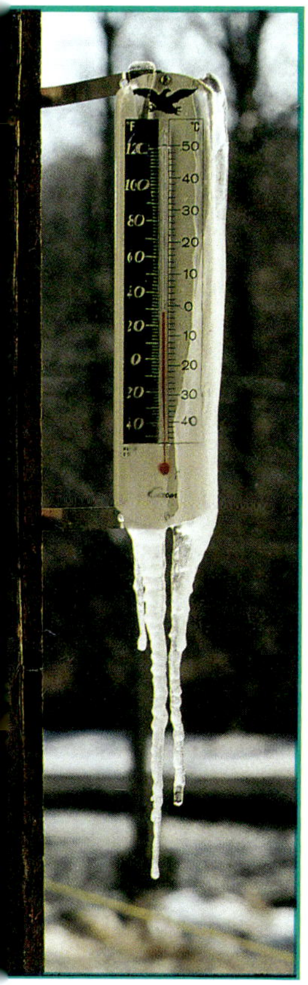

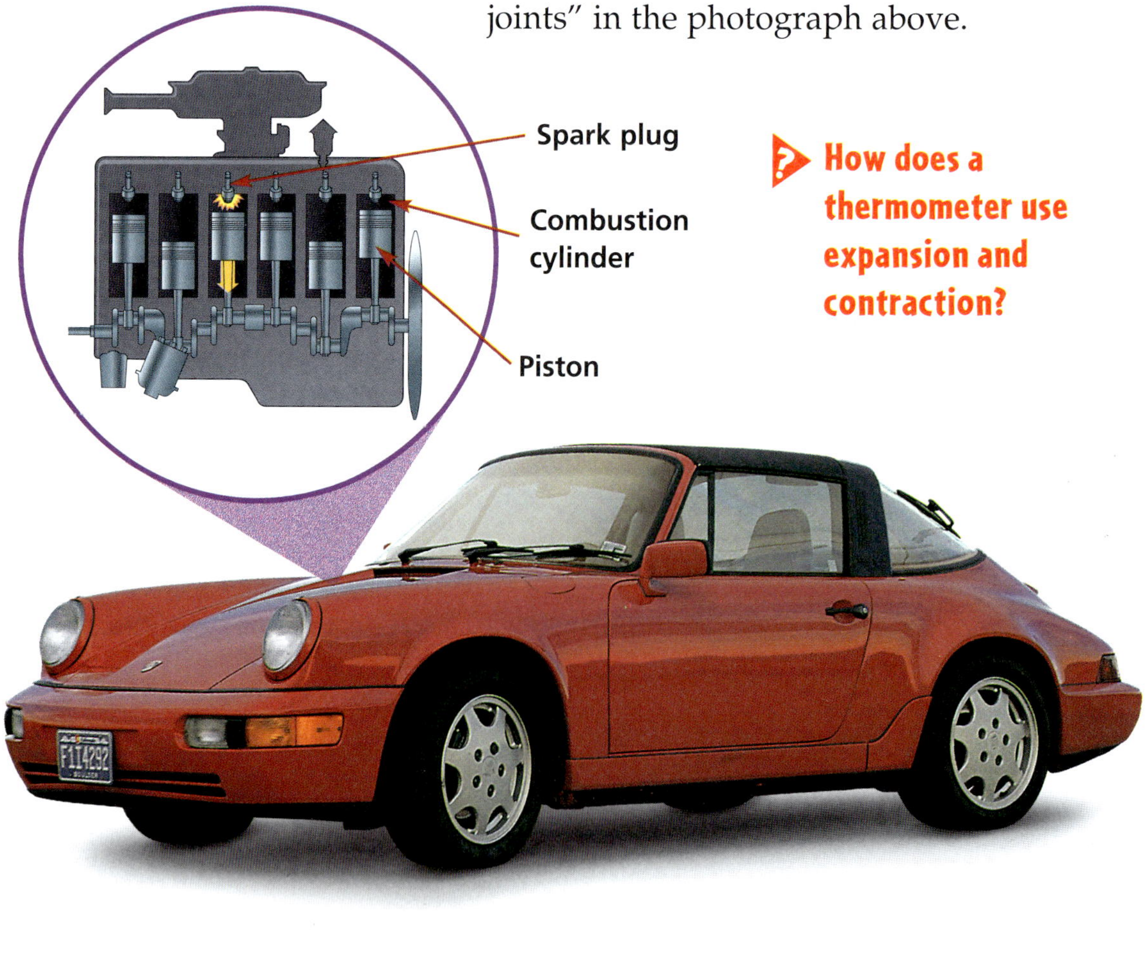

How does a thermometer use expansion and contraction?

Lesson Review

Why It Matters

You sit, write, and climb on solids. Liquids allow you to bathe, swim, and drink. Gases are what you breathe every day. They are what allow you to smell odors at a distance. You learned that gases always fill the full volume of their containers. Did you realize that you notice this property of gases every time you are in your room and smell food cooking in the kitchen?

Think and Write

1. Explain what happens to the temperature of ice as it melts.

2. Acetone freezes at 95.35° below 0°C and boils at 56.2°C. At 42°C what state of matter would acetone be in? At 84°C?

3. Gases can be easily squeezed into a smaller volume. Why is this so?

4. On a hot, damp summer day, drops of water will form on the outside of a glass containing an ice cold drink. Explain how this happens.

5. **Critical Thinking** Water boils at 100°C at sea level. High up in the mountains, water boils at a lower temperature. Why does it take longer to cook potatoes high up in the mountains than it does to cook potatoes at sea level?

L·I·N

LITERATURE LIN

Read ***Chilled to the Bone*** to learn about icy places. Try the activities in the end of the book.

ART LINK

Draw a chart. Make a list of all the things you do before you go to bed at night. How many of these things involve solids? Liquids? Organize the things you use according to the three states of matter. Draw a chart showing how you use matter in its different states.

MATH LINK

Use conversions. Scientists use the Celsius scale to measure temperature. Most people in America, however, measure temperature in Fahrenheit. You can change Celsius into Fahrenheit by multiplying the temperature in Celsius by 9, dividing that number by 5, and then adding 32. Using this method, try to calculate the melting and boiling temperatures of water in Fahrenheit.

TECHNOLOGY LINK

At the Computer Visit **www.mhscience02.com** for more links.

Neon

Neon is a colorless, odorless gas. But something magical happens when electrical current passes through neon. The gas and electricity create brightly colored light.

French chemist Georges Claude discovered neon light around 1910. It wasn't long before glassmakers made fanciful signs using neon. The signs were so beautiful, businesses started using them. Theaters, diners, car dealerships and other businesses used neon signs to advertise. Some signs were huge. One sign for chewing gum was eight stories high and one block long! Some signs had moving tubes to create animated scenes.

To make neon signs, glassblowers heat glass tubes and bend the softened glass into different shapes or letters. Then, neon gas is pumped into the tubes, and they are sealed shut. Wires conduct electrical current into the tubes through electrodes. Electricity speeds back and forth between electrodes at both ends of the tubes. The electrons in the neon start to vibrate. As they vibrate, they release excess energy as light.

Neon light glows bright red. Gases similar to neon create different colors. Argon gas, for example, makes bright green light. With different combinations of gases, certain chemicals, and colored glass, neon artists can create more than a hundred colors. Though different materials are used, they're all called "neon signs."

Bright neon lights have another important use. Airplane pilots use lights on land to guide them to safe landings. The lights are often neon lights because they can penetrate fog. Pilots can see neon lights from far away!

What Did I Learn?

1. What is the first step in making a neon light?

- **A** Neon gas is pumped in a glass tube.
- **B** A glassblower heats a glass tube over a flame.
- **C** The inside of a glass tube is coated with colored powder.
- **D** A glass tube is bent into a certain shape.

2. What color light does neon gas make?

- **F** red
- **G** green
- **H** blue
- **J** yellow

AT THE COMPUTER Visit www.mhscience02.com to learn more about neon and other elements.

Chapter 10 Review

Vocabulary

Fill each blank with the best word or words from the list.

atom, E26
boiling point, E37
density, E8
electron, E27
insulate, E14
mass, E6
molecule, E30
nucleus, E27
proton, E27
state of matter, E36
weight, E7

1. An atomic particle that has a positive charge is called a(n) _____.

2. A substance made of different atoms linked together is called a(n) _____.

3. _____ is a measure of the force of gravity between Earth and an object.

4. A(n) _____ is the smallest unit of an element.

When a compound reaches its **5.** _____, its **6.** _____ changes.

A(n) **7.** _____ is a negatively charged particle in the space outside an atom's **8.** _____.

9. _____ is a measure of matter's **10.** _____ divided by its volume.

Test Prep

11. An object's ability to float depends on its _____.

A size
B temperature
C insulation
D density

12. Water can turn from liquid to gas by evaporating or _____.

F condensing
G pouring
H boiling
J freezing

13. Mass is the measure of the _____.

A amount of material in an object
B weight of an object
C space an object takes up
D density of an object

14. The molecules of a _____ tend to be packed tightly in an organized way.

F gas
G solid
H liquid
J neutron

15. The number of _____ an atom has determines what element it is.

A electrons

B neutrons

C protons

D charges

Concepts and Skills

16. Process Skills: Make a Model Scientists use a variety of models to understand and explain the natural world. A formula such as H_2O is a model for water. Tell what the formula means. Give another example of a chemical formula, and tell what it means.

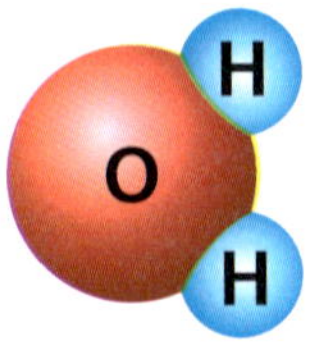

17. Reading in Science What is the main difference between mass and weight? Support your answers with any facts or details necessary.

18. Scientific Methods Which do you think would evaporate faster—pure water or salt water? Why? Describe an experiment that would test your idea.

19. Critical Thinking Are all molecules compounds? Explain your answer.

20. Product Ads Teflon is an artificial compound. It is a "nonstick" plastic. What products might advertise the use of this material?

CHAPTER 11

Forms of Matter and Energy

Did You Ever Wonder?

Where does the steel used to build bridges and skyscrapers come from? Steel is a mixture of several different elements, including iron, carbon, and nickel. Is the process of making steel a physical change or a chemical change? How are the properties of steel different from the properties of the metals that make it up?

LESSON 4

Mixtures and Solutions

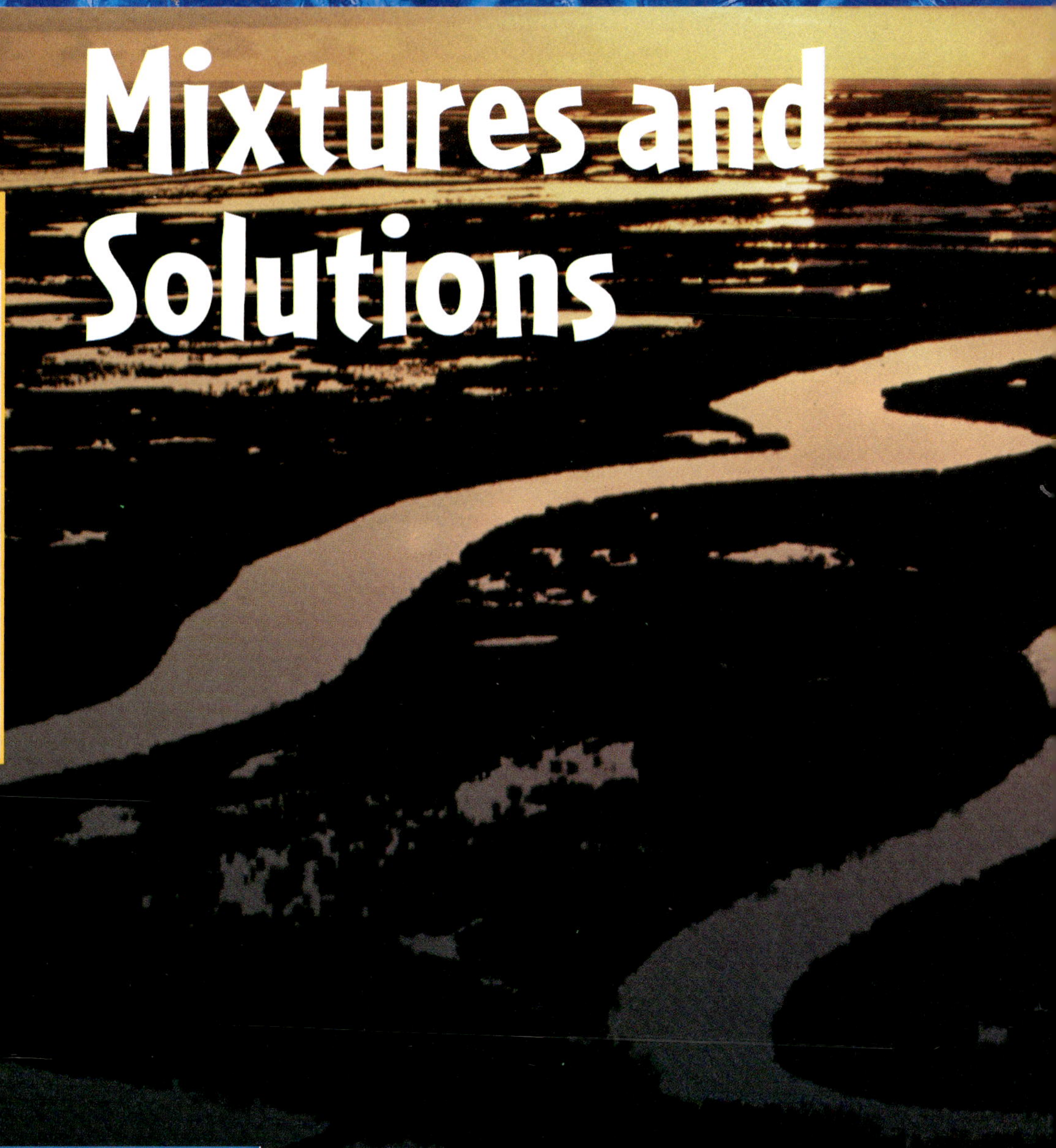

Vocabulary

mixture, E52
solution, E54
colloid, E54
suspension, E59
emulsion, E60
aerosol, E60
gel, E60
foam, E60

Get Ready

Why do people call the Mississippi River the "muddy Mississippi"? What happens when the muddy Mississippi flows into the Gulf of Mexico?

The flowing water of the river joins with standing water in the gulf. The river drops much of what it is carrying.

The Mississippi is made of things mixed together. How many other examples can you give of things that are mixed together?

Process Skill

You observe when you use one or more of the senses to identify or learn about an object or event.

Explore Activity

How Can You Take Apart Things That Are Mixed Together?

Procedure: Design Your Own

BE CAREFUL! Wear goggles. Do not taste your sample.

1. **Observe** Examine the sample your teacher gives you. It is made of different substances. One of the substances is table salt. What else does it seem to be made of? Record your observations.

2. **Experiment** Design and carry out an experiment to separate the various ingredients in your sample.

Drawing Conclusions

1. **Infer** How many parts or substances were mixed into your sample? How did you reach that conclusion?

2. You knew one substance was salt. What properties of salt might help you separate it from the rest? Could you separate salt first? Why or why not?

3. How did you separate out the substances? How did you use the properties of these substances to separate them?

4. **Going Further: Experiment** What if you were given white sand and sugar mixed together? How would you separate the two ingredients?

Materials

- sample of substances mixed together
- hand lens
- toothpicks
- magnet
- paper (coffee) filters
- 2 cups or beakers
- water
- goggles

Read to Learn

Main Idea Substances can combine to form mixtures.

What Is a Mixture?

The iron filings and yellow sulfur powder in the first photo have been stirred together. The two materials were *physically* combined. The result is a **mixture**.

The substance shown in the second photograph, iron disulfide, also contains both iron and sulfur. However, now the iron and sulfur are *chemically* combined, and a new substance is formed, a compound.

How do mixtures and compounds differ? Compounds are produced by chemically combining substances. Mixtures are produced by a physical combination of substances. In mixtures the parts simply blend together without forming new substances. Differences in chemical and physical properties of substances are used to separate mixtures and identify compounds.

A compound has different properties from the substances it contains. For example, iron disulfide is not magnetic, while pure iron is. In contrast, the parts of a mixture keep their original properties. Even though the iron has been mixed with sulfur in the first picture, it remains magnetic. You could use a magnet to remove the iron filings from the mixture.

When iron filings and yellow sulfur powder are stirred together to make a *mixture*, the substances keep their original properties. The iron remains magnetic. You could use a magnet to remove the iron filings.

This is *iron disulfide*, a mineral known as iron pyrite, or "fool's gold." Iron disulfide is a compound of iron and sulfur. When a *compound* forms, it has different properties from the substances it contains. Unlike iron, iron disulfide is not magnetic.

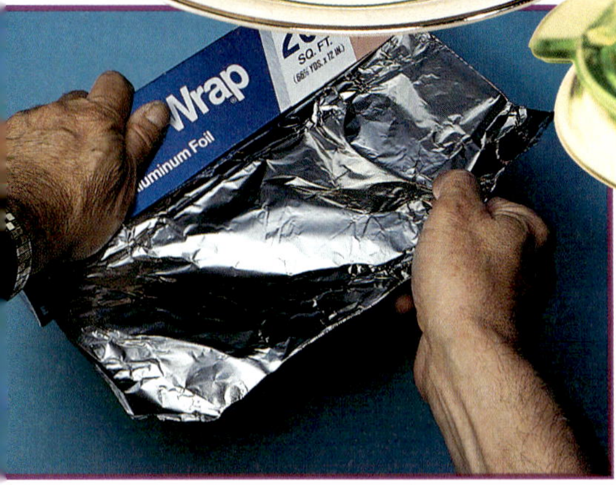

Here are a number of household materials. Which are mixtures? Which are either elements or compounds?

What if you stir one spoonful of sugar into a glass of water to make a sugar-water mixture? A friend could stir two spoonfuls of sugar into the same amount of water. You would both have the same kind of mixture. However, your friend's drink would have a much sweeter taste.

Like the sugar water, any type of mixture can contain varying amounts of the parts that make it up. Salt water could be barely salty or very salty. Granola cereal could have many or few raisins. Tea could be strong or weak, and so on.

On the other hand, compounds are always made up in the same way. For example, about two-fifths of the mass of any sample of table salt is sodium, and three-fifths is chlorine.

What is the difference between compounds and mixtures?

How Can Mixtures Be Classified?

Mixtures are not pure substances because they contain more than one element or compound. If the substances in a mixture are blended completely, the mixture looks the same everywhere, or is *homogeneous* (hoh·muh·JEE·nee·uhs). We call such mixtures **solutions**. There are many different types of solutions. Look at the table on page E55 for examples of some common solutions.

On the other hand, the parts of a mixture may be only partly blended. The mixture may look "speckled," either to your eye or through a microscope. This type of mixture is said to be *heterogeneous* (het·uhr·uh·JEE·nee·uhs). Most mixtures are heterogeneous. Rivers contain a mixture of water, rock, and soil. Stones are heterogeneous, too.

Some mixtures are neither solutions nor heterogeneous mixtures. These mixtures are called **colloids**. Colloids have properties in between those of solutions and heterogeneous mixtures. Like solutions, there are many types of colloids. The chart on page E55 shows some of these.

What are three types of mixtures?

A lunch of a chicken salad sandwich, tea, and gelatin dessert with whipped cream contains each type of mixture. Can you tell which one is which?

Types of Solutions

Substance	Dissolved In	Examples
Liquid	liquid gas solid	cranberry juice in water water dissolved in air mercury in silver (dental fillings)
Gas	liquid gas	carbon dioxide in soda oxygen and nitrogen in air
Solid	liquid solid gas	salt in water copper and zinc mixed in brass mothballs

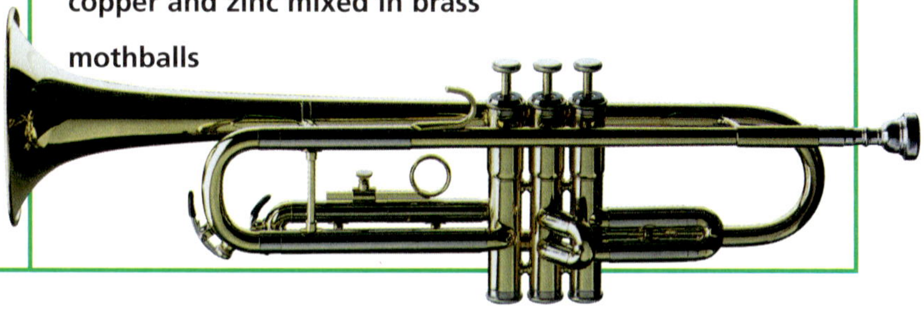

Types of Colloids

Substance	Mixed In	Examples
Liquid	liquid gas solid	mayonnaise clouds jam
Gas	liquid solid	shaving cream marshmallows
Solid	liquid gas	toothpaste smog

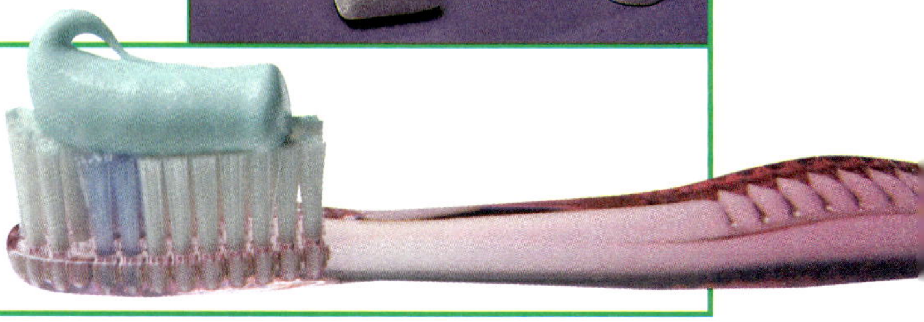

What Kinds of Solutions Are There?

You are already familiar with many solutions. In fact, you are surrounded by them all the time. The atmosphere contains a very important solution—air. Seawater is another type of solution.

Solutions are usually transparent or are evenly colored. They never settle into layers. They are the same all the way through.

Not all solutions are liquid. The flask contains a solution of two gaseous compounds, NO_2 and N_2O_4. NO_2 is red-brown, while N_2O_4 is colorless.

Solutions come in many different forms. Air is an example of a gaseous solution. Nitrogen, oxygen, and a small amount of other gases mix evenly together. One breath of air is always made up of 78 percent nitrogen and 20 percent oxygen gas.

Seawater is an example of a liquid solution. Tea and your favorite fruit punch are other examples. These solutions are all made from solids that dissolve in a liquid—water. Liquid solutions can also be made by mixing two liquids together, as in nail polish remover. Mixing a liquid with a gas, as in a bottle of soda, is another way to form a liquid solution.

Solutions may also be solid. Alloys are solid solutions. They are made by mixing two or more metals together. Bronze, steel, and brass are all alloys.

The properties of an alloy can be varied by changing the amounts of pure metals it contains. The stainless steel used in silverware uses only a slightly different mixture of elements than the

This bridge is made of an alloy, steel.

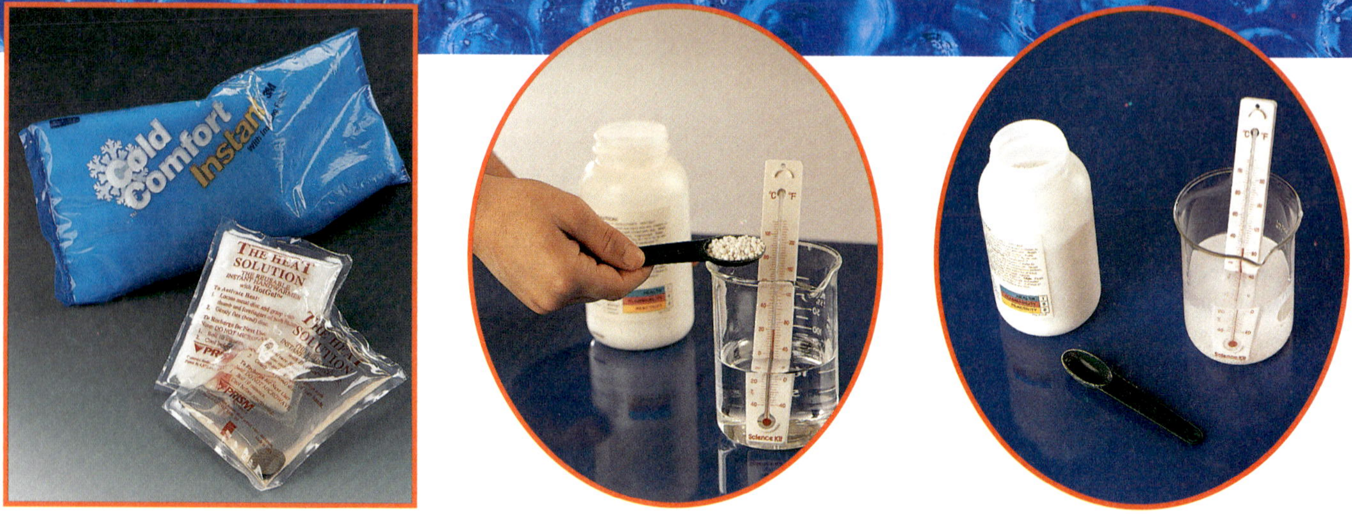

Heat is released when calcium chloride dissolves in water. Hot packs can be used to warm your hands on a cold day for this reason.

high-strength steel you might find in construction.

Solutes and Solvents

Solutions may form in many different ways. However, no matter how they form, all solutions have two parts. The substance that makes up the smaller part of a solution is called the *solute*. The substance that makes up the larger amount is the *solvent*. The solute dissolves in the solvent to form a homogeneous mixture. All solutions

consist of at least one solute and one solvent.

Think about the examples on page E56. What is the solvent in fruit punch? What is the solute in seawater? Think about which of the substances is in the greater amount.

Water is an important solvent. Many different kinds of compounds can dissolve in water, such as salts, minerals, proteins, and sugars. Nutrients from food dissolve and are carried through your body because of the water in blood.

Some solute and solvent pairs give off or absorb heat when they are combined. Hot and cold packs use this property of solutions. Calcium chloride is a salt that releases a great deal of heat when it is mixed with water. A hot pack often contains a small pouch of this salt in a sealed package of water. When the package is struck, the pouch of salt breaks open. This allows the salt to dissolve. Heat is then released.

What are five types of solutions?

FOR SCHOOL OR HOME

Solubility

1. **Measure** Add 100 mL of water to each of three cups. Place a sugar cube in one of the cups, and stir until the cube is dissolved. Record the time it took to dissolve.
2. **Predict** Carefully break a second sugar cube into two pieces. How long do you think it will take to dissolve? Place the two pieces in a second cup of water, and stir until they dissolve. Record the time they took to dissolve.
3. **Use Variables** Fold a piece of paper around a sugar cube, and carefully break the cube into many pieces. Pour the pieces into the third cup of water, and stir until dissolved. Record the dissolving time.
4. **Interpret Data** Construct a graph that illustrates your findings. Which sugar cube dissolved the fastest?
5. What conclusion can you make regarding dissolving time based on the experiment?

What Is Solubility?

Have you ever tried making fruit punch from a mix? How easy is it to get all of the mix to dissolve? Solutes act differently in different solvents. This property describes *solubility.* Solubility explains the ability of a solute to dissolve in a solvent.

Many things affect solubility. Temperature is an example. Most solutes dissolve more quickly when a solvent is hot. Sugar is more soluble in hot tea than in cold, iced tea.

The amount and type of solute and solvent also affect solubility. Some substances do not dissolve in others. Oil does not dissolve in water. It is *insoluble* in water. It does dissolve in other substances, like dish detergent, however. The structure of a substance determines its solubility in different solvents.

Most solute-solvent combinations have a limit of how much solute will dissolve in a volume of solvent. After that limit is reached, no more solute will dissolve. You may observe this when you add sugar to a glass of lemonade. After a few teaspoons, the sugar settles to the bottom of the glass, and no more sugar will dissolve.

What are some factors that affect solubility?

What Are Heterogeneous Mixtures Like?

Rocks are an example of heterogeneous mixtures. Tomato sauce, casseroles, and taco salads are also familiar examples.

Heterogeneous mixtures are even more common than solutions. Heterogeneous mixtures, unlike solutions, settle into layers in a fluid. Oil-and-vinegar salad dressing separates when it is left alone, for example.

Heterogeneous mixtures are either cloudy or opaque. They are not evenly mixed. Think of a pot of chicken soup. One ladle may have a lot of carrots. The next may have few carrots and a lot of rice. One part of a mixture may have more of one substance than another.

Mixtures like clay and water, with particles that are easily seen, are called **suspensions**. Suspensions form when one substance is insoluble, or does not dissolve in a solvent.

Rocks are heterogeneous mixtures. They are composed of pieces or layers of different minerals.

What are the characteristics of heterogeneous mixtures?

Heterogeneous Mixtures Can Settle into Layers

Freshly shaken mixtures of clay and water, and oil and water

The mixtures after they were allowed to stand for a length of time

The fog in this scene is a colloid called an aerosol. Aerosols have either liquid drops or solid particles spread through a gas. Fog is made of tiny drops of water suspended in air.

What Types of Colloids Are There?

Milk is not transparent, so it cannot be a solution. It does not settle out into layers, so it is not a heterogeneous mixture. Milk is a colloid. Like milk, all colloids have properties between those of solutions and heterogeneous mixtures.

The photograph on page E61 shows what milk looks like under a microscope—droplets of fat spread throughout water. Other colloids are similar. They have particles of one material scattered through another. The particles are big enough to block or scatter light but not big enough to settle out.

There are many types of colloids. Milk is an example of an **emulsion**, a liquid (fat) spread through another liquid (water).

Another type of colloid is called an **aerosol**. Aerosols have either liquid drops or solid particles spread through a gas. Fog is made of tiny drops of water suspended in air.

Many food products are colloids. Gelatin dessert is a **gel**. A gel is a solid spread through a liquid. The solid in the gelatin is protein. The liquid in the gelatin is water.

Whipped cream is a **foam**. A foam is a gas spread through a liquid. The gas in the whipped cream is air. The

liquid in the whipped cream is water and fat. Marshmallows are a solid foam—a gas spread through a solid. The gas in the marshmallows is air. The solid in the marshmallows is a sweetened gelatin.

What are four types of colloids?

FOR SCHOOL OR HOME

Kitchen Colloids

1. Pour some whipping cream into a bowl. Set this bowl in a bed of ice in another bowl. Let the cream and bowl chill.
2. **Experiment** Use a whisk to whip the cream until it becomes a fluffy texture.
3. **Observe** Let the cream warm, and continue beating it. Observe how it changes. Record your observations.
4. **Define** What kind of colloid is the whipped cream in step 2?
5. **Interpret Data** What is it made of?
6. **Infer** In step 3 you made a colloid. What is this colloid commonly known as? What do you think it is made of?

How Can Mixtures Be Separated?

We can separate the parts of mixtures using methods called physical separations. A physical separation gets the parts of a mixture away from one another without changing their identities.

We can use the different properties of matter to separate mixtures. Density, magnetism, and boiling and melting temperatures are all helpful tools.

The illustrations on these pages show examples of physical separation methods. Study them to see the steps and equipment needed.

What properties might you use to separate mixtures?

The mud particles cannot pass through the pores in the paper, but the water molecules can. The mud collects in the paper, while the water drips through.

1 To separate a mixture of sand and salt, pour in water and stir. The salt dissolves, but the sand doesn't.

2 Use a filter to separate the sand from the salt water.

3 Then let the water evaporate to get back the salt.

Separating Sand and Wood Chips

To separate sand and wood chips, first pour in water. Stir briefly.

The wood chips float to the top, while the sand settles to the bottom. The wood chips can be skimmed off and dried. The water can be poured off, and the sand dried.

Separating Alcohol and Water

You could separate alcohol and water by heating them in this apparatus.

Alcohol and water are heated. Alcohol boils at a lower temperature than water, so at the beginning, more of the vapor will be alcohol than water.

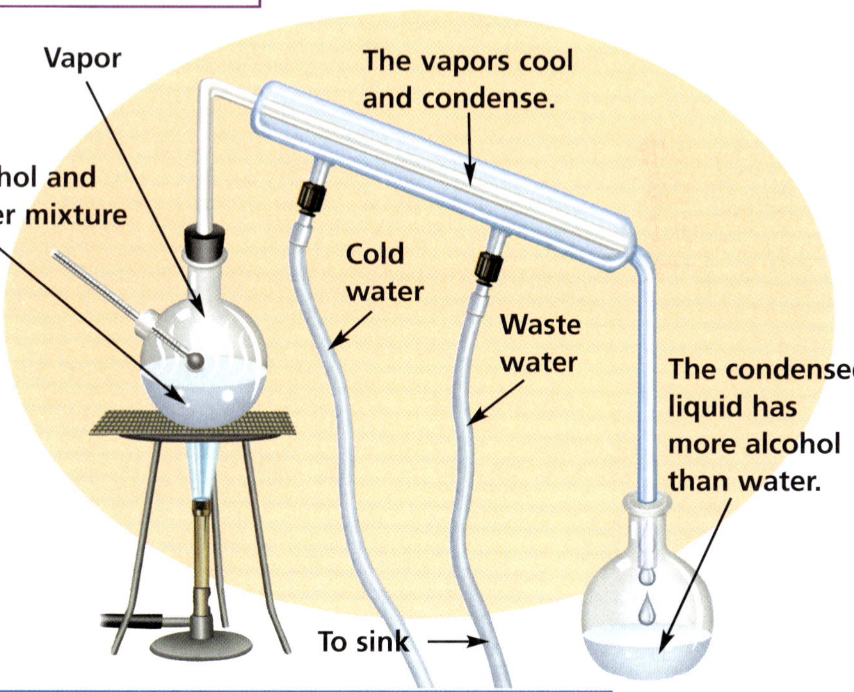

READING Diagrams

1. What is one way to separate two substances in a mixture?
2. Could you separate sand and wood chips the same way you separate sand and salt? Explain.
3. Make a list of three ways to separate parts of a mixture.

Which Resources Come from Mixtures?

Many of Earth's resources exist as mixtures. Ores are mixtures that provide us with metals and minerals. Seawater is a mixture that can be used as a resource for fresh water, thanks to desalination—another separation process.

Crude oil, our major energy source, is a mixture, too. The diagram below shows a process called *distillation*. We use this process to separate important chemicals out of crude oil.

First, the crude oil is heated until it becomes a gas. Then, the vapors are sent to the tower. There they rise and cool. As they cool, they condense to form liquids.

The substances with large molecules and high boiling points quickly cool into a liquid. The substances with small molecules and low boiling points rise higher in the tower before condensing. The condensed liquids are drawn off as shown.

READING **Cause and Effect** **How can we get resources from mixtures?**

Distillation

Crude oil is heated until it becomes a gas. The vapors are sent to the tower. There they rise, cool, and condense to form liquids. Substances with smaller molecules and lower boiling points rise higher in the tower before condensing.

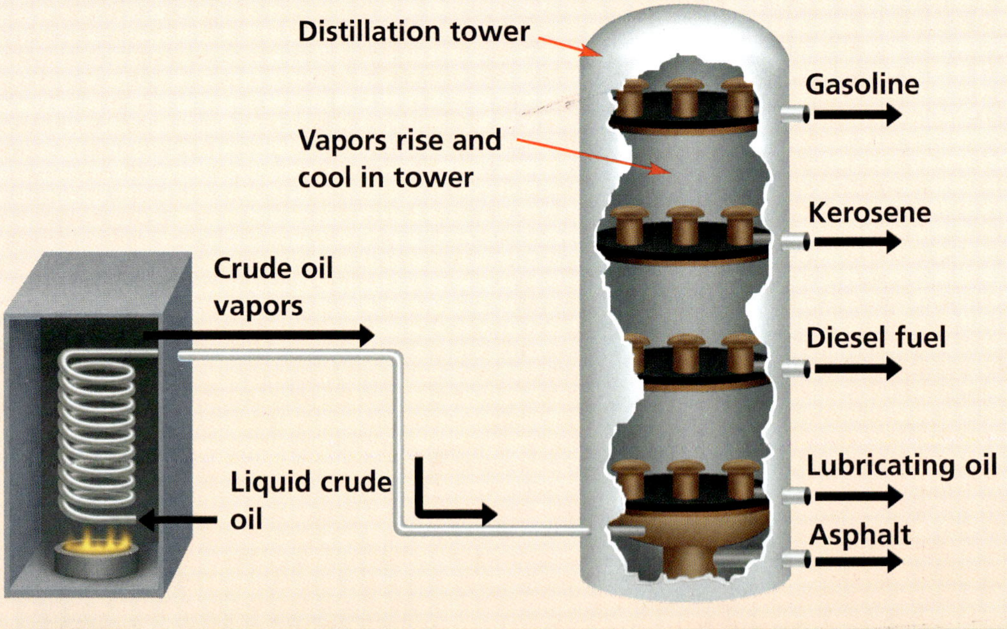

Lesson Review

Why It Matters

Many things you use every day—from the air you breathe to the milk you drink to the steel in your bicycle—are mixtures. Some mixtures need to have just the right amounts of their ingredients each time. For example, you need a certain amount of oxygen in the air you breathe. The amount of iron, carbon, and other metals in steel determines its properties, such as hardness and resistance to rusting.

As you go through your day, think of all the mixtures you use and why they are important to you.

Think and Write

1. How do the properties of sugar and water alone compare with the properties of a sugar-water solution?
2. How are mixtures different from compounds?
3. Air is a mixture of oxygen and nitrogen gas. What type of mixture is air? Why?
4. Oil paints are made of colored particles spread through an oil. Are oil paints solutions, heterogeneous mixtures, or colloids? How do you know?
5. **Critical Thinking** Describe the steps you could follow to separate a mixture of sawdust and salt.

L·I·N·K·S

ART LINK

Make a collage. Cut pictures of mixtures from magazines. Paste them on a board. Tell your classmates which are solutions, colloids, and heterogeneous mixtures.

MATH LINK

Make a graph. Air is a solution of gases. Research what the gases are and how much of each gas is in air. Show the results in a graph.

WRITING LINK

Write a poem. Many meals are made from a mixture of foods, like salad, casserole, and pizza. Sometimes the mixture tastes better than the ingredients by themselves. Write a poem about a dish like this. Tell about all the ingredients that are part of this mixture.

TECHNOLOGY LINK

Science Newsroom CD-ROM Choose *Here's the Solution* to learn how the three types of mixtures are similar.

At the Computer Visit **www.mhscience02.com** for more links.

Got Milk? Got Butter?

The success of mammals on Earth is helped by what they feed their newborns: milk produced by their mothers. Humans also raise other large mammals to produce milk for them.

A mammal's milk is seven-eighths water, but the other eighth has nearly everything needed for good health! Some food value comes from the lactose, or milk sugar, dissolved in it.

Milk has a lot of fat globs. Because they're lighter than water, the globs rise to the top of a container. Gravity pulls the heavier liquid down. The fat globs merge to become cream. Milk with little or no fat is skim milk.

Many people prefer skim or low-fat milk. The fat in milk contributes to weight problems, heart disease, and possibly other diseases.

Milk you buy has vitamins D and A added to make it more nutritious. It's been pasteurized—heated to kill disease-causing bacteria. The heating also makes some milk proteins inactive and slows down the spoiling.

Milk is homogenized by putting it through a fine screen to break fat globs into tiny specks. They're so small that the movement of the other molecules in milk keeps them from rising. For that reason cream doesn't form at the top of homogenized milk.

By constantly moving cream in a closed container, you cause the fat globs to merge. Drain off the thin, watery stuff and you've got . . . butter!

Automatic Milking Machine

Write ABOUT IT

1. What other foods are vitamins added to? Why do you think that is done?
2. Fat is used to make cells' outer membranes. How does this explain why mammals' milk is high in fat?

AT THE COMPUTER

Visit www.mhscience02.com to learn more about milk products.

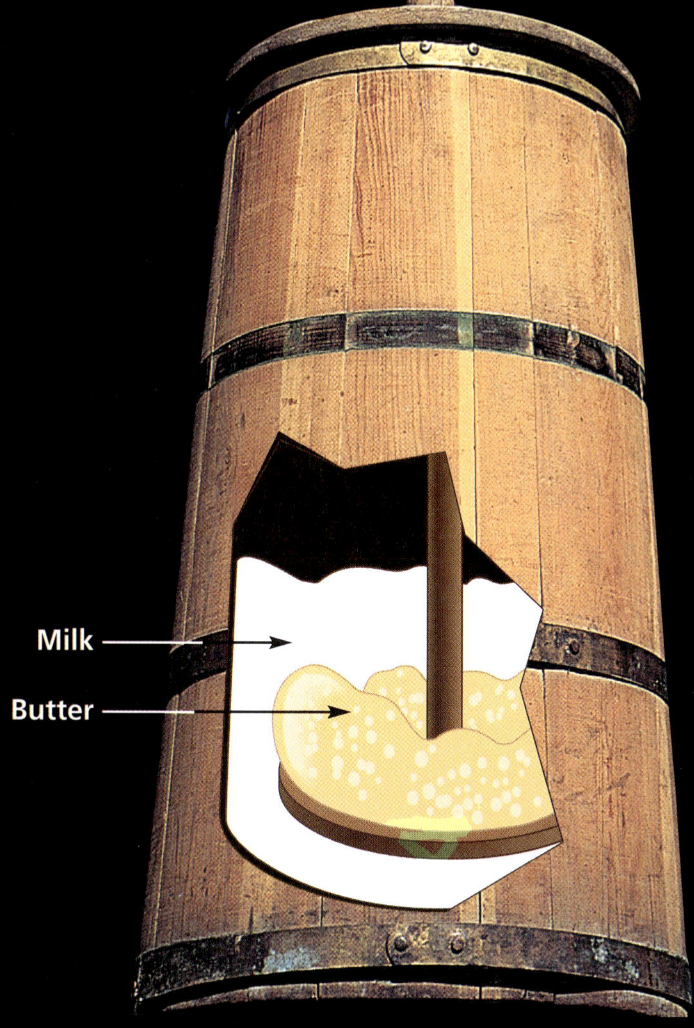

An old-fashioned churn stirs up milk to form butter.

LESSON 5

Chemical Changes

Vocabulary

- **physical change,** E70
- **chemical change,** E71
- **chemical reaction,** E71
- **reactant,** E71
- **product,** E71

Get Ready

How can you tell changes occur? Metal rusts. Milk sours. Bread dough rises when baking powder is mixed into it. A runny egg hardens when it is cooked. What are other changes going on around you?

Process Skill

You infer when you form an idea from facts or observations.

Explore Activity

How Can You Recognize a Change?

Procedure

BE CAREFUL! Wear goggles.

1 Copy this grid on wax paper with a marking pen. Using a spoon, put a pea-sized amount of cornstarch in each of the three boxes in the first row.

2 **Observe** Use a dropper to add five drops of water to the cornstarch in the first column. Stir with a toothpick. Record your observations.

3 **Experiment** Using a different dropper, add five drops of vinegar to the cornstarch in the second column. Stir with a new toothpick. Record your observations.

4 **Observe** Use a third dropper to add five drops of iodine solution to the cornstarch in the third column. Record your observations.
CAUTION: Iodine can stain and is poisonous.

5 **Experiment** Repeat steps 1–4 for baking powder, baking soda, and salt.

Drawing Conclusions

1 **Infer** In which boxes of the grid do you think substances changed into new substances? Explain your answers.

2 **Going Further: Infer** Your teacher will give you samples of two unknown powders. Use what you have learned to identify these powders. Report on your findings.

	Water	Vinegar	Iodine Solution
Cornstarch			
Baking powder			
Baking soda			
Salt			

Materials

- baking soda
- baking powder
- cornstarch
- salt
- iodine solution
- vinegar
- water
- wax paper
- permanent marker
- 4 toothpicks
- 3 droppers
- 4 plastic spoons
- 7 small cups
- goggles

Read to Learn

Main Idea **Matter can undergo chemical as well as physical changes.**

What Are Physical and Chemical Changes?

Different kinds of changes are going on all the time. In a **physical change**, matter changes in size, shape, or state without also changing identity.

In Lesson 3 you learned about the states of matter. Change of state is an example of a physical change. A substance can change from solid to liquid to gas. The substance does not change its chemical identity in this process. Its state simply changes. The photograph below shows why a change of state is a physical change.

You also learned in Lesson 4 about mixtures. Combining two substances to form a solution is another example of physical change. The two substances do not lose their identities. They can be physically separated from each other to give back the original substances. The photograph above shows this kind of physical change.

When baking soda mixes with water, the baking soda seems to disappear. However, when the water evaporates, baking soda is left behind. This is a physical change.

A change of state is a physical change. When the steam—gaseous water—hits the dish, it cools and turns back into liquid water.

The photo on page E68 shows a **chemical change**. Chemical changes occur when atoms link together in new ways. The changes cause new compounds to form. The new compounds have properties different from the original substances from which they were formed.

The reaction between vinegar and baking soda is an example of a chemical change. When these two materials are mixed, gas bubbles form. A change in the linking pattern of the atoms in the vinegar and baking soda causes a new substance—carbon dioxide—to form. Other new substances form, too. However, you cannot see them because they remain in the liquid.

Chemical changes are often referred to as **chemical reactions**. The original substances are called the **reactants**. The new substances produced by the chemical reaction are called the **products**. During chemical reactions the atoms in the reactants rearrange to form products with different properties. In the reaction between baking soda and vinegar, the baking soda and the vinegar are the reactants. The carbon dioxide, water, and a chemical called sodium acetate are the products.

READING

Cause and Effect
What happens during a chemical change?

What happens when baking soda and vinegar mix?

STARTING SUBSTANCES				NEW SUBSTANCES
$NaHCO_3$	+	CH_3COOH	→	$H_2O + CO_2 + NaC_2H_3O_2$
Baking soda	+	Acetic acid (part of vinegar)	→	Water + Carbon dioxide + Sodium acetate

What Are the Signs of a Chemical Change?

Chemical reactions often show one or more signs that a chemical change has occurred. These signs include a color change, formation of a gas, and formation of light and heat. The reactions on these pages show some of these signs.

Does a chemical reaction occur when reddish brown iodine is placed on a potato? The iodine reacts with starch in the potato. The white starch and iodine change to a bluish black color.

When reddish blueberry juice is mixed with a solution of baking soda, it turns to a greenish color. The green color results from a chemical change in the molecules of the blueberry juice.

The bubbles you see when lemon juice is added to a solution of baking soda are a sign of a chemical change. Carbon dioxide gas forms by the reaction between acid in the lemon juice and the sodium bicarbonate in the baking soda.

Have you ever put hydrogen peroxide on a cut to kill germs? The bubbles tell you that a chemical change is occurring.

What happens when propane gas is released from a tank? It reacts with oxygen in the air. The light and heat produced are signs of this chemical reaction.

What are three signs of a chemical change?

Color Change

When iodine is dropped onto a potato, a color change is observed.

The reaction of blueberry juice and baking soda shows a change of color.

Formation of a Gas

When hydrogen peroxide comes into contact with bodily fluids, it reacts and gives off pure oxygen gas. The oxygen gas, in turn, kills germs in the cut and guards against infection.

Carbon dioxide gas forms when lemon juice is added to a baking soda solution.

Formation of Light and Heat

When propane mixes with oxygen, a chemical reaction occurs.

When you light a match, it gives off light and heat all on its own. This tells you that a chemical change is occurring.

What Are Some Familiar Chemical Changes?

Rust

Tarnish

As a cake bakes, several chemical changes occur. Heat turns the baking soda (sodium bicarbonate) in the cake dough into sodium carbonate, steam, and carbon dioxide gas. The sodium carbonate is a harmless solid that remains in the cake. The steam helps make the cake moist. The bubbles of carbon dioxide help the dough expand and make the cake light and fluffy. The heat of the oven also triggers other chemical reactions in the cake batter. These strengthen the cake and keep it from collapsing after it is baked.

The red powder covering the wheelbarrow above is iron oxide. Iron oxide is commonly known as rust. Rust forms when iron atoms in steel react with oxygen from the air. The reaction is very complex and needs moisture to occur. Steel objects are most likely to rust if they get wet and are not dried right away.

Rocket engines use chemical reactions that produce lots of heat. This space shuttle's main engines are powered by liquid hydrogen and liquid oxygen. When the two react together, they make water vapor and the energy the shuttle needs. The shuttle is also equipped with launch boosters that use a solid fuel. When the solid fuel burns, aluminum powder is converted to aluminum oxide.

The silver spoon in the photo is partly covered with a tarnish of silver sulfide. The silver sulfide forms when silver reacts with sulfur or hydrogen sulfide in foods or the air. You can even tarnish silver by wrapping it with a rubber band. Sulfur added to strengthen the rubber causes the tarnish to form. Polishes can be used to remove the tarnish and restore the silver's shiny appearance.

What are three examples of chemical changes?

Process Skill BUILDER

SKILL Experiment

Preventing Rust

You've learned that steel forms rust when exposed to oxygen and moisture. Rusting can ruin metal objects. Can you find a way to stop or slow rusting? In this activity you will experiment to try to find the answer. In order to experiment, you need to do the following things. Form a hypothesis. Design a control. Carry out your experiment. Analyze and communicate your results.

Materials

- steel nails and sand-paper
- paper cups
- dilute salt water
- goggles

Procedure

BE CAREFUL! Wear goggles.

1. **Hypothesize** The photograph shows a method for making a steel nail rust. Think of a way to protect a steel nail from rusting under such conditions. Write down an explanation of why you think your method will work.
2. **Experiment** To test your method of rust protection, you need a control nail kept under normal conditions. Each experimental nail will have just one condition (variable) change. For example, what if you wanted to make a nail rust? You might leave one nail in a clean, empty jar (the control). You might put another in water. You might put a third in lemon juice. The amount of rusting that occurs is called the *dependent variable*. Write out how you will set up the experimental and control nails for your experiment.
3. **Experiment** Carry out your experiment, and record your observations.

Drawing Conclusions

1. **Infer** Write out a description of how well your hypothesis agreed with your results. Be sure to compare the experimental nail with the control nail.
2. **Communicate** Why did you need a control in this experiment?

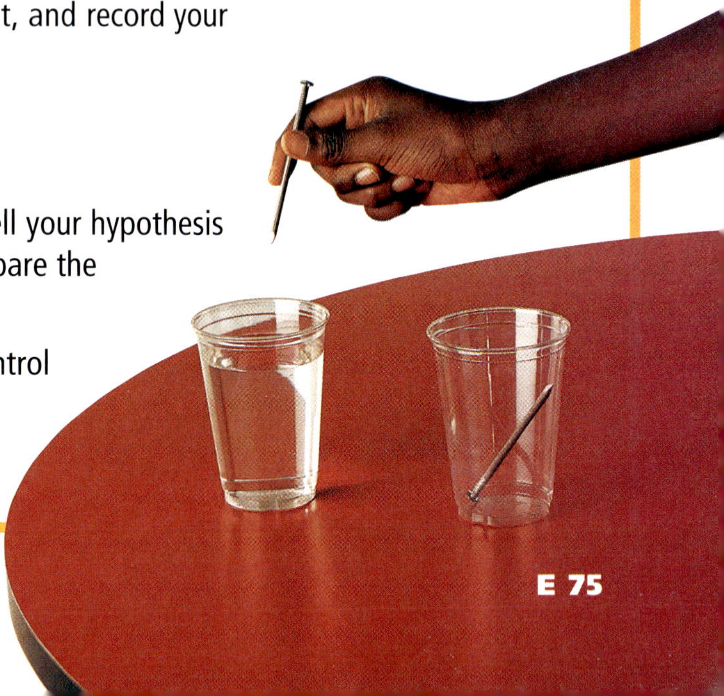

Which Are Easier to Reverse – Chemical or Physical Changes?

You would probably agree that turning carbon dioxide gas, water, and sodium acetate back into baking soda and vinegar would be difficult. Simply stirring the three ingredients together would not give you baking soda and vinegar. In general, chemical changes are difficult to reverse. Imagine trying to "unburn" toast or "unspoil" milk!

On the other hand, physical changes can sometimes be easily reversed. Although this is not always true. For example, melting an ice cube can easily be reversed by cooling it until it freezes again. Stirring sugar into water can be reversed by letting the water evaporate.

What changes occur when toast burns? What happens when a candle burns?

However, it would not be so easy to put pieces of paper back together after cutting them from a single page. Still, if a change seems very easy to reverse, it is more likely to be a physical change.

The photograph of a burning candle shows that many changes are happening. Wax melts, runs down the side, and turns solid again. However, some of the wax turns into carbon dioxide gas and steam when it combines with oxygen in the air. This change releases enough heat to make the candle flame you see.

Why are chemical changes more difficult to reverse than physical changes?

Lesson Review

Why It Matters

Chemical changes bake your cakes and let your bread rise. They turn fuels into heat to warm your home. Chemical changes even turn the food you eat into energy to keep you going. In what other ways are chemical changes important to you?

Visit **www.mhscience02.com** to do a research project on chemical changes.

Think and Write

1. Is the rusting of a nail a chemical or a physical change?
2. Is the melting of ice a chemical or a physical change? Why?
3. When a match burns, what evidence is there that a chemical change is occurring?
4. **Experiment** What if you wanted to find out if a cake bakes better with baking soda or baking powder? Design an experiment to test your ideas. Why might you want to use a control?
5. **Critical Thinking** What could you do to protect a bike from rusting?

L·I·N·K·S

LITERATURE LINK

Read *Let's Go Spelunking!* to learn about a trip to Howe Caverns. Try the activities at the end of the book.

SOCIAL STUDIES LINK

Research the Statue of Liberty. The Statue of Liberty is a famous statue in New York Harbor. What does it look like today? What did it look like 100 years ago? What is the statue made of? What could have happened to make the statue appear the way it does today?

TECHNOLOGY LINK

Science Newsroom CD-ROM Choose *The Action of Reaction* to learn more about physical and chemical changes.

At the Computer Visit **www.mhscience02.com** for more links.

Can Chemical Reactions Make Food Safe or Unsafe?

Why do mold and bacteria grow in foods and spoil them? Are the foods unsafe to eat? What can be done to prevent microorganisms like molds and bacteria from spoiling foods? All the answers involve chemical reactions.

Like all living organisms, molds and bacteria require food. They can "eat" the same foods we eat and multiply in the food. They cause chemical reactions to occur in food, making it spoil.

In some cases, molds and bacteria can be harmful, perhaps even deadly, to people who eat foods in which these microorganisms have grown. Bacteria from contaminated food can multiply in the digestive tract of a person, causing vomiting, diarrhea, and intestinal bleeding. Hamburger, for example, may be contaminated with a bacterium known as *E. coli* O157:H7. Each year, *E. coli* O157:H7 causes about 73,000 illnesses and about 60 deaths in the United States.

To help prevent bacteria and molds from spoiling foods, food manufacturers may add chemicals to kill microorganisms. Sodium propionate, for example, is a chemical often added to cheeses and baked goods to keep molds from growing. Manufacturers also package foods in airtight containers and bags to prevent spoiling.

While food manufacturers take steps to keep the foods you eat safe, what can you do at home? Chemical reactions slow down as the temperature is lowered. Keeping foods in the refrigerator or freezer is a primary means of preventing the growth of bacteria and molds. The cold temperatures slow down the chemical reactions that make food spoil. Foods such as lunch meats and potato salads should not be kept out of the refrigerator for a long time.

The cheese in the photograph has spots of mold growing on it.

and Society

NATIONAL GEOGRAPHIC

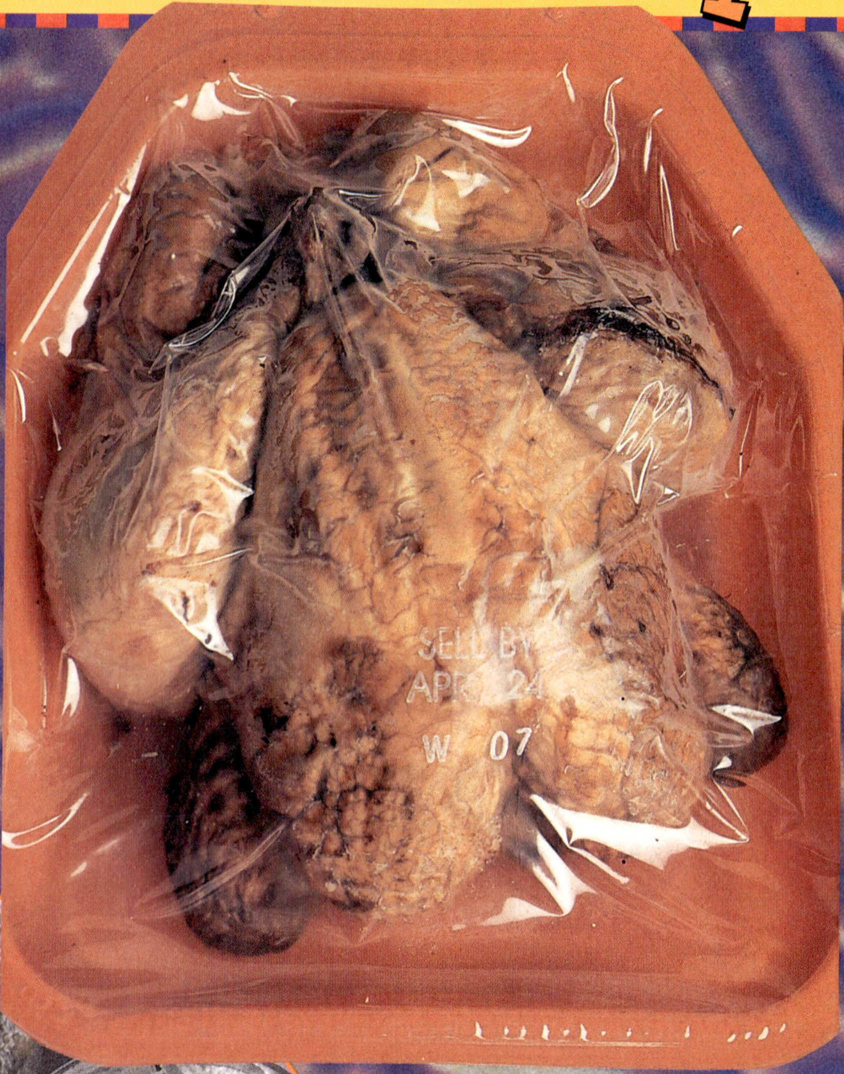

AT THE COMPUTER

Visit www.mhscience02.com to learn more about bacteria and mold.

Vacuum-sealed containers prevent bacteria from contaminating food.

Write ABOUT IT

1. How can molds and bacteria cause food to spoil?
2. What are some harmful effects of eating food contaminated with bacteria such as *E. coli*?

LESSON 6

Acids and Bases

Vocabulary

acid, E82
base, E82
neutral, E82
indicator, E84
acidity, E86
alkalinity, E86
pH, E86

Get Ready

Have you ever tried to suck on a lemon? It might have made your cheeks pucker! Lemons taste very sour. Why is this?

Have you ever seen ammonia being used to mop the floor? Why is it a good cleaning agent?

The answer to these questions is that these substances are either acids or bases. What are acids and bases? Are there any other substances in your house that contain an acid or base? How can you find out?

Process Skill

You observe when you use one or more of the senses to identify or learn about an object.

Explore Activity

Which Are Acids and Which Are Bases?

Procedure

BE CAREFUL! Wear goggles, gloves, and an apron.

1. **Predict** Which solutions do you think are acids and which are bases? Write your predictions in a chart like the one shown below.

2. **Observe** Vinegar is an acid. Put a small amount in a cup, and mark the cup with a label. Test by dipping a piece of red litmus paper into the vinegar. Record the result in your table. Repeat with a piece of blue litmus paper. Litmus paper is a material that allows you to tell which solutions are acids and which are bases.

3. **Classify** Test all of your other solutions in the same way, and record your results.

Sample	Predict: Acid or Base?	Affect on Red Litmus	Affect on Blue Litmus	Result: Acid or Base?
Vinegar	ACID			ACID
Baking soda				
Lemon juice				

Drawing Conclusions

1. Which samples are acids? How do you know?

2. Which samples are bases? How do you know?

3. **Measure** Now test each sample with a small strip of pH paper. Match the color of the paper to the color scale on the holder, and find the pH.

4. **Going Further: Interpret Data** Look at your data. Do acids have higher or lower pH values than bases? Which sample is most acidic? Which is most basic? How do you know?

Materials

- red and blue litmus paper
- wide-range pH paper
- plastic cups
- labels
- goggles
- gloves
- apron
- household solutions

Read to Learn

Main Idea Many important substances in our lives are acids or bases.

What Are Acids and Bases?

How do you know whether something is an **acid** or a **base**? Vinegar, orange juice, and lemon juice are acids. An acid tastes sour and turns blue litmus paper red. Bases, like ammonia and baking soda, taste bitter and turn red litmus paper blue. (You should never test acids and bases by tasting them, however.)

In Lesson 5 you learned about chemical reactions. When you mixed vinegar, an acid, with baking soda, a base, a chemical reaction occurred. Acids and bases can react with each other to form water and a salt.

In a reaction acids "give away" hydrogen particles, or *hydronium ions*. Bases give off *hydroxide ions*.

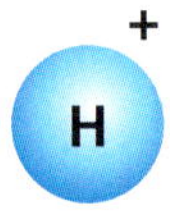

This is a simplified hydronium ion. Acids release them in solution.

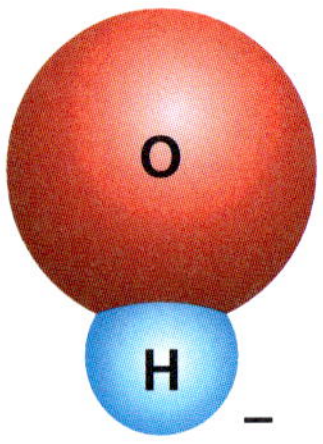

Bases release hydroxide ions, such as this, in solution.

Hydroxide ions are particles that are made up of one oxygen atom and one hydrogen atom linked together. Hydronium and hydroxide ions combine to make water. What is left of the acid and base also combines to make a new substance—a salt.

If you place a blue and a red strip of litmus paper in a glass of water, both strips will stay the same color. This tells you that water is neither acidic nor basic. A solution that is neither acidic nor basic is **neutral**. Water is a neutral substance.

When hydrochloric acid is added to a base, sodium hydroxide, a chemical reaction occurs to produce water and sodium chloride (table salt).

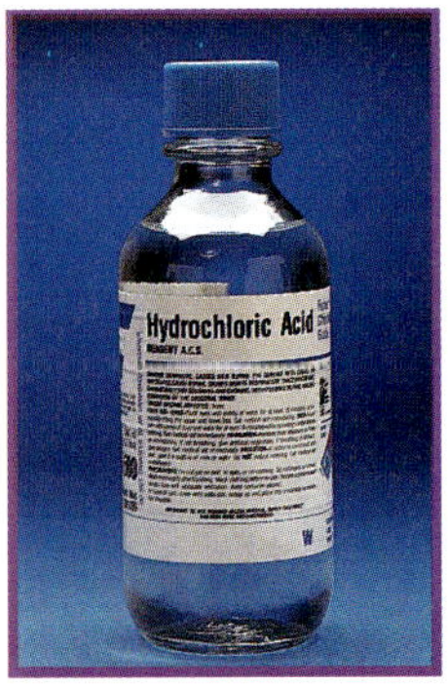

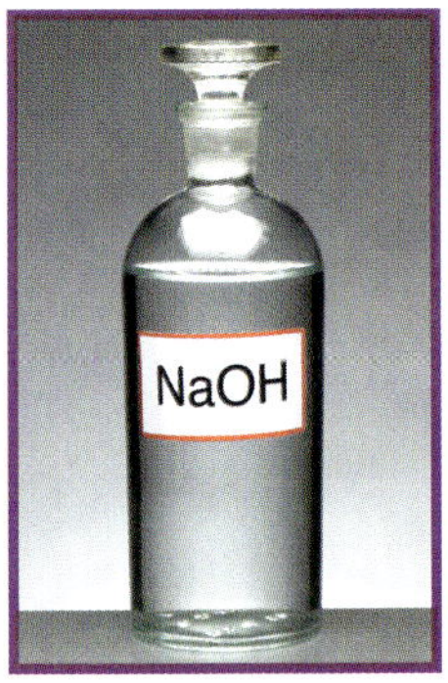

HCl + NaOH → NaCl + H_2O

You can make an acid neutral by mixing it with a base. Likewise, you can make a base neutral by mixing it with an acid. Acids and bases react to form neutral compounds.

The chemical properties, or reactivity, of acids and bases are what make them useful and important. You may know not to add lemon to hot tea with milk. This is because the acid in the lemon can react with the milk, causing it to sour. Acids react strongly with metals, as well. Statues can corrode from the acid found in rain and the atmosphere. The acid in rain is also harmful to plant and animal life.

Acids aren't only harmful, however. Acids are used in batteries to help make electricity. They are used in industry to produce plastics, metals, explosives, textiles, and dyes. They are also used for many functions in your body. All living things use amino acids, for example, to build proteins. All of an organism's muscles and tissues are made up mostly of proteins.

Bases can also be reactive. You may have experienced a bloody nose from smelling ammonia. Ammonia is a strong base that can be corrosive. Bases are often used in cleansers. They can break down grease and oil. Soap is a base you use every day.

Baking soda and baking powder are bases used in cooking. They are often used in baking to make cakes rise. When these bases mix with an acid, carbon dioxide gas is produced. The carbon dioxide gas that is released helps to make cakes become airy and rise.

This statue of George Washington has been corroded by acid in rain.

READING **Cause and Effect**
What happens when an acid is added to a base?

How Can You Tell if Something Is an Acid or a Base?

Litmus paper has a different color in acids than it does in bases. Litmus is an example of an **indicator**. An indicator is a substance whose color changes when it is mixed with an acid or a base. You can use litmus paper to tell which household materials are acids and which are bases.

Many indicators come from plants. Litmus, for example, is made from certain lichens. Another common vegetable indicator is phenolphthalein (fee·nawl·THAL·ee·in). Phenolphthalein is colorless in acid and pink in base.

Red cabbage juice is another indicator. Add acid to red cabbage juice, and the juice turns maroon. If there is a lot of acid, the juice turns pink. A neutral substance does not change the color. A base turns it green. A very basic substance turns it yellow.

Many household materials can act as indicators. These materials include blueberry juice, beet juice, carrot juice, grape juice, red cabbage, purple hollyhock flowers, and blue iris flowers. Each has one color in an acid and another color in a base.

What is an indicator?

Hydrangeas have pink flowers in basic soil and blue flowers in acidic soil. Are these flowers indicators?

Cabbage juice is an indicator because it changes color in acids and bases. Litmus paper can also be used as an indicator.

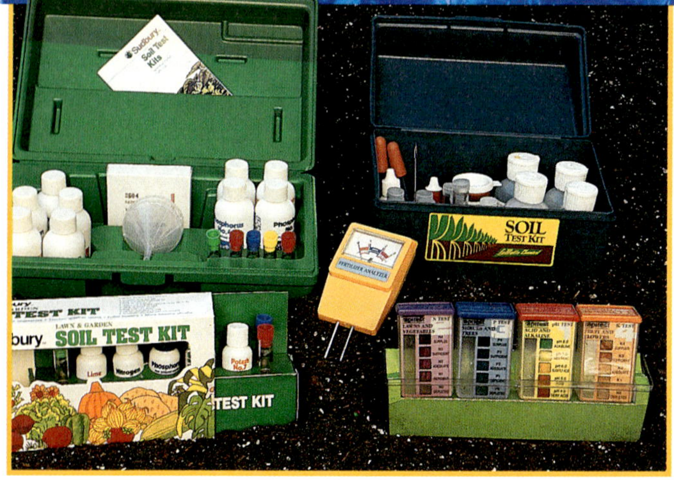

FOR SCHOOL OR HOME

Mystery Writing with a Base

1. Using a cotton swab, write a short message to your partner on a piece of paper with a baking soda solution.
2. Put the paper aside, and allow it to completely dry. After it is dry, give it to your partner.
3. Can you read the message your partner gave you? You probably cannot. Use another cotton swab and gently "paint" the paper with grape juice.
4. **Observe** What happened when you painted the paper with the grape juice?
5. **Infer** Is the grape juice an indicator? Why or why not?

How Can Indicators Be Useful?

The photograph shows a test kit that can be used to find how acidic the soil is. Doing so is important because certain plants grow well only when soil is slightly acidic. The test kit has paper strips that are soaked with an indicator. When a strip is placed in moist soil, it turns a certain color. Matching the color of the strip against the colored scale on the container reveals how acidic the soil is.

Indicators are important in many situations other than gardening. For example, swimming pool water must be routinely checked with a test kit. Aquarium owners or pond owners periodically have to check how acidic the water is to make sure it is healthy for the fish and plants.

What are some ways indicators are used?

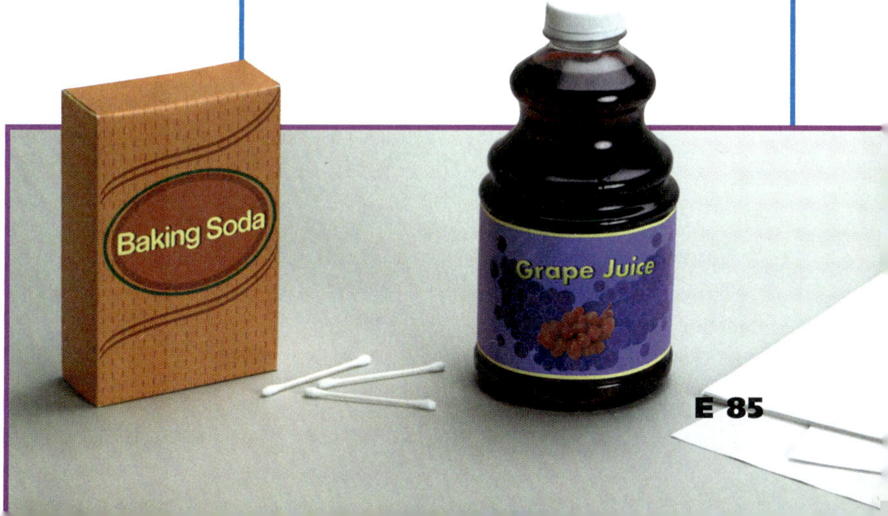

Are All Acids and Bases the Same?

Are all acids equally acidic? Are all bases equally basic? No. Acids and bases have different strengths. The strength of an acid is called its **acidity**. The strength of a base is called its **alkalinity**.

Hydrochloric acid, a laboratory chemical, is much more acidic than citric acid, the acid found in citrus fruits like oranges and lemons. Hydrochloric acid, therefore, has a higher acidity.

Acidity and alkalinity depend on how many hydronium and hydroxide ions are in a solution. The diagram below compares the solution of a strong acid with a weak acid, and a strong base with a weak base.

A scientist named Soren Sorenson developed a scale in 1909 to compare acidic and basic solutions. This scale is called the *pH scale*. The **pH** of a solution tells how acidic or basic the solution is. It measures acidity and alkalinity. Scientists still use this scale today.

The pH of most solutions lies between pH 1 and pH 14. A pH of 1 means that there are a lot of hydronium ions in a solution. The solution is very acidic. A pH of 14 means that there are a lot of hydroxide ions in a

The first solution is a stronger acid than the second because it has more hydronium ions. The third solution is a weaker base than the fourth solution because it has fewer hydroxide ions. Alkalinity increases as the pH increases from 7 to 14. Acidity increases as the pH decreases from 7 to 0.

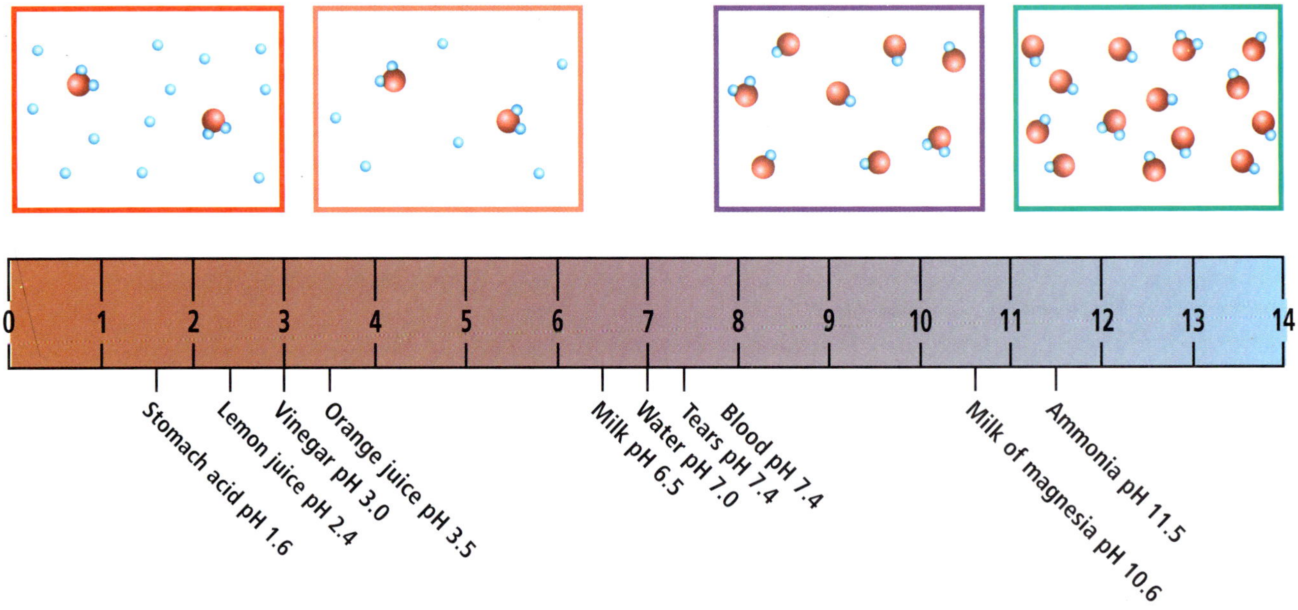

pH meter

solution. The solution is very basic. A pH of 7 means that the solution is neutral.

Scientists often use a pH meter to determine the acidity or alkalinity of a solution. Strips of paper called pH paper are also commonly used. This paper changes to a different color depending on the exact pH of a solution.

Your blood has a pH of 7.4. Doctors can use this pH to diagnose certain diseases. The blood of a person with diabetes, for example, has a pH that is lower than normal.

How can acidity and alkalinity be measured?

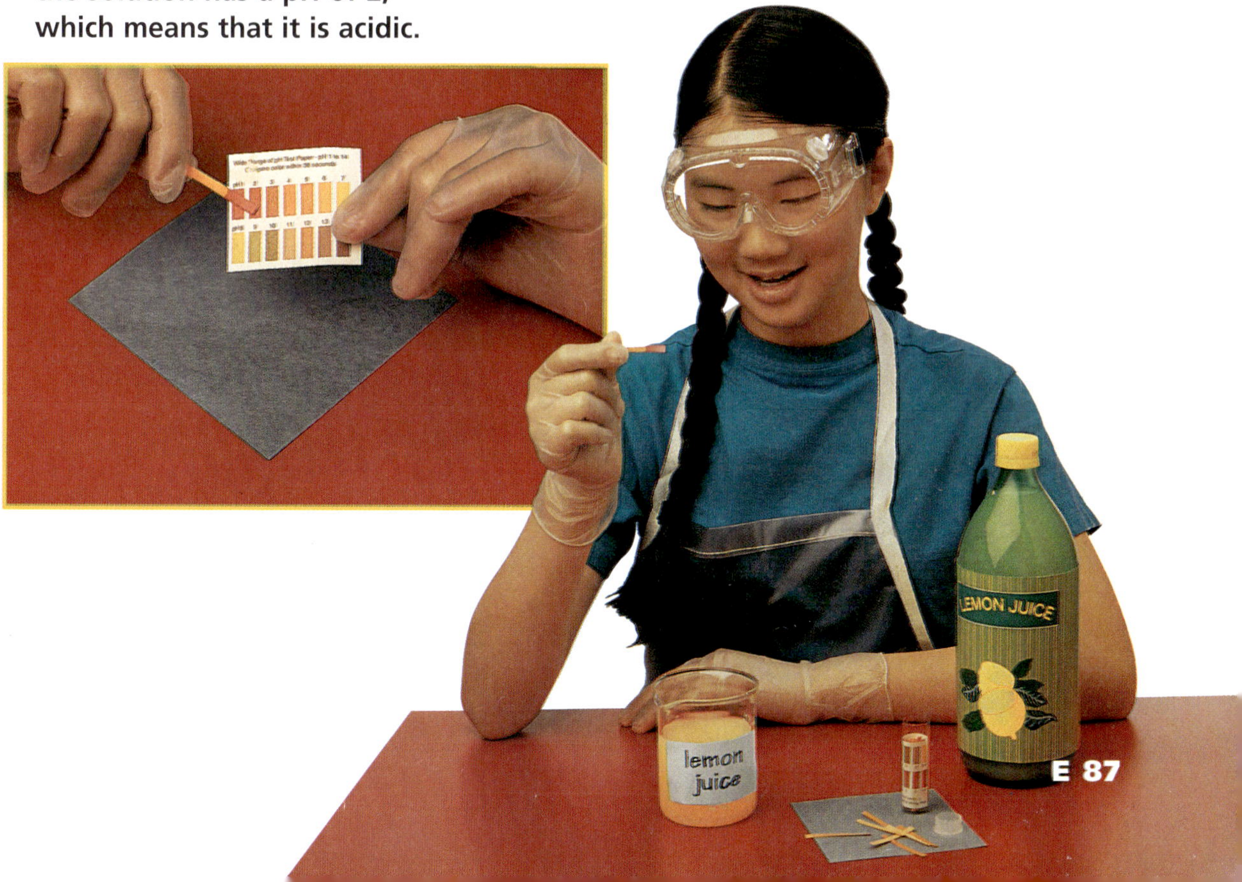

The color match indicates that the solution has a pH of 2, which means that it is acidic.

How Can Acids and Bases Be Used?

Acids and bases are used in many different ways every day. They can be used in your home as cleaning agents. Bleach contains acids, for example. Ammonia, drain cleaners, and window cleaning solutions all contain bases. Bases are good cleaning agents because they dissolve grease, fats, and oils.

Many foods get their flavor from acids. Tomatoes, grapefruit, lemons, and limes all contain acids.

Acids and bases are used in scientific laboratories and in industry to make plastics and textiles. Cotton is often treated with a base to make it look shiny.

The reaction of acids and bases is very useful. You have learned that acids and bases react to make neutral compounds. You may have even experienced this kind of reaction in your own body! Have you ever taken an antacid or milk of magnesia for an upset stomach? Your stomach contains acids to help you digest food. In fact, the pH of your stomach is usually between 1 and 2.

Sometimes there is too much acid in your stomach, causing the pH to go even lower. This may happen when you eat foods that are very acidic or when you are very nervous. The decrease in pH can cause a stomachache.

Products like antacids are basic. When you take them, they react with the extra acid in your stomach. They help increase the pH of your stomach back to its normal level and make you feel better.

How can acids and bases be useful?

Lesson Review

Why It Matters

Acids and bases make up many of the compounds around you. They clean your clothes and help you to digest food. Oranges are acidic. Eating oranges is obviously not dangerous. However, there are other acids and bases that must be treated with care. Use these materials safely. Wear protective eyewear and cover your skin when working with these acids and bases. Understanding pH lets you know how strong these substances are.

Think and Write

1. What kind of particles do acids produce?
2. What are the properties of a base?
3. Your friend wonders if a cleanser is an acid or a base. What test could you do to help him answer the question?
4. What numerical scale describes acidity? How does this scale work?
5. **Critical Thinking** A friend calls you and says he accidentally spilled some acid. Describe what you would tell him to do to clean up the spill safely.

L·I·N·K·S

MATH LINK

Solve a problem. An acid with a pH of 3 is 10 times more acidic than an acid with a pH of 4. How much more acidic is an acid with a pH of 1 than an acid with a pH of 3? With a pH of 4?

ART LINK

Draw a picture. Use lemon juice to paint a picture. Let the lemon juice dry, and then "develop" your picture with grape juice.

HEALTH LINK

Research swimming pools. You learned that swimming pools are checked for their acidity level. Why is this? Use the Internet or an encyclopedia to learn more.

TECHNOLOGY LINK

At the Computer Visit **www.mhscience02.com** for more links.

LESSON 7

Matter and Energy

Vocabulary

kinetic energy, E95
potential energy, E95
conduction, E97
convection, E97
radiation, E97

Get Ready

If you were scuba diving and saw this animal, what would you do? Swim the other way! It is an electric ray. It produces enough electricity to power a small motor.

Luckily, you don't need an electric ray to run appliances for you. Batteries let you carry electricity with you wherever you go. Rays don't run out of electricity, however. Do batteries run out?

Process Skill

You interpret data when you use the information that has been gathered to answer questions or solve a problem.

Explore Activity

How Well Do Batteries Provide Energy?

Materials
- battery
- flashlight bulb
- 2 wires

Procedure

1. **Experiment** Connect one end of a wire to the light bulb. Connect the other end of the wire to the battery. Do the same for the other wire. Record what time the light bulb went on. Record the type, size, and brand of battery you used.
2. **Observe** Examine the light bulb every 15 minutes to see if it is still lit. Record the time the light bulb goes off.
3. Repeat the experiment using another type or brand of battery.

Drawing Conclusions

1. **Use Numbers** Divide the time each battery lasted by the cost of that type of battery. Share your results with your classmates.
2. Make a graph of the class's results. Which batteries lasted the longest? Which batteries cost the least per hour of use? Were some brands longer lasting? Were some brands cheaper to use than others?
3. **Infer** Are the cheapest batteries the best buy? Are the longest lasting batteries the best buy?
4. **Going Further: Interpret Data** When might you choose the longest lasting batteries? The least expensive batteries? The batteries that cost the least per hour of use? Explain.

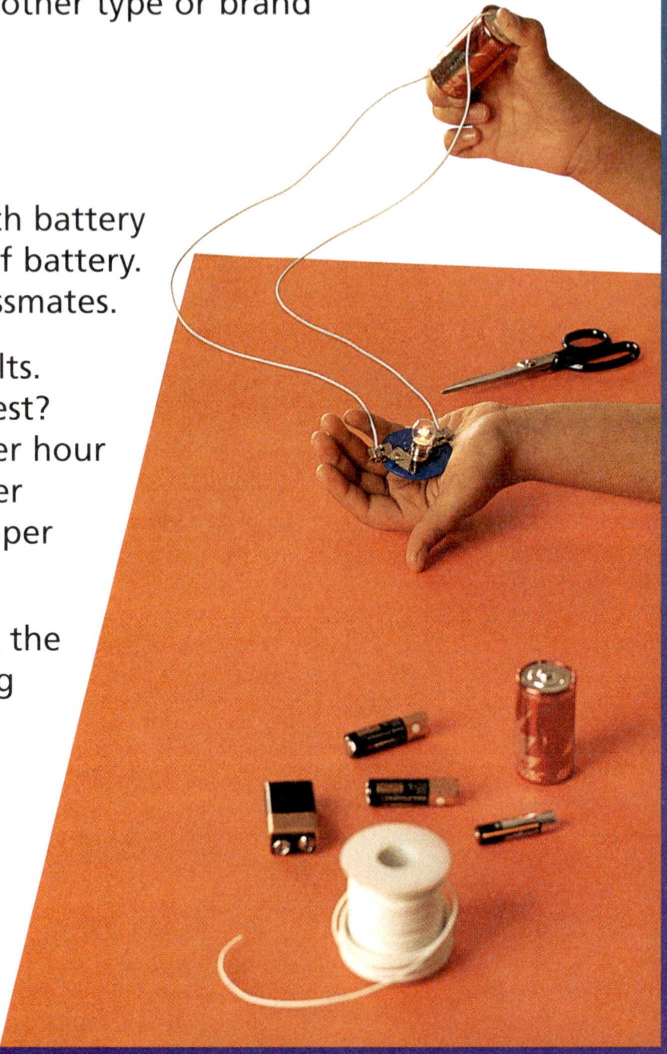

Read to Learn

Main Idea Energy has different forms.

What Is Electrical Energy?

You know that a battery can produce enough power to light up a light bulb. How does it do this? What is the "power" in a battery? Where does it come from?

A battery provides electrical energy. Chemicals inside the battery react. These reactions produce electrons. As you learned in Lesson 2, an electron is one of the particles that make up an atom. Each electron carries energy, giving the battery its "power".

When a battery is connected to a light bulb with wires, a closed circuit is formed. A closed circuit means that there is a continuous path for electrons to travel through. The diagram below shows a closed circuit.

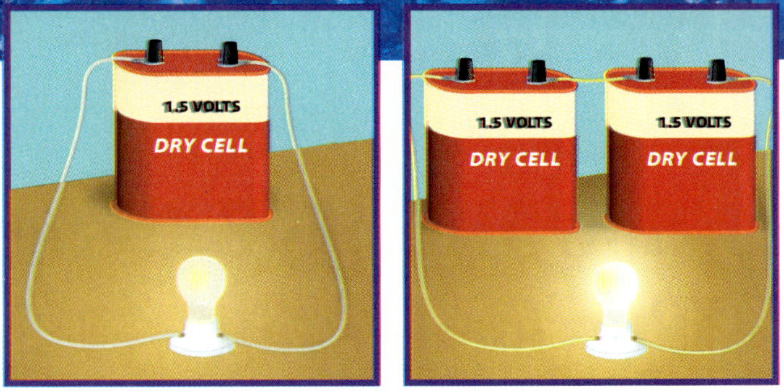

In some cases the amount of electrical energy in a circuit may not be great enough to light certain bulbs. For example, a flashlight battery could not light up a 60-watt light bulb from a lamp. Electrical energy can be measured by the size of the bulb it can light.

Electrons flow from the battery to the light bulb through wires. Some of the energy is given up to the wire in the light bulb, called the *filament*. The filament gets hot enough to glow and give off light. The electrical energy is changed into light and heat.

The rest of the electrons flow back into the battery. They can be sent through the circuit again.

Electrical Energy

READING Diagrams

Describe the path electrons take in a closed circuit.

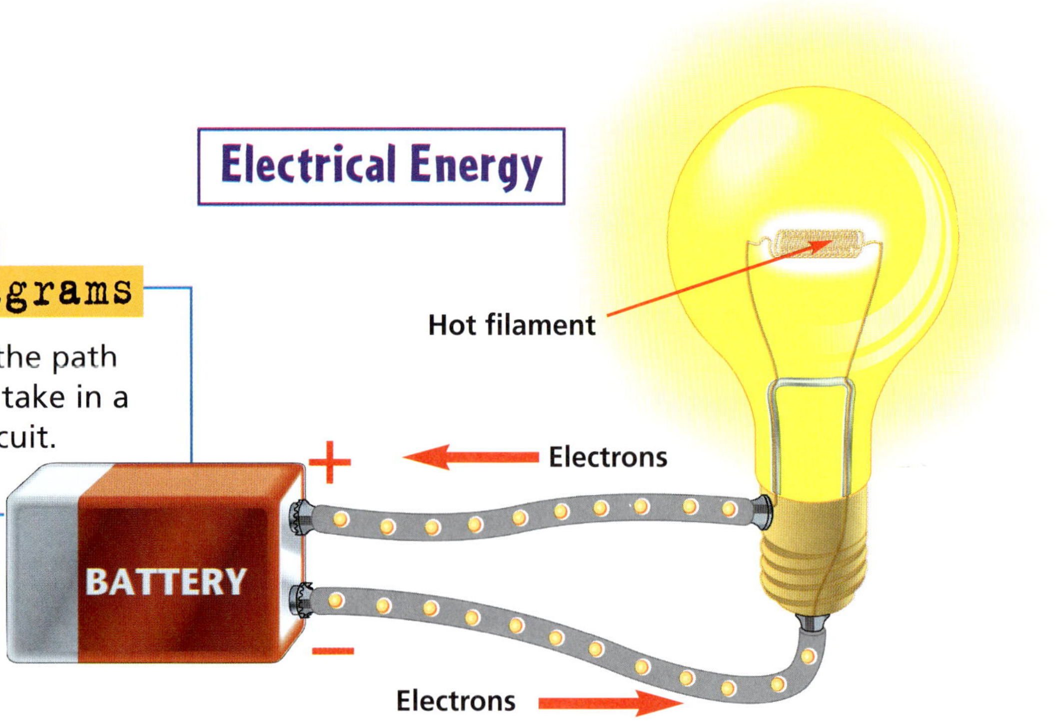

After a time the chemicals in a battery have all reacted, and no more electrons can be produced. This causes the battery to go dead.

Measuring Electrical Energy

Electrical energy can be measured in a number of ways. The circuit with two batteries has twice as many electrons flowing as the circuit with one battery. The bulb is brighter when two batteries are present. The brightness of a bulb can measure electrical energy.

We can also use different kinds of meters to measure electrical energy. An *ammeter* measures *amperes*, or *amps*. It tells us how many electrons flow each second. The *voltmeter* measures *volts*. Volts are another measure of electrical energy.

READING **Cause and Effect**
How does a battery produce electrical charge?

FOR SCHOOL OR HOME

Measuring Electricity

1. Wrap fine varnished wire around a compass. Use sandpaper to remove the coating from the ends of the wire.
2. Turn the compass until the needle is lined up with the coils of wire.
3. Keeping the compass this way, connect the ends of the wire to a circuit of a battery and small light bulb. See the photograph.
4. **Observe** What happens to the compass needle as you connect and disconnect the circuit? Record your observations.
5. How did you know when electricity was flowing in the circuit?
6. **Observe** When electricity was flowing, what did the compass needle do?
7. **Infer** How do you think the needle would move if you used a less powerful battery?

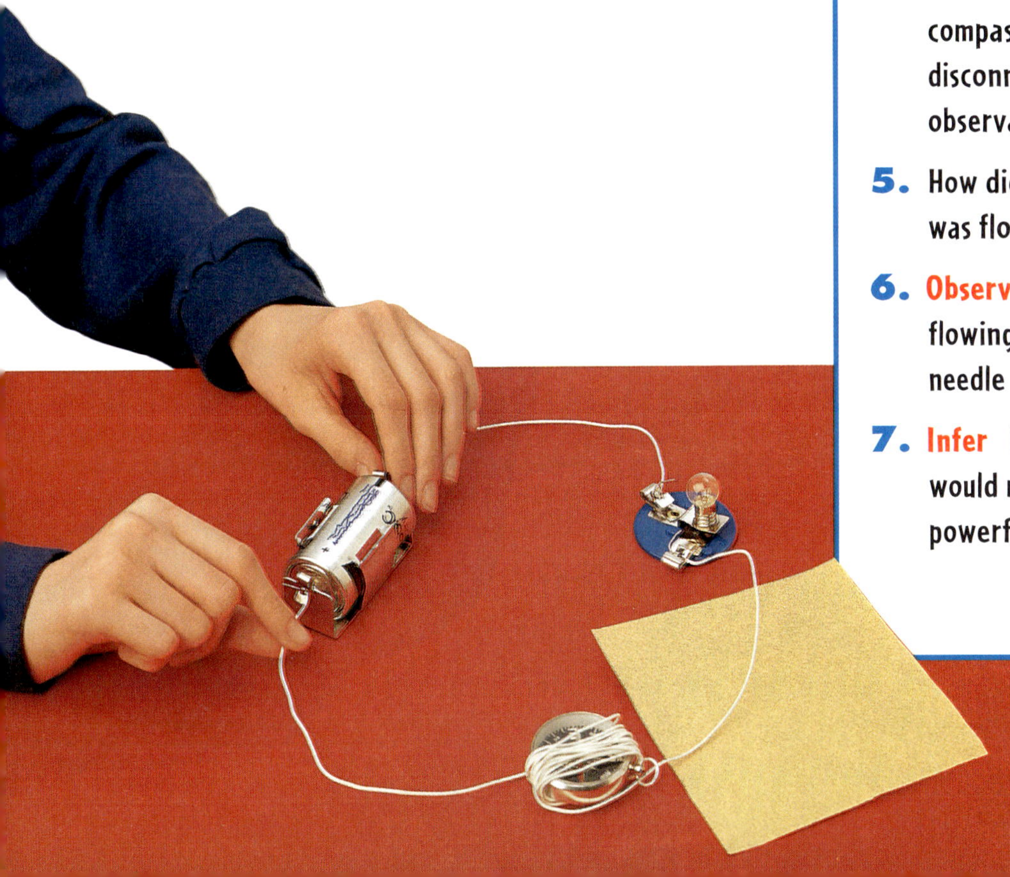

What Are Other Forms of Energy?

You've seen how chemical changes in a battery can produce electrical energy. You've also seen how that electrical energy can produce light and heat. All of these things are forms of energy. What exactly is energy? We know energy has many forms, but defining energy can be a little difficult.

A good place to start in talking about energy is to look at what energy can do. Energy is a measure of how much work something can produce. To scientists work means using a force—a push or a pull—to move an object. Energy is the ability to do work.

Energy is not a type of matter. Matter is something you can often touch or see—solids, liquids, gases. Energy may be thought of as the ability to move matter around.

We can describe energy by its source or by how it is carried. For example, the energy produced by a chemical reaction is called chemical energy. Some typical forms of energy are shown in the table on page E95.

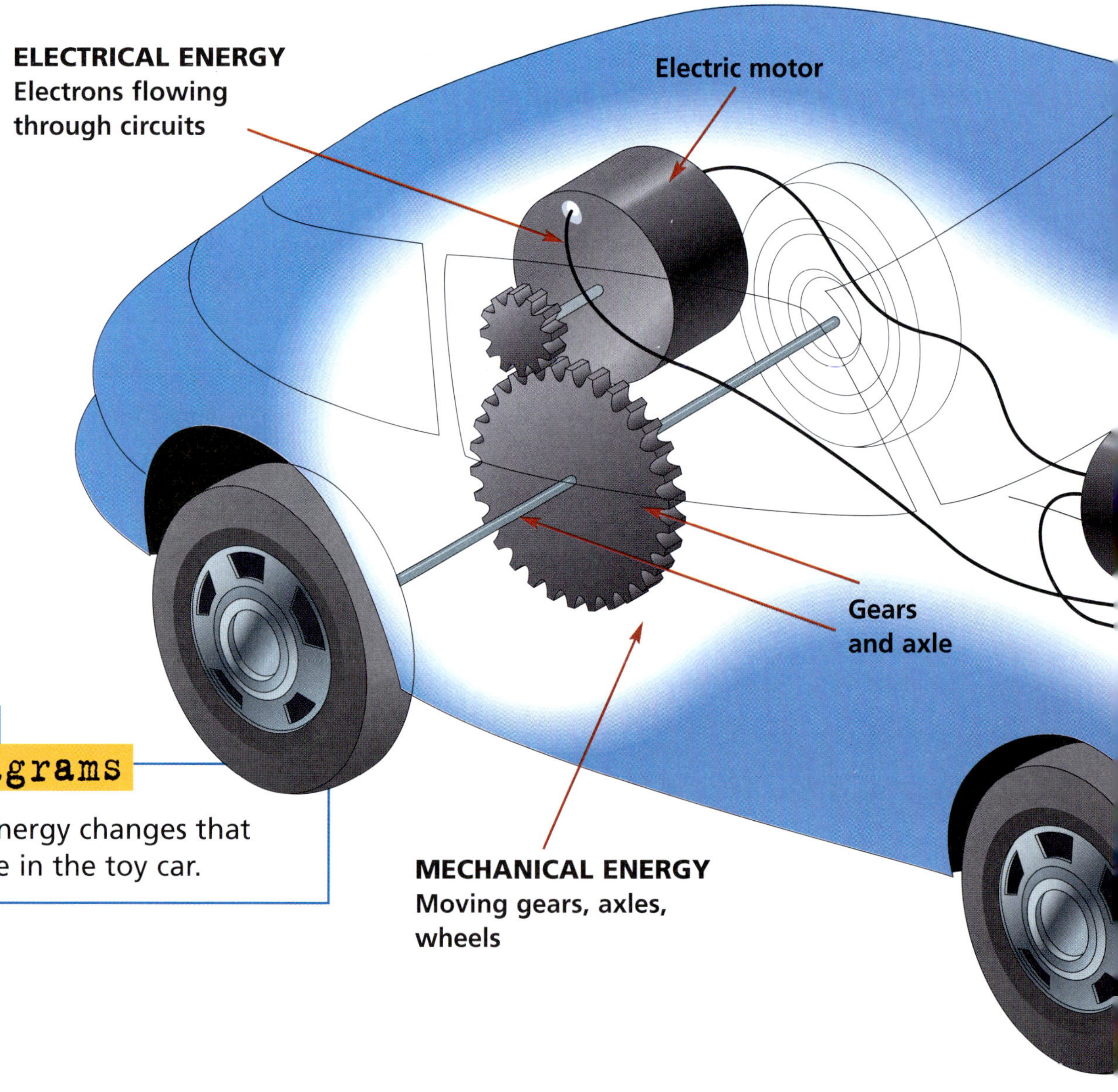

READING Diagrams

List the energy changes that take place in the toy car.

Kinetic and Potential Energy

Look at the toy car in the diagram. Electrical energy is being used by the headlights. Electrons are being produced by the battery and are moved through a circuit. When something moves, its energy is called **kinetic energy**. Electrical energy is an example of kinetic energy. Any object that is in motion has kinetic energy.

When the headlights are turned off, the battery stops working. Electrons stop moving, and no new electrons are produced. No energy is being used. However, energy is stored in the chemicals in the battery. This energy is waiting to be used. We refer to stored energy as **potential energy**. Chemical energy is an example of potential energy.

Matter always has at least one of these energy forms.

What are the two main forms of energy?

Energy Forms

Form of Energy	Description
Chemical	stored in links between atoms
Mechanical	sum of the kinetic and potential energy of a system
Electrical	movement of electrons
Thermal	motion of atoms and molecules
Radiant	the energy of light

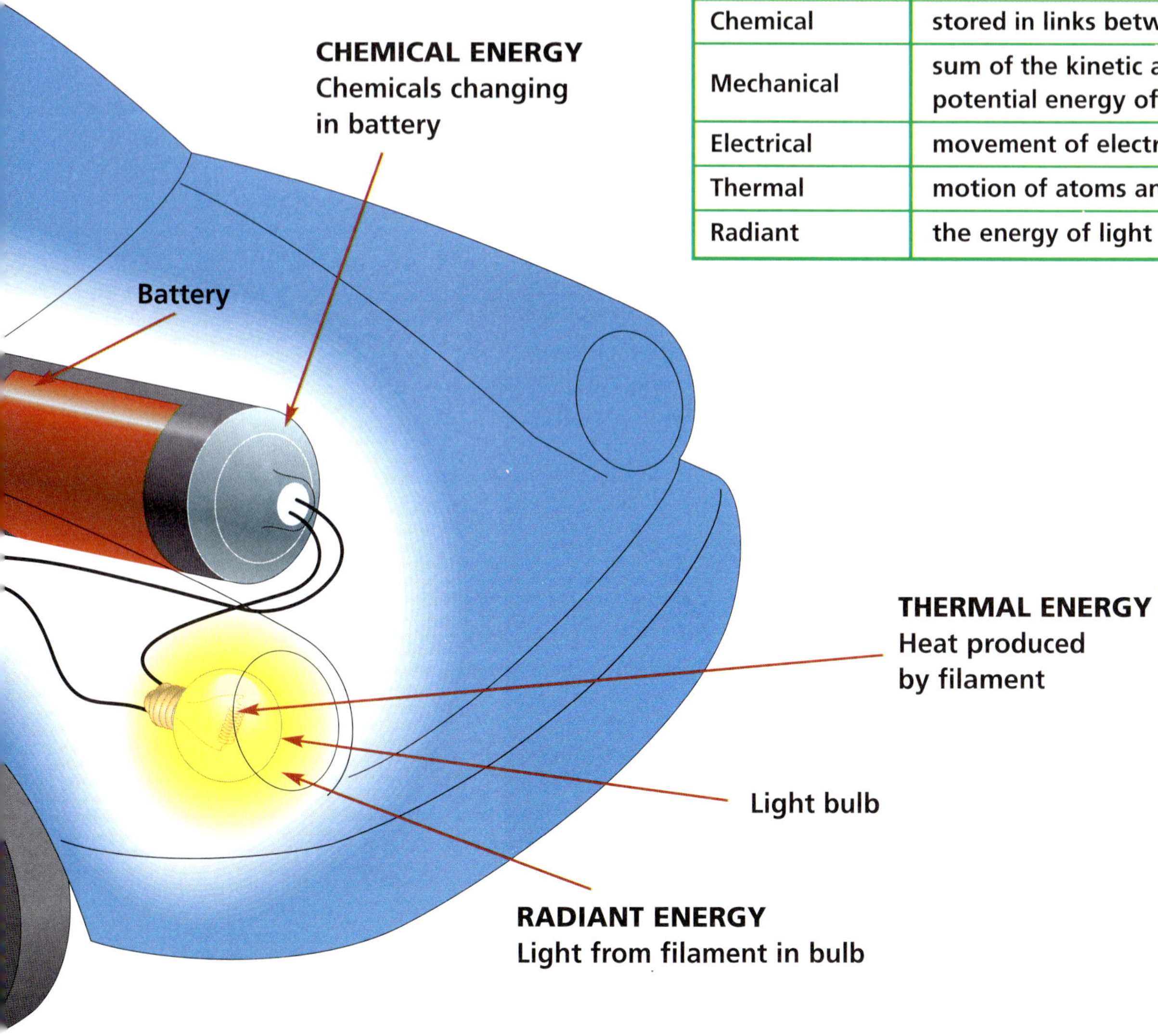

How Can We Describe Thermal Energy?

Have you ever used a thermometer to measure temperature? You have learned that thermal energy is a form of energy that describes the motion of atoms and molecules. Temperature tells us how fast the particles in matter are moving. High temperatures mean the molecules are moving fast and have a lot of energy. Lower temperatures mean the molecules are moving more slowly and have less energy. The movement of molecules is what makes things feel hot or cold.

Heat is the transfer of thermal energy from one object to another. Heat flows when an object is warmer than its surroundings. Heat always flows from hotter materials to cooler materials, never the other way. Heat flows until objects and their surroundings have the same temperature.

When you hold your hands around a mug of hot chocolate, your body gets warmed. This happens because heat flows from the hot mug into your skin. Thermal energy is transferred from the cup to your hands. Your body gains energy, and your temperature rises as a result. Energy is lost from the mug, however. Its temperature decreases.

How are temperature and heat related?

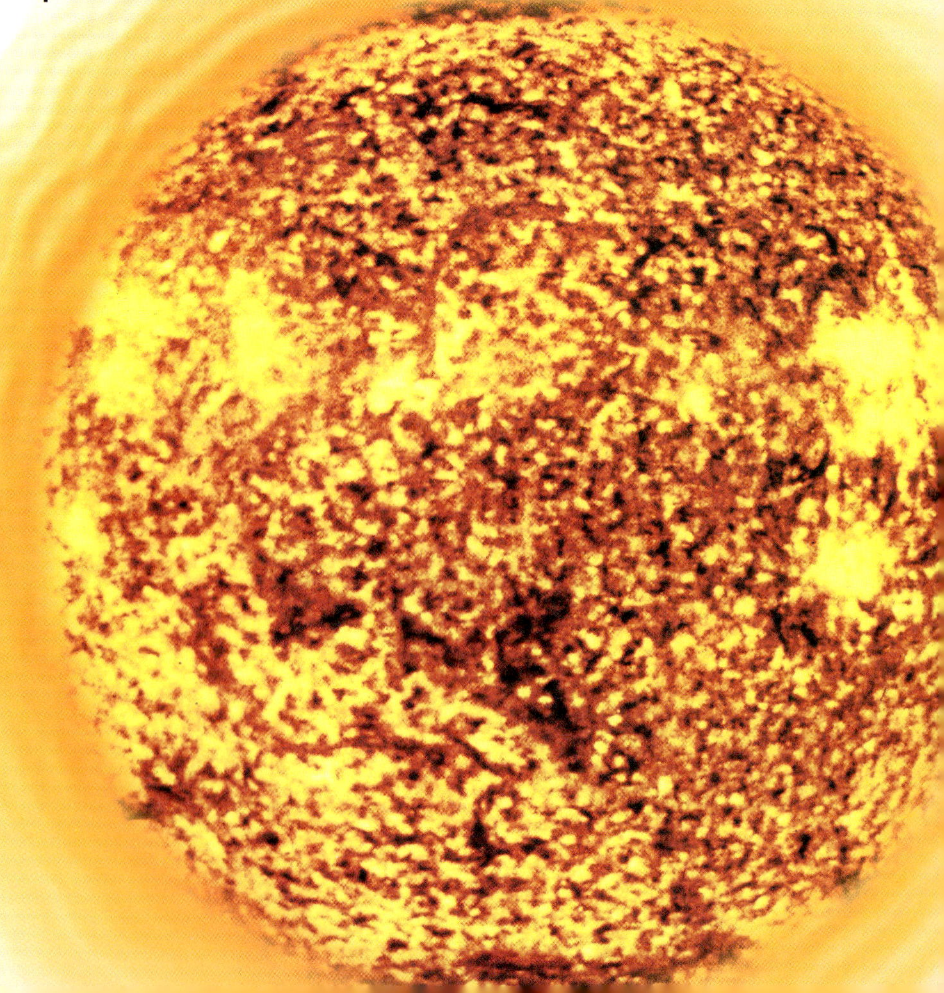

The Sun is the most important source of heat for life on our planet.

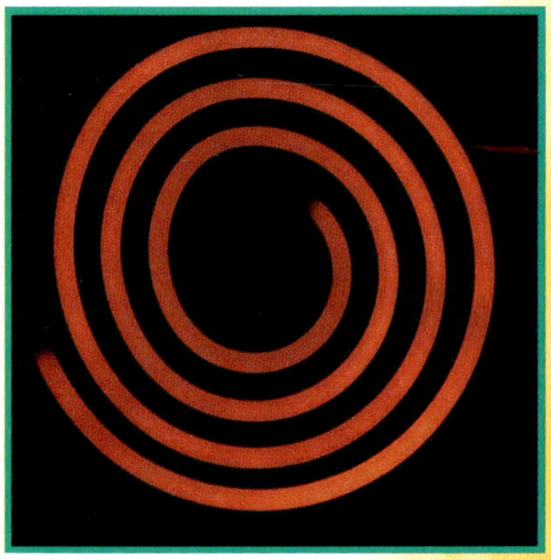

These heating coils in an oven are warmed by an electric current. The space inside the oven is warmed by heat flowing from the hot coils.

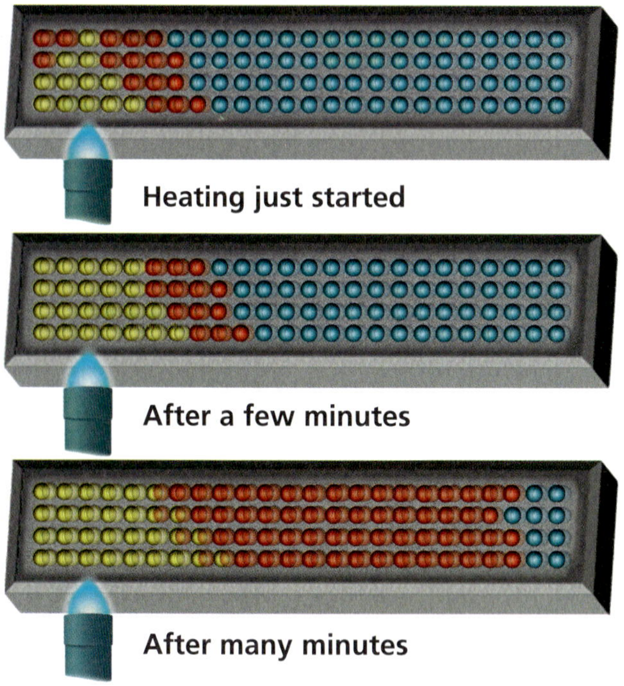

How Does Heat Move?

When heat flows, it can move in three ways—conduction, convection, and radiation. In **conduction** thermal energy flows through objects without the movement of any matter. Conduction is the way your hand is warmed by a mug of hot chocolate. It usually occurs in solids and between objects that are touching.

In **convection** thermal energy is transferred by the movement of matter. Convection occurs in liquids and gases. In convection hot parts of a material rise, while cooler parts sink. There is a flow of material and heat.

A pot of water is heated by convection, for example. As water is heated on a stove, the water near the burner gets hot and rises to the top of the pan. The cooler water near the top then sinks and gets warmed. Thermal energy is transferred by a cycle of rising and sinking matter.

In **radiation** heat is transferred through electromagnetic rays. Matter is not needed at all in this energy transfer. All objects around us give off radiation. Radiation can travel through space. Radiation from the Sun warms Earth, for example.

What are three ways that heat can move?

In convection, cooler materials sink while warmer materials rise in a cycle of motion.

What Materials Conduct Heat Well?

The photograph shows very hot tea in a foam cup. A metal spoon has been sitting in the tea for some time. The outside of the cup is slightly warm. However, the spoon's handle is almost too hot to hold. Why has more heat flowed into the handle of the spoon than into the walls of the cup?

As you learned in Lesson 1, some materials are better at conducting heat than others. The metal spoon is a good conductor of heat. However, the foam cup is a poor conductor of heat. As a result, heat flows quickly from the hot bowl of the spoon to its handle. However, heat flows very slowly from the tea into the foam.

Metals are the best conductors of heat. Why do metals conduct heat so well?

Heat is carried through a material by the motion of molecules. When a metal is heated at one end, the molecules move about rapidly. They collide with their neighbors, spreading the motion through the material. The spreading of the motion warms up other parts of the material.

The molecules in solids are packed very closely together. This makes transferring energy easier.

In Chapter 10 you learned that the molecules in gases are spread apart. They cannot transfer heat between one another as easily as in liquids and solids. This explains why air is such a poor conductor of heat. Gases are the poorest thermal conductors of all. Look at the table to see how well common materials conduct heat.

How Materials Conduct Heat

Material	How Many Times Better than Air It Conducts Heat
Wood	5
Water	23
Brick	25
Glass	42
Rock	67
Aluminum	8,300
Copper	15,300

What materials are the best conductors?

Lesson Review

Why It Matters

Energy comes in many forms. The air in your home is warmed by convection of thermal energy. There is energy stored in batteries and energy stored in the food you eat. The Sun gives us light and heat as well. You depend on various forms of energy to live, move, and have a comfortable life.

Think and Write

1. Describe how a battery makes a light bulb glow. Identify the different forms energy takes.
2. Why is energy not a form of matter?
3. How does thermal energy get from place to place?
4. Insulating windows have two layers of glass with air sealed in between. Why is this layer of air important?
5. **Critical Thinking** Two flashlights have the same kind of bulb. One glows more dimly than the other. Why do you think this is so?

L·I·N·K·S

SOCIAL STUDIES LINK

Research electricity. Who discovered electricity? When was this important discovery made? What was used to light and heat houses before electrical energy? Use the Internet or an encyclopedia for your research. Write a report.

ART LINK

Make a collage. Cut pictures of different types of energy from a magazine. Identify the source of energy being used. Paste your pictures onto a poster. Present your poster to the class.

WRITING LINK

Write a poem. Make up a poem to explain how you use different types of energy every day.

TECHNOLOGY LINK

At the Computer Visit **www.mhscience02.com** for more links.

Chapter 11 Review

Vocabulary

Fill each blank with the best word or words from the list.

acid, E82
alkalinity, E86
base, E82
chemical change, E71
colloid, E54
conduction, E97
convection, E97
kinetic energy, E95
mixture, E52
potential energy, E95
radiation, E97
solution, E54

1. A(n) ______ is a mixture that looks the same everywhere, even under a microscope.

2. A(n) ______ turns blue litmus paper red.

3. In a(n) ______ two chemicals react to form a new substance.

4. The Sun's energy is transferred to Earth by ______.

5. An object that is moving has ______.

6. In ______ energy is transferred without the movement of matter.

7. A(n) ______ has properties between a solution and heterogeneous mixture.

8. Stored energy is called ______.

9. Energy is usually transferred by ______ in liquids and gases.

10. The strength of a base is called its ______.

Test Prep

11. In a chemical reaction, there may be a ______.

A color change
B formation of a gas
C heat change
D all of the above

12. All of the following are poor conductors of heat EXCEPT ______.

F wood
G glass
H copper
J air

13. An example of a physical change is ______.

A ice melting
B bread baking
C a match burning
D a nail rusting

14. Heat always flows ______.

- **F** from lighter materials to heavier materials
- **G** from heavier materials to lighter materials
- **H** from cooler materials to hotter materials
- **J** from hotter materials to cooler materials

15. ______ may be used as an indicator.

- **A** cabbage juice
- **B** litmus paper
- **C** a pH meter
- **D** all of the above

Concepts and Skills

16. Reading in Science What signs are there that baking bread is a chemical change?

17. Process Skills: Experiment A friend says he removed tarnish from a silver spoon by putting it in the bottom of an aluminum pot containing a hot baking-soda solution. What really removed the tarnish? Describe how you would perform experiments to find out.

18. Critical Thinking A certain material can be separated by physical changes. Can it be a single compound? Why or why not?

19. Scientific Methods What are two things you might see during a chemical change?

20. Safety Whenever you use a cleaning material, you should read the label carefully. Some kinds of cleaning materials should never be used together. What may be one reason for this?

Chemist

Dr. Mario Molina

Massachusetts Institute of Technology

The rise of pollution in our world has led to the need for new kinds of scientists. Environmental chemists like Dr. Mario Molina study the effects of chemicals on the environment. Dr. Molina has been especially interested in the effect of pollution on Earth's ozone layer.

When he received his first toy microscope and chemistry set as a child, Dr. Molina turned his family's bathroom into a laboratory! He knew then that he wanted to become a research chemist. Dr. Molina received his doctorate in chemistry from the University of California in 1972.

Dr. Molina decided to study a group of chemicals called chlorofluorocarbons, or CFCs. CFCs are compounds that were used in aerosol sprays, refrigerators, and air conditioners.

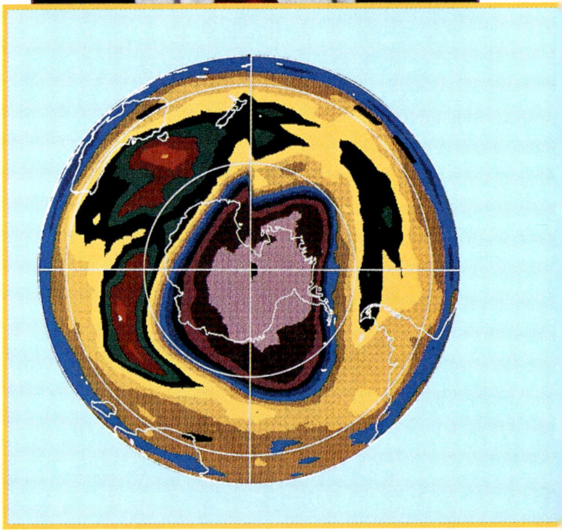

When exposed to radiation, CFCs break down into chlorine, fluorine, and carbon atoms. The chlorine atom is very reactive. It breaks down ozone. A single chlorine atom can destroy as many as 100,000 ozone molecules! This is especially destructive because the amount of ozone in the atmosphere is very limited and because ozone provides us with needed protection from the Sun.

More research showed that enough ozone had been destroyed by CFCs to create a "hole" in the ozone layer over Antarctica. Almost all the nations of the world agreed to a ban on the production of CFCs starting in 1996. Thanks to Dr. Molina, people around the world are working to ensure that the ozone layer continues to help protect life on Earth.

Careers IN SCIENCE

Environmental Engineer

If you're interested in chemistry, you may want to be an environmental engineer. An environmental engineer studies ways to eliminate, control, or prevent pollution in our environment. Some try to clean polluted lakes and rivers. Environmental engineers usually split their time between the laboratory and the field.

To become an environmental engineer, you need a college degree, usually in environmental engineering. An advanced degree is required for research and teaching. A license is also required for engineers working in the area of public health and safety.

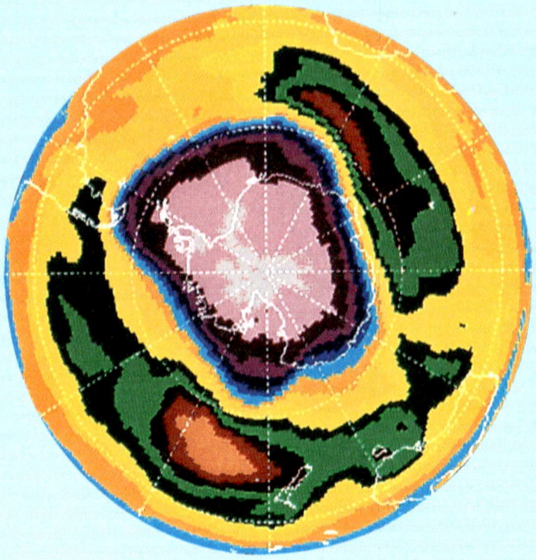

Computer-enhanced images of ozone hole over Antarctica

Write ABOUT IT

1. What three elements make up CFCs?
2. How is chlorine especially destructive to ozone?

AT THE COMPUTER

Visit www.mhscience02.com to learn more about careers.

PROBING the PROPERTIES

Your goal is to describe objects in a collection in terms of their properties.

What to Do

1. List each object in your collection. Leave space next to each name where you can list the object's properties.
2. List as many properties as you can observe for each object.
3. Measure the mass of each object, and record it on your list.

Analyze Your Results

What are all of the objects in your collection made of?

TESTING FOR pH

Your goal is to put eight unknown solutions in order from most acidic to most basic.

What to Do

1. Use eight unknown solutions, pH paper, a pH scale, a pencil, and paper. Dip a piece of pH paper into each solution. Compare the color of the pH paper with the pH scale. Record each pH in a table.
2. Make a new table that shows the order of the solutions from most acidic to most basic. Include the pH of each solution.

Analyze Your Results

1. Which solutions are acids? Which solutions are bases?
2. If you have an upset stomach, it might be because you have too much acid in your stomach. Why are medicines taken for a stomachache usually bases?

For Your Reference

Science Handbook

Health Handbook

Units of Measurement

Units of Measurement

Table of Measurements

International System of Units (SI)

Temperature

Water freezes at 0°C and boils at 100°C.

Length and Distance

1,000 meters (m) = 1 kilometer (km)
100 centimeters (cm) = 1 meter
10 millimeters (mm) = 1 centimeter

Volume

1,000 milliliters (mL) = 1 liter (L)
1 cubic centimeter (cm^3) = 1 milliliter

Mass

1,000 grams (g) = 1 kilogram (kg)

English System of Units

Temperature

Water freezes at 32°F and boils at 212°F.

Length and Distance

5,280 feet = 1 mile
3 feet = 1 yard
12 inches = 1 foot

Volume of Fluids

4 quarts = 1 gallon
2 pints = 1 quart
2 cups = 1 pint
8 fluid ounces = 1 cup

Weight

2,000 pounds = 1 ton
16 ounces = 1 pound

Use a Hand Lens

You use a hand lens to magnify an object, or make the object look larger. With a hand lens, you can see details that would be hard to see without the hand lens.

Magnify a Piece of Cereal

1. Place a piece of your favorite cereal on a flat surface. Look at the cereal carefully. Draw a picture of it.
2. Look at the cereal through the large lens of a hand lens. Move the lens toward or away from the cereal until it looks larger and in focus. Draw a picture of the cereal as you see it through the hand lens. Fill in details that you did not see before.
3. Look at the cereal through the smaller lens, which will magnify the cereal even more. If you notice more details, add them to your drawing.
4. Repeat this activity using objects you are studying in science. It might be a rock, some soil, or a seed.

Observe Seeds in a Petri Dish

Can you observe a seed as it sprouts? You can if it's in a petri dish. A petri dish is a shallow, clear, round dish with a cover.

1. Line the sides and bottom of a petri dish with a double layer of filter paper or paper towel. You may have to cut the paper to make it fit.
2. Sprinkle water on the paper to wet it.
3. Place three or four radish seeds on the wet paper in different areas of the dish. Put the lid on the dish, and keep it in a warm place.
4. Observe the seeds every day for a week. Use a hand lens to look for a tiny root pushing through the seed. Record how long it takes each seed to sprout.

Use a Microscope

Hand lenses make objects look several times larger. A microscope, however, can magnify an object to look hundreds of times larger.

Examine Salt Grains

1. Look at the photograph to learn the different parts of your microscope.
2. Place the microscope on a flat surface. Always carry a microscope with both hands. Hold the arm with one hand, and put your other hand beneath the base.
3. Move the mirror so that it reflects light up toward the stage. Never point the mirror directly at the Sun or a bright light. Bright light can cause permanent eye damage.
4. Place a few grains of salt on the slide. Put the slide under the stage clips. Be sure that the salt grains you are going to examine are over the hole in the stage.
5. Look through the eyepiece. Turn the focusing knob slowly until the salt grains come into focus.
6. Draw what the grains look like through the microscope.
7. Look at other objects through the microscope. Try a piece of leaf, a human hair, or a pencil mark.

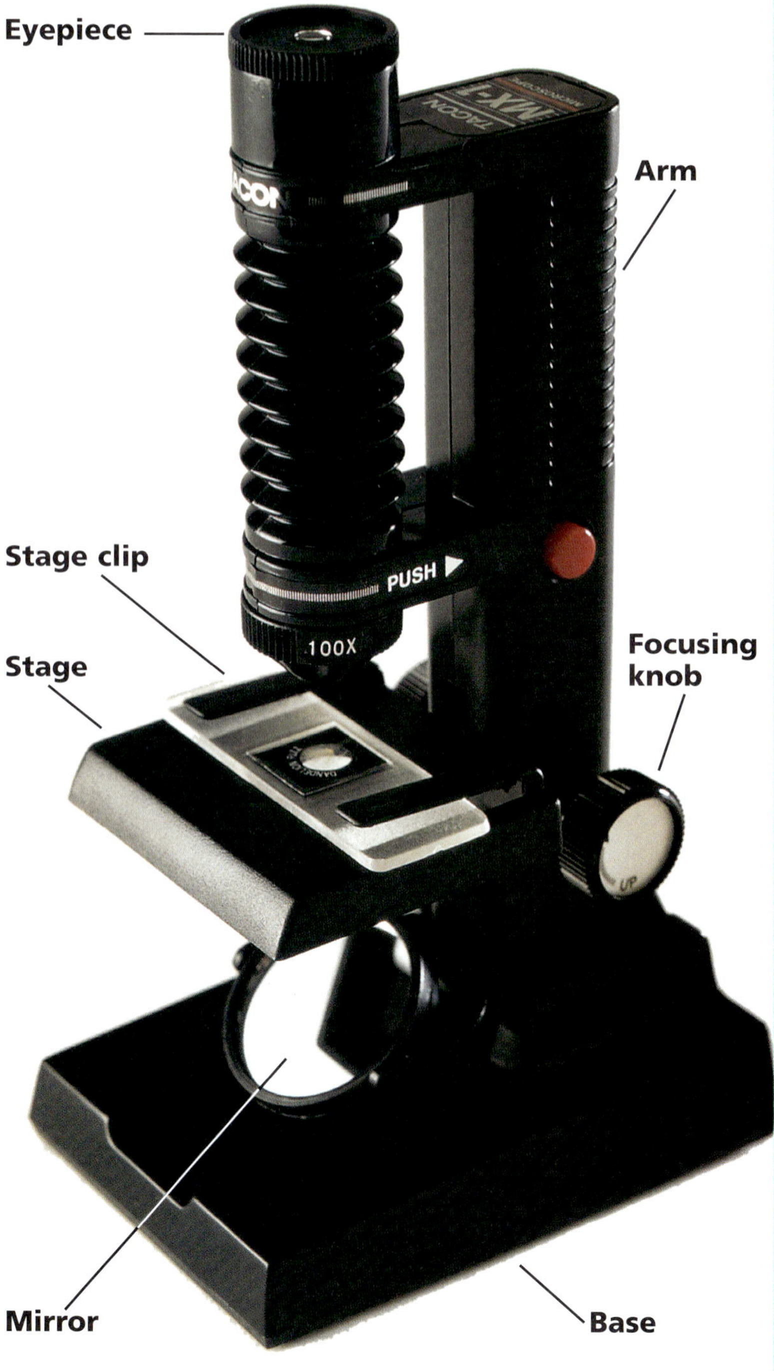

Measure Time

You use timing devices to measure how long something takes to happen. Some timing devices you use in science are a clock with a second hand and a stopwatch. Which one is more accurate?

Comparing a Clock and Stopwatch

1. Look at a clock with a second hand. The second hand is the hand that you can see moving. It measures seconds.
2. Get an egg timer with falling sand or some device like a wind-up toy that runs down after a certain length of time. When the second hand of the clock points to 12, tell your partner to start the egg timer. Watch the clock while the sand in the egg timer is falling.
3. When the sand stops falling, count how many seconds it took. Record this measurement. Repeat the activity, and compare the two measurements.
4. Switch roles with your partner.
5. Look at a stopwatch. Click the button on the top right. This starts the time. Click the button again. This stops the time. Click the button on the top left. This sets the stopwatch back to zero. Notice that the stopwatch tells time in minutes, seconds, and hundredths of a second.
6. Repeat the activity in steps 1–3, using the stopwatch instead of a clock. Make sure the stopwatch is set to zero. Click the top right button to start timing the reading. Click it again when the sand stops falling. Make sure you and your partner time each other twice.

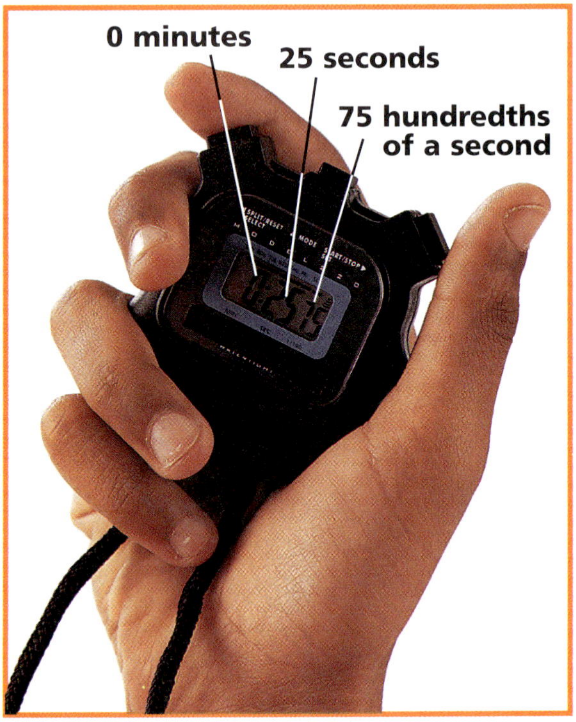

More About Time

1. Use the stopwatch to time how long it takes an ice cube to melt under cold running water. How long does an ice cube take to melt under warm running water?
2. Match each of these times with the action you think took that amount of time.

   a. 0:00:14:55
   b. 0:24:39:45
   c. 2:10:23:00

   1. A Little League baseball game
   2. Saying the Pledge of Allegiance
   3. Recess

Measure Length

Find Length with a Ruler

1. Look at this section of a ruler. Each centimeter is divided into 10 millimeters. How long is the paper clip?
2. The length of the paper clip is 3 centimeters plus 2 millimeters. You can write this length as 3.2 centimeters.
3. Place the ruler on your desk. Lay a pencil against the ruler so that one end of the pencil lines up with the left edge of the ruler. Record the length of the pencil.
4. Trade your pencil with a classmate. Measure and record the length of each other's pencil. Compare your answers.

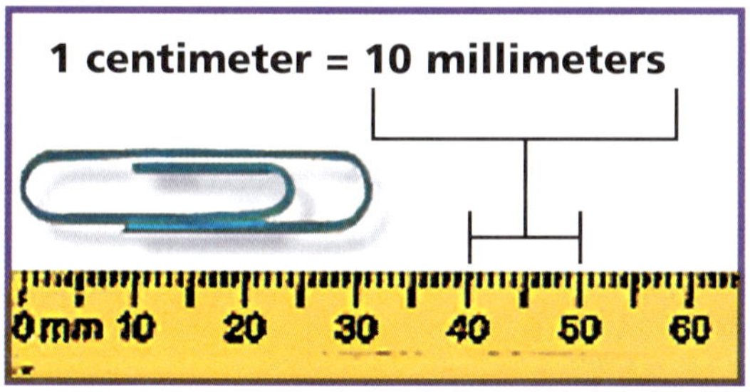

Measuring Area

Area is the amount of surface something covers. To find the area of a rectangle, multiply the rectangle's length by its width. For example, the rectangle here is 3 centimeters long and 2 centimeters wide. Its area is 3 cm x 2 cm = 6 square centimeters. You write the area as 6 cm^2.

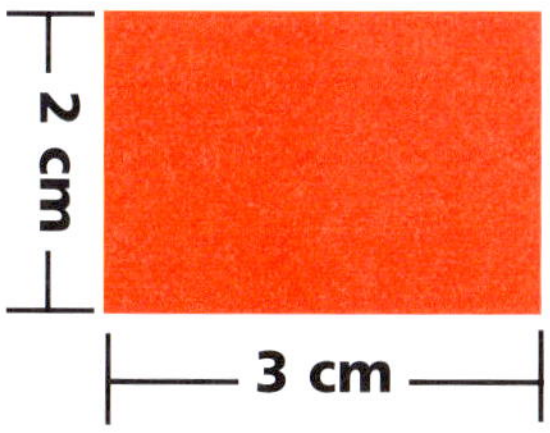

1. Find the area of your science book. Measure the book's length to the nearest centimeter. Measure its width.
2. Multiply the book's length by its width. Remember to put the answer in cm^2.

Find Length with a Meterstick

1. Line up the meterstick with the left edge of the chalkboard. Make a chalk mark on the board at the right end of the meterstick.
2. Move the meterstick so that the left edge lines up with the chalk mark. Keep the stick level. Make another mark on the board at the right end of the meterstick.
3. Continue to move the meterstick and make chalk marks until the meterstick meets or overlaps the right edge of the board.
4. Record the length of the chalkboard in centimeters by adding all the measurements you've made. Remember, a meterstick has 100 centimeters.

Estimating Length

Try estimating the length of objects in the room. Then measure the length, and compare the estimation with the measurement.

Measure Mass

Mass is the amount of matter an object has. You use a balance to measure mass. To find the mass of an object, you balance it with objects whose masses you know. Let's find the mass of a box of crayons.

Measure the Mass of a Box of Crayons

1. Place the balance on a flat, level surface. Check that the two pans are empty and clean.
2. Make sure the empty pans are balanced with each other. The pointer should point to the middle mark. If it does not, move the slider a little to the right or left to balance the pans.
3. Gently place a box of crayons on the left pan. This pan will drop lower.
4. Add masses to the right pan until the pans are balanced.
5. Add the numbers on the masses that are in the right pan. The total is the mass of the box of crayons, in grams. Record this number. After the number write a *g* for "grams."

Estimating Mass

Once you become familiar with the mass of objects, you can try estimating the masses of objects. Then you can compare the estimation with the actual mass.

More About Mass

The mass of your crayons was probably less than 100 grams. You may not have enough masses to balance a pineapple. It has a mass of about 1,000 grams. That's the same as 1 kilogram, because *kilo* means "1,000."

1. How many kilograms do all these masses add up to?
2. Which of these objects have a mass greater than 1 kilogram?

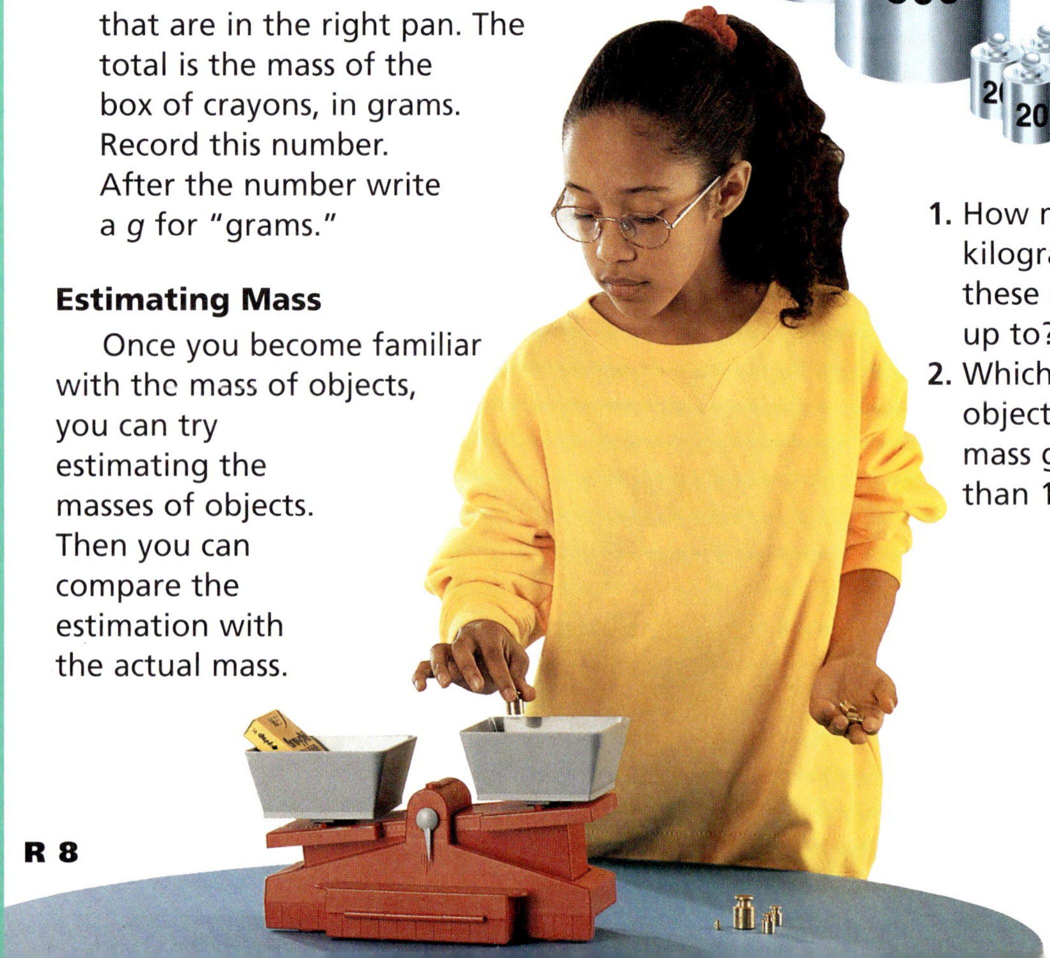

Measure Volume

Volume is the amount of space something takes up. In science you usually measure the volume of liquids by using beakers and graduated cylinders. These containers are marked in milliliters (mL).

Measure the Volume of a Liquid

1. Look at the beaker and at the graduated cylinder. The beaker has marks for each 25 mL up to 200 mL. The graduated cylinder has marks for each 1 mL up to 100 mL.
2. The surface of the water in the graduated cylinder curves up at the sides. You measure the volume by reading the height of the water at the flat part. What is the volume of water in the graduated cylinder? How much water is in the beaker? They both contain 75 mL of water.
3. Pour 50 mL of water from a pitcher into a beaker.
4. Now pour the 50 mL of water into a graduated cylinder.

Find the Volume of a Solid

Here's a way to find the volume of a solid, such as a rock.

1. Start with 50 mL of water in a graduated cylinder.
2. Place a small rock in the water. The water level rises.
3. Measure the new water level. Subtract 50 mL from the new reading. The difference is the volume of the rock. Record the volume in cm^3.

Estimating Volume

Once you become familiar with the volumes of liquids and solids, you can estimate volumes. Estimate the amount of liquid in a glass or can. Estimate the volume of an eraser.

Measure Weight/Force

You use a spring scale to measure weight. An object has weight because the force of gravity pulls down on the object. Therefore, weight is a force. Weight is measured in newtons (N) like all forces.

Measure the Weight of an Object

1. Look at your spring scale to see how many newtons it measures. See how the measurements are divided. The spring scale shown here measures up to 5 N. It has a mark for every 0.1 N.
2. Hold the spring scale by the top loop. Put the object to be measured on the bottom hook. If the object will not stay on the hook, place it in a net bag. Then hang the bag from the hook.
3. Let go of the object slowly. It will pull down on a spring inside the scale. The spring is connected to a pointer. The pointer on the spring scale shown here is a small bar.
4. Wait for the pointer to stop moving. Read the number of newtons next to the pointer. This is the object's weight. The mug in the picture weighs 4 N.

More About Spring Scales

You probably weigh yourself by standing on a bathroom scale. This is a spring scale. The force of your body stretches a spring inside the scale. The dial on the scale is probably marked in pounds—the English unit of weight. One pound is equal to about 4.5 newtons.

A bathroom scale, a grocery scale, and a kitchen scale are some other spring scales you may have seen.

Measure Temperature

You use a thermometer to measure temperature—how hot or cold something is. A thermometer is made of a thin tube with colored liquid inside. When the liquid gets warmer, it expands and moves up the tube. When the liquid gets cooler, it contracts and moves down the tube. You may have seen most temperatures measured in degrees Fahrenheit (°F). Scientists measure temperature in degrees Celsius (°C).

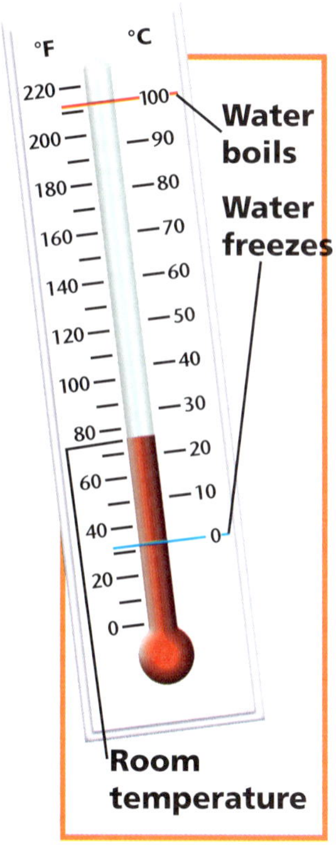

Read a Thermometer

1. Look at the thermometer shown here. It has two scales—a Fahrenheit scale and a Celsius scale.
2. What is the temperature shown on the thermometer? At what temperature does water freeze?

What Is Convection?

1. Fill a large beaker about two-thirds full of cool water. Find the temperature of the water by holding a thermometer in the water. Do not let the bulb at the bottom of the thermometer touch the sides or bottom of the beaker.
2. Keep the thermometer in the water until the liquid in the tube stops moving—about 1 minute. Read and record the temperature in °C.
3. Sprinkle a little fish food on the surface of the water in the beaker. Do not knock the beaker, and most of the food will stay on top.
4. Carefully place the beaker on a hot plate. A hot plate is a small electric stove. Plug in the hot plate, and turn the control knob to a middle setting.
5. After 1 minute measure the temperature of water near the bottom of the beaker. At the same time, a classmate should measure the temperature of water near the top of the beaker. Record these temperatures. Is water near the bottom of the beaker heating up faster than near the top?
6. As the water heats up, notice what happens to the fish food. How do you know that warmer water at the bottom of the beaker rises and cooler water at the top sinks?

Use Calculators

Sometimes after you make measurements, you have to analyze your data to see what it means. This might involve doing calculations with your data. A calculator helps you do time-consuming calculations.

Find an Average

After you collect a set of measurements, you may want to get an idea of a typical measurement in that set. What if, for example, you are doing a weather project? As part of the project, you are studying rainfall data of a nearby town. The table shows how much rain fell in that town each week during the summer.

Week	Rain (cm)
1	2.0
2	1.4
3	0.0
4	0.5
5	1.2
6	2.5
7	1.8
8	1.4
9	2.4
10	8.6
11	7.5

What if you want to get an idea of how much rain fell during a typical week in the summer? In other words, you want to find the average for the set of data. There are three kinds of averages—mean, median, and mode. Does it matter which one you use?

Find the Mean

The mean is what most people think of when they hear the word *average*. You can use a calculator to find the mean.

1. Make sure the calculator is on.
2. Add the numbers. To add a series of numbers, enter the first number and press +. Repeat until you enter the last number. See the hints below. After your last number, press =. Your total should be 29.3.
3. While entering so many numbers, it's easy to make a mistake and hit the wrong key. If you make a mistake, correct it by pressing the clear entry key, CE. Then continue entering the rest of the numbers.
4. Find the mean by dividing your total by the number of weeks. If 29.3 is displayed, press ÷ 1 1 =. Rounded up to one decimal point, your mean should be 2.7.

Hints:

- If the only number to the right of the decimal point is 0, you don't have to enter it into the calculator. To enter 2.0, just press 2.
- If the only number to the left of the decimal point is 0, you don't have to enter it into the calculator. To enter 0.5, just press . 5.

Find the Median

The median is the middle number when the numbers are arranged in order of size. When the rainfall measurements are arranged in order of size, they look like this.

0.0
0.5
1.2
1.4
1.4
1.8 — The median is 1.8. This number is in the middle; there are five numbers above it and five numbers below it.
2.0
2.4
2.5
7.5
8.6

Find the Mode

The mode is the number that occurs most frequently. From the ranked set of data above, you can see that the most frequent number is 1.4. It occurs twice. Here are your three different averages from the same set of data.

Average Weekly Rainfall (cm)

Mean	2.7
Median	1.8
Mode	1.4

Why is the mean so much higher than the median or mode? The mean is affected greatly by the last two weeks when it rained a lot. A typical week for that summer was much drier than either of those last two weeks. The median or mode gives a better idea of rainfall for a typical week.

Find the Mean, Median, and Mode

The table shows the length of 15 peanuts. Find the mean, median, and mode for this set of data. Which do you think best represents a typical peanut?

Peanut	Length (mm)
1	32
2	29
3	30
4	31
5	33
6	26
7	28
8	27
9	29
10	29
11	32
12	31
13	23
14	36
15	31

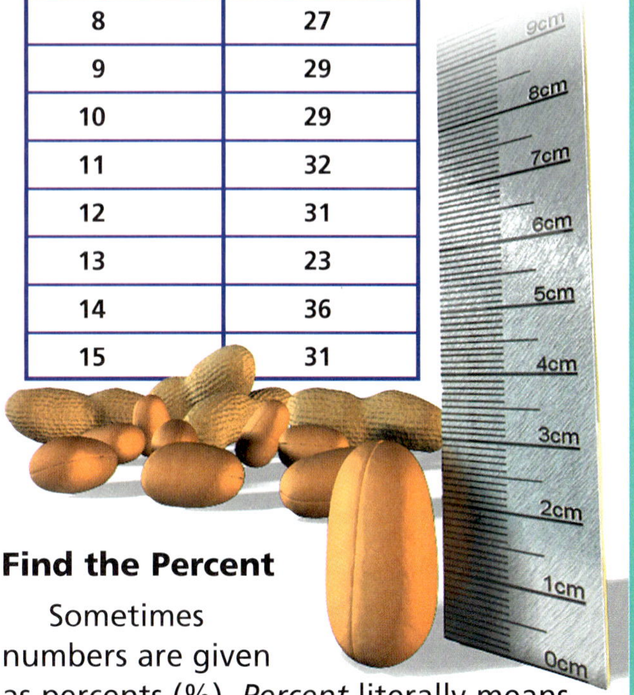

Find the Percent

Sometimes numbers are given as percents (%). *Percent* literally means "per hundred." For example, 28% means 28 out of 100. What if there are about 14,000 trees in the forest and 28% are over 50 years old? How many of them are over 50 years old? Use your calculator. You want to find 28% of 14,000. Press [1][4][0][0][0] [×] [2][8][%]. The answer should be 3,920.

Use Computers

A computer has many uses. The Internet connects your computer to many other computers around the world, so you can collect all kinds of information. You can use a computer to show this information and write reports. Best of all you can use a computer to explore, discover, and learn.

You can also get information from CD-ROMs. They are computer disks that can hold large amounts of information. You can fit a whole encyclopedia on one CD-ROM.

Use Computers for a Project

Here is how one group of students uses computers as they work on a weather project.

1. The students use instruments to measure temperature, wind speed, wind direction, and other parts of the weather. They input this information, or data, into the computer. The students keep the data in a table. This helps them compare the data from one day to the next.

Use Technology

2. The teacher finds out that another group of students in a town 200 kilometers to the west is also doing a weather project. The two groups use the Internet to talk to each other and share data. When a storm happens in the town to the west, that group tells the other group that it's coming their way.
3. The students want to find out more. They decide to stay on the Internet and send questions to a local TV weather forecaster. She has a Web site and answers questions from students every day.

4. Meanwhile some students go to the library to gather more information from a CD-ROM. The CD-ROM has an encyclopedia that includes movie clips. The clips give examples of different kinds of storms.
5. The students have kept all their information in a folder called Weather Project. Now they use that information to write a report about the weather. On the computer they can move around paragraphs, add words, take out words, put in diagrams, and draw weather maps. Then they print the report in color.

Make Graphs to Organize Data

When you do an experiment in science, you collect information. To find out what your information means, you can organize it into graphs. There are many kinds of graphs.

Bar Graphs

A bar graph uses bars to show information. For example, what if you do an experiment by wrapping wire around a nail and connecting the ends of the wire to a battery? The nail then becomes a magnet that can pick up paper clips. The graph shows that the more you wrap the wire around the nail, the more paper clips it picks up. How many paper clips did the nail with 20 coils pick up? With 50 coils?

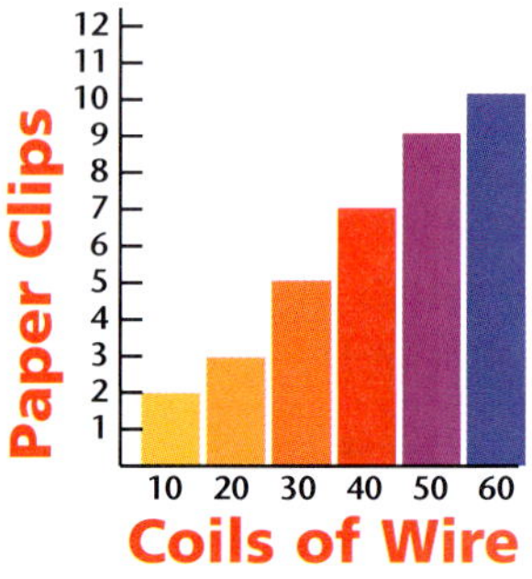

Pictographs

A pictograph uses symbols, or pictures, to show information. What if you collect information about how much water your family uses each day? The table shows what you find.

You can organize this information into the pictograph shown here. The pictograph has to explain what the symbol on the graph means. In this case each bottle means 20 liters of water. A half bottle means half of 20, or 10 liters of water.

1. Which activity uses the most water?
2. Which activity uses the least water?

Activity	Water Used Each Day (L)
Drinking	10
Showering	180
Bathing	240
Brushing teeth	80
Washing dishes	140
Washing hands	30
Washing clothes	280
Flushing toilet	90

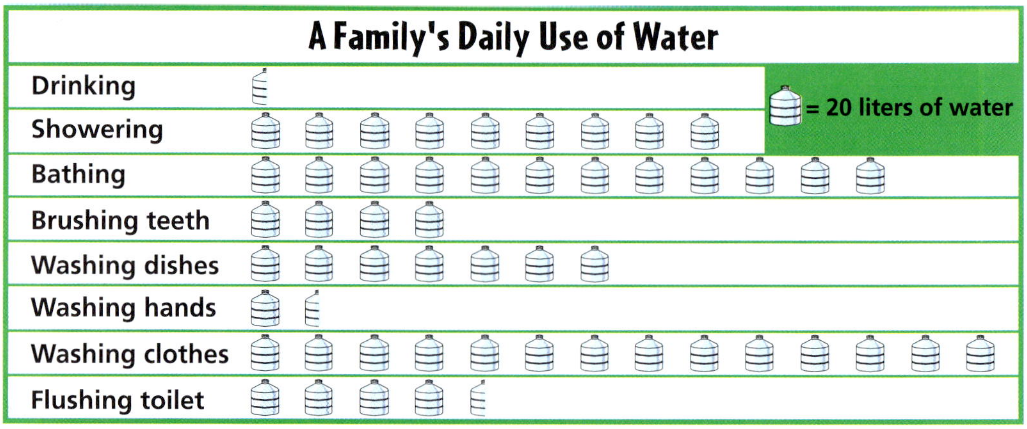

Represent Data

Circle Graphs

A circle graph is helpful to show how a complete set of data is divided into parts. The circle graph here shows how water is used in the United States. What is the single largest use of water?

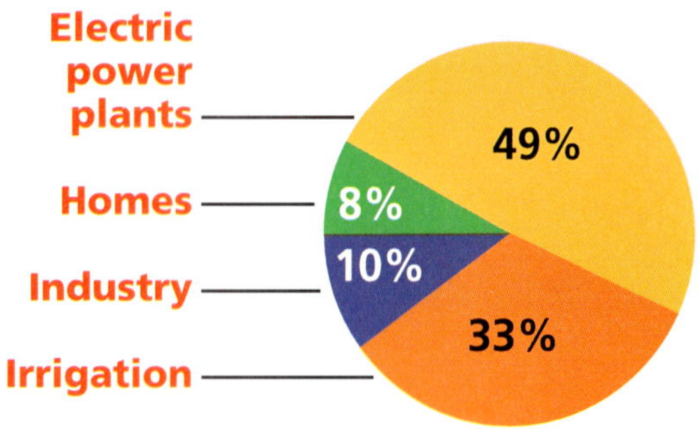

Line Graphs

A line graph shows information by connecting dots plotted on the graph. It shows change over time. For example, what if you measure the temperature out of doors every hour starting at 6 A.M.? The table shows what you find.

Time	Temperature (°C)
6 A.M.	10
7 A.M.	12
8 A.M.	14
9 A.M.	16
10 A.M.	18
11 A.M.	20

You can organize this information into a line graph. Follow these steps.

1. Make a scale along the bottom and side of the graph. The scales should include all the numbers in the chart. Label the scales.
2. Plot points on the graph. For example, place your finger at the "6 A.M." on the bottom line. Place a finger from your other hand on the "10" on the left line. Move your "6 A.M." finger up and your "10" finger to the right until they meet, and make a pencil point. Plot the other points in this way.
3. Connect the points with a line.

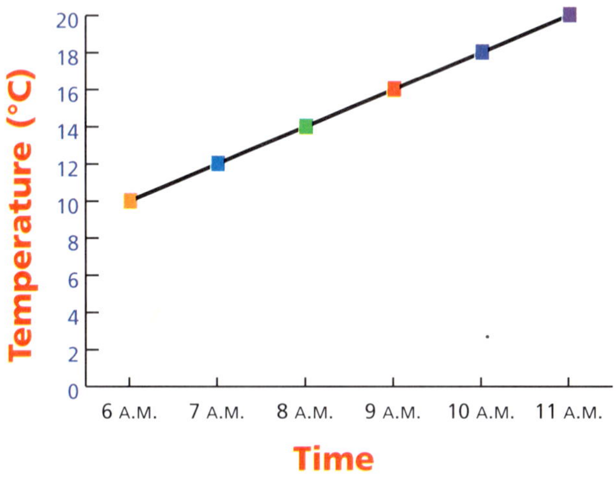

The line graph to the right organizes measurements you collected so that you can easily compare them.

1. Between which two weeks did the plant grow most?
2. When did plant growth begin to level off?

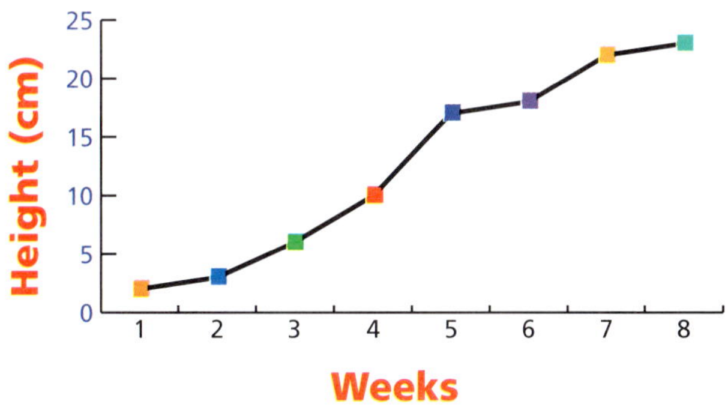

Make Maps to Show Information

Locate Places

A map is a drawing that shows an area from above. Most maps have coordinates—numbers and letters along the top and side. Coordinates help you find places easily. For example, what if you wanted to find the library on the map? It is located at B4. Place a finger on the letter B along the side of the map, and another finger on the number 4 at the top. Then move your fingers straight across and down the map until they meet. The library is located where the coordinates B and 4 meet, or very nearby.

1. What color building is located at F6?
2. The hospital is located three blocks north and two blocks east of the library. What are its coordinates?
3. Make a map of an area in your community. It might be a park or the area between your home and school. Include coordinates. Use a compass to find north, and mark north on your map. Exchange maps with classmates, and answer each other's questions.

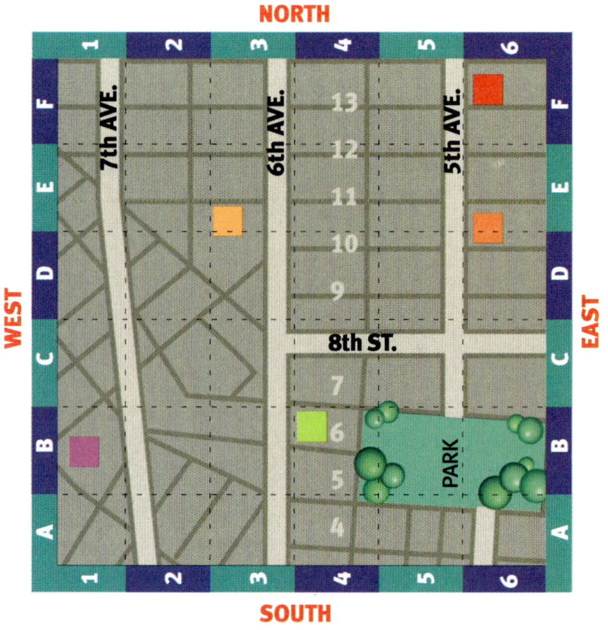

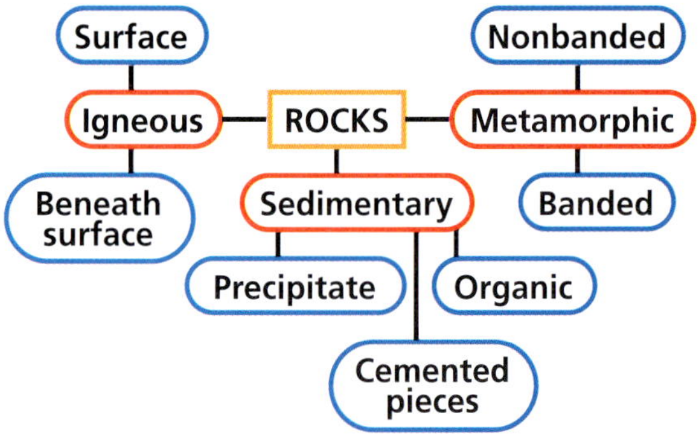

Idea Maps

The map below shows how places are connected to each other. Idea maps, on the other hand, show how ideas are connected to each other. Idea maps help you organize information about a topic.

The idea map above connects ideas about rocks. This map shows that there are three major types of rock—igneous, sedimentary, and metamorphic. Connections to each rock type provide further information. For example, this map reminds you that igneous rocks are classified into those that form at Earth's surface and far beneath it.

Make an idea map about a topic you are learning in science. Your map can include words, phrases, or even sentences. Arrange your map in a way that makes sense to you and helps you understand the ideas.

Represent Data

Make Tables and Charts to Organize Information

Tables help you organize data during experiments. Most tables have columns that run up and down, and rows that run across. The columns and rows have headings that tell you what kind of data goes in each part of the table.

A Sample Table

What if you are going to do an experiment to find out how long different kinds of seeds take to sprout? Before you begin the experiment, you should set up your table. Follow these steps.

1. In this experiment you will plant 20 radish seeds, 20 bean seeds, and 20 corn seeds. Your table must show how many radish seeds, bean seeds, and corn seeds sprouted on days 1, 2, 3, 4, and 5.

2. Make your table with columns, rows, and headings. You might use a computer to make a table. Some computer programs let you build a table with just the click of a mouse. You can delete or add columns and rows if you need to.
3. Give your table a title. Your table could look like the one here.

Make a Table

Now what if you are going to do an experiment to find out how temperature affects the sprouting of seeds? You will plant 20 bean seeds in each of two trays. You will keep each tray at a different temperature, as shown below, and observe the trays for seven days. Make a table you can use for this experiment.

Make a Chart

A chart is simply a table with pictures as well as words to label the rows or columns.

HEALTH Handbook

The Skeletal System

The body has a supporting frame, called a skeleton, which is made up of bones. The skeleton has several jobs.

- It gives the body its shape.
- It protects organs in the body.
- It works with muscles to move the body.

Each of the 206 bones of the skeleton is the size and shape best fitted to do its job. For example, long and strong leg bones support the body's weight.

CARE!

- **Exercise to keep your skeletal system in good shape.**
- **Don't overextend your joints.**
- **Eat foods rich in vitamins and minerals. Your bones need the minerals calcium and phosphorus to grow strong.**

The Skeleton

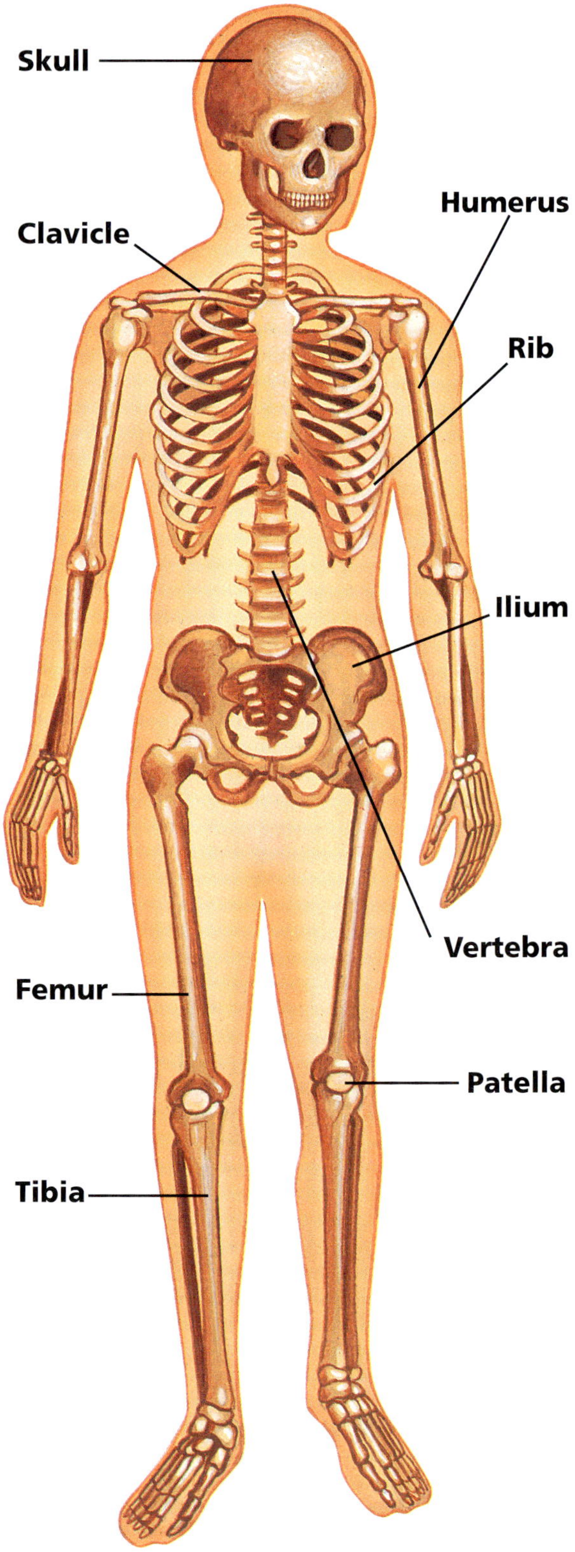

Joints

The skeleton has different types of joints. A joint is a place where two or more bones meet. Joints can be classified into three major groups—immovable joints, partly movable joints, and movable joints.

Types of Joints

Immovable Joints

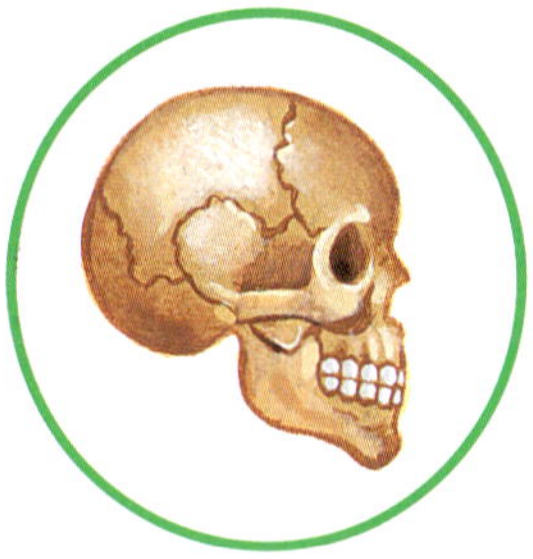

Head

Immovable joints are places where bones fit together too tightly to move. Nearly all the 29 bones in the skull meet at immovable joints. Only the lower jaw can move.

Partly Movable Joints

Partly movable joints are places where bones can move only a little. Ribs are connected to the breastbone with these joints.

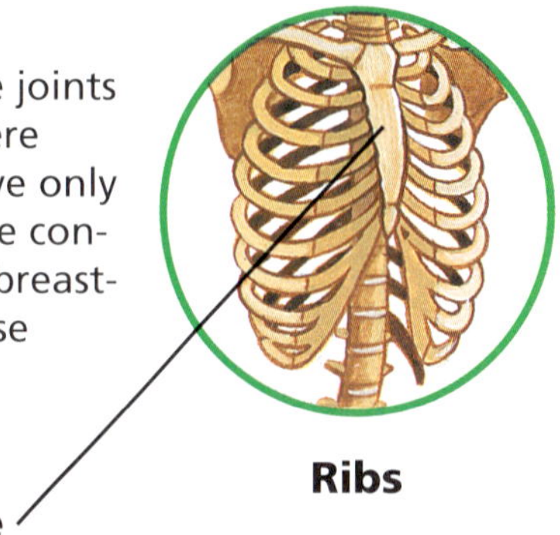

Ribs

Movable Joints

Movable joints are places where bones can move easily.

Gliding joint

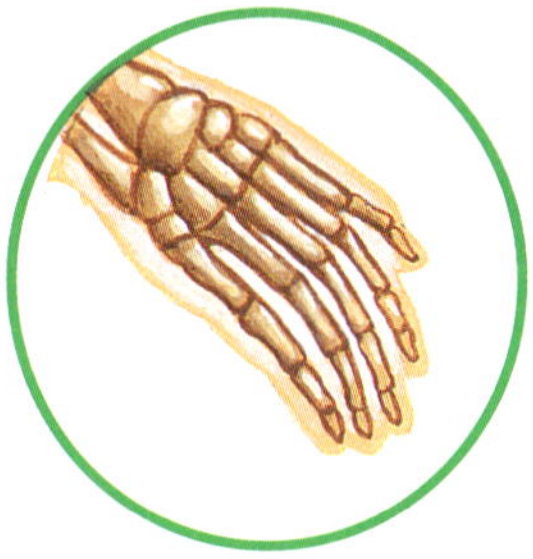

Hand and wrist

Small bones in the wrists and ankles meet at gliding joints. The bones can slide against one another. These joints allow some movement in all directions.

Ball-and-socket joint

The hips are examples of ball-and-socket joints. The ball of one bone fits into the socket, or cup, of another bone. These joints allow bones to move back and forth, in a circle, and side to side.

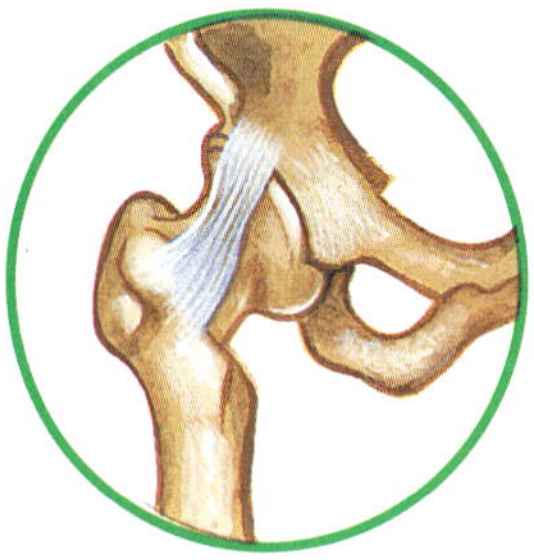

Hip

Hinge joint

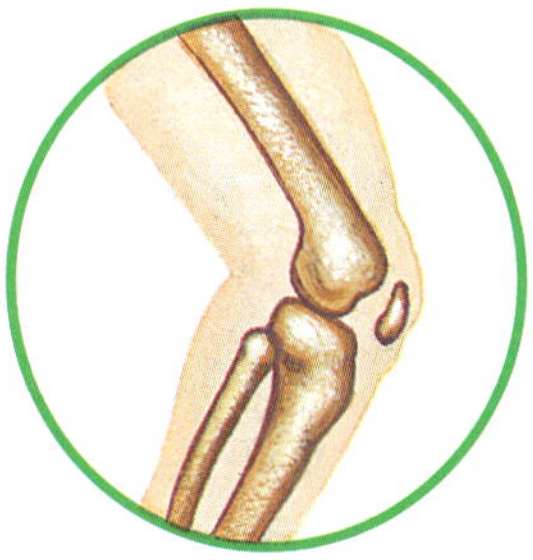

Knee

The knees are hinge joints. A hinge joint is similar to a door hinge. It allows bones to move back and forth in one direction.

Pivot joint

The joint between the skull and neck is a pivot joint. It allows the head to move up and down, and side to side.

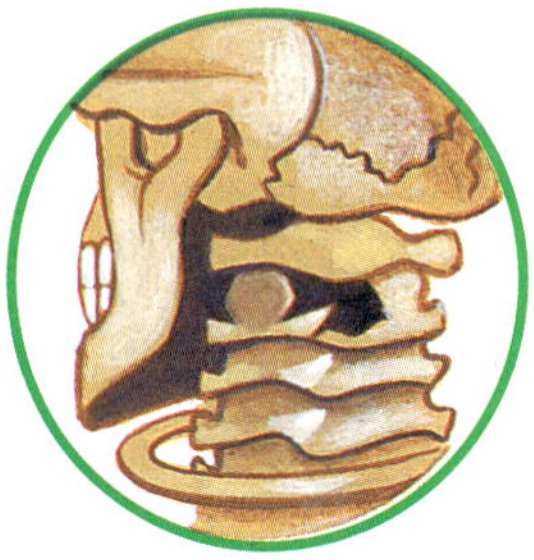

Neck

The Muscular System

Three types of muscles make up the body—skeletal muscle, cardiac muscle, and smooth muscle.

The muscles that are attached to and move bones are called skeletal muscles. These muscles are attached to bones by a tough cord called a tendon. Skeletal muscles pull bones to move them. Muscles do not push bones.

Cardiac muscles are found in only one place in the body—the heart. The walls of the heart are made of strong cardiac muscles. When cardiac muscles contract, they squeeze blood out of the heart. When cardiac muscles relax, the heart fills with more blood.

Smooth muscles make up internal organs and blood vessels. Smooth muscles in the lungs help a person breathe. Those in the blood vessels help control blood flow around the body.

CARE!

- **Exercise to strengthen your muscles.**
- **Eat the right foods.**
- **Get plenty of rest.**
- **Never take steroids unless your doctor tells you to.**

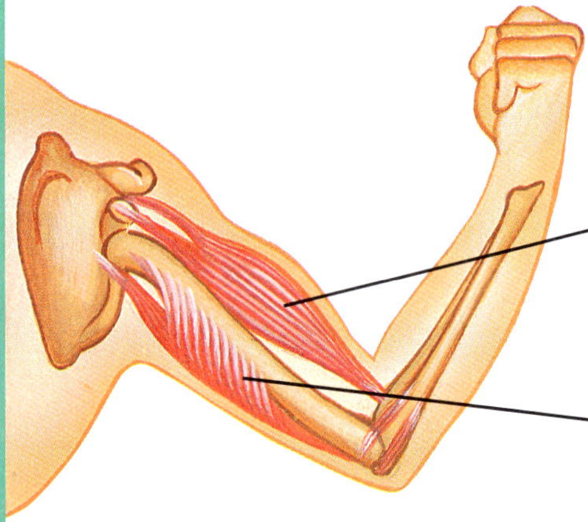

1. A message from you brain causes this muscle, called the biceps (BIGH·seps), to contract. When a muscle contracts, it becomes shorter and thicker. As the biceps contacts, it pulls on the arm bone it is attached to.
2. Most muscles work in pairs to move bones. This muscle, called the triceps (TRIGH·seps), relaxes when the biceps contacts. When a muscle relaxes, it becomes longer and thinner.

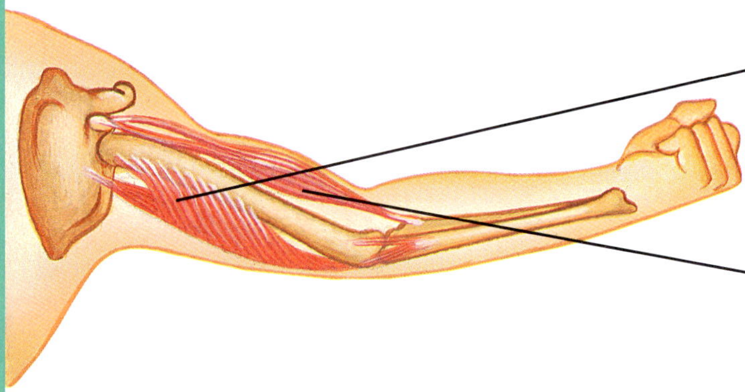

3. To straighten your arm, a message from your brain causes the triceps to contract. When the triceps contracts, it pulls on the bone it is attached to.
4. As the triceps contracts, the biceps relaxes. Your arm straightens.

The Circulatory System

The circulatory system consists of the heart, blood vessels, and blood. Circulation is the flow of blood through the body. Blood is a liquid that contains red blood cells, white blood cells, and platelets. Red blood cells carry oxygen and nutrients to cells. White blood cells work to fight germs that enter the body. Platelets are cell fragments that make the blood clot.

The heart is a muscular organ about the size of a fist. It beats about 70 to 90 times a minute, pumping blood through the blood vessels. Arteries carry blood away from the heart. Some arteries carry blood to the lungs, where the cells pick up oxygen. Other arteries carry oxygen-rich blood from the lungs to all other parts of the body. Veins carry blood from other parts of the body back to the heart. Blood in most veins carries the wastes released by cells and has little oxygen. Blood flows from arteries to veins through narrow vessels called capillaries.

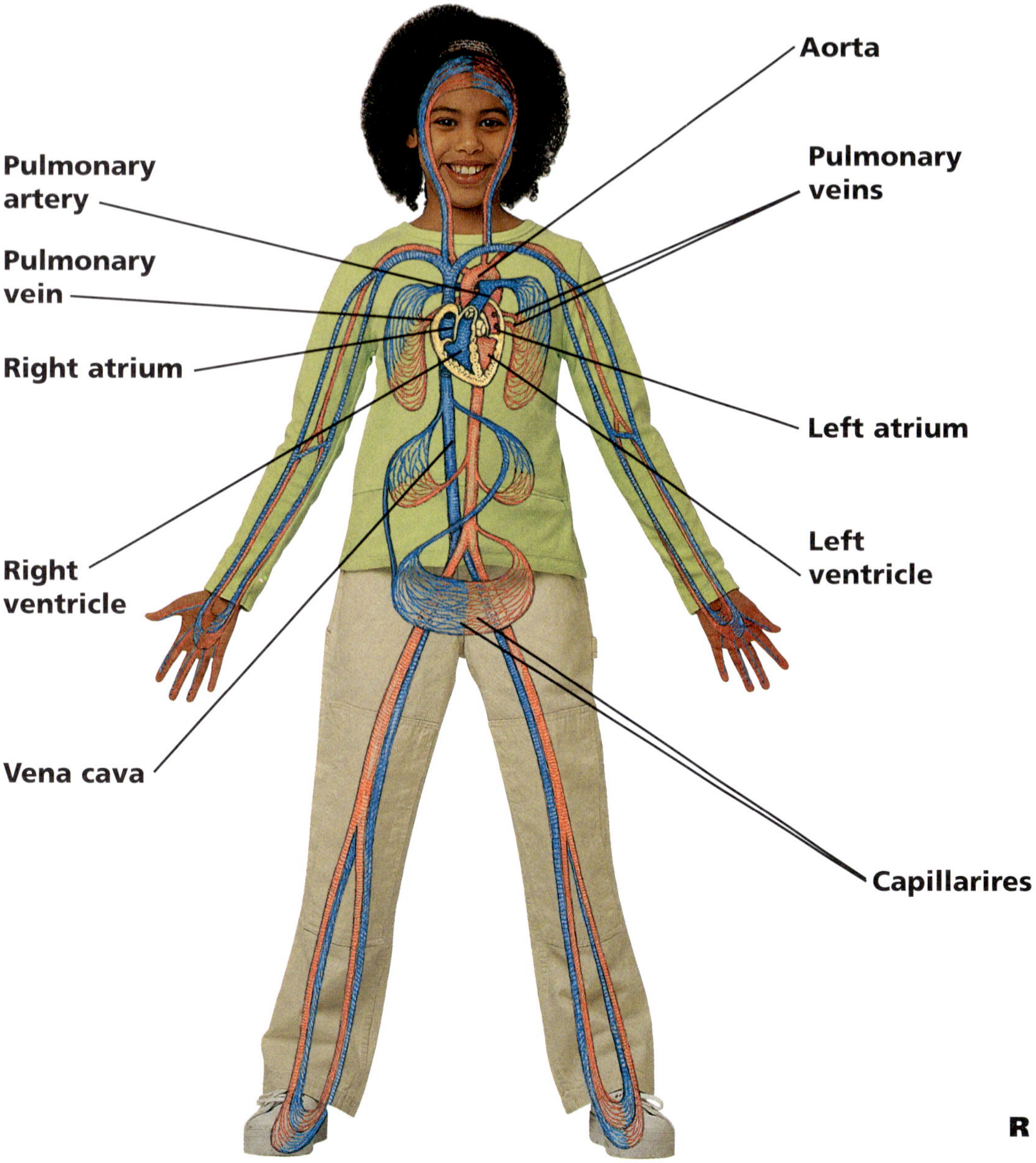

The Heart

The heart has two sides, right and left, separated by a thick muscular wall. Each side has two chambers for blood. The upper chamber is the atrium. The lower chamber is the ventricle. Blood enters the heart through the vena cava. It leaves the heart through the aorta.

The pulmonary artery carries blood from the body into the lungs. Here carbon dioxide leaves the blood to be exhaled by the lungs. Fresh oxygen enters the blood to be carried to every cell in the body. Blood returns from the lungs to the heart through the pulmonary veins.

CARE!

- **Don't smoke. The nicotine in tobacco makes the heart beat faster and work harder to pump blood.**
- **Never take illegal drugs, such as cocaine or heroin. They can damage the heart and cause heart failure.**

How the Heart Works

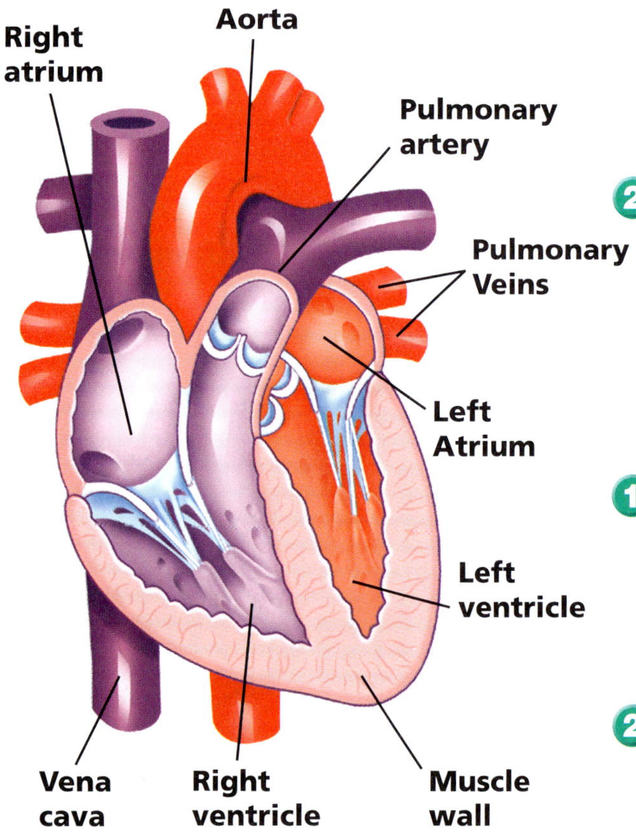

To the Lungs

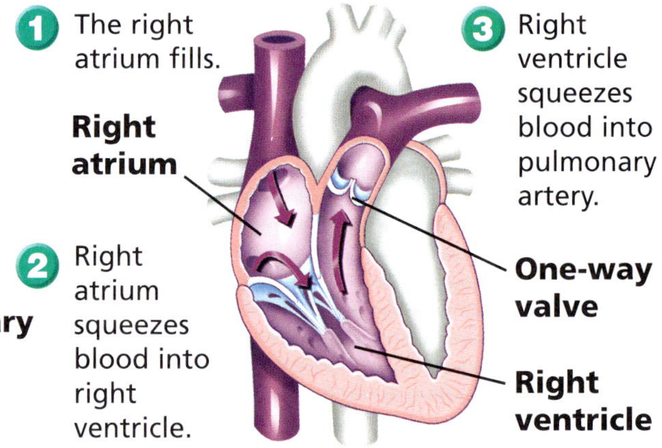

From the Lungs

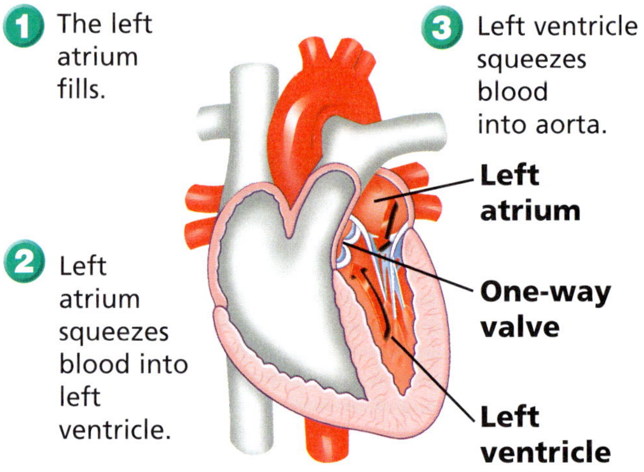

The Respiratory System

The process of getting and using oxygen in the body is called respiration. When a person inhales, air is pulled into the nose or mouth. The air travels down into the trachea. In the chest the trachea divides into two bronchial tubes. One bronchial tube enters each lung. Each bronchial tube branches into smaller tubes called bronchioles.

At the end of each bronchiole are tiny air sacs called alveoli. The alveoli exchange carbon dioxide for oxygen.

Oxygen comes from the air a person breathes. Two main muscles control breathing. One is located between the ribs. The other is a dome-shaped sheet of muscle called the diaphragm.

To inhale, the diaphragm contracts and pulls down. Other muscles pull the ribs up and out. This makes more room in the chest. Air rushes into the lungs and fills the space.

To exhale, the diaphragm relaxes and returns to its dome shape. The lungs get smaller and force the air out.

CARE!

- **Don't smoke. Smoking damages your respiratory system.**
- **Exercise to strengthen your breathing muscles.**
- **If you ever have trouble breathing, tell an adult at once.**

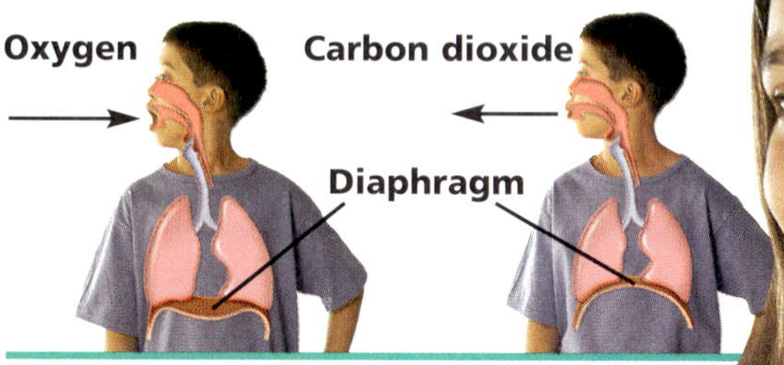

The air you breathe is about 21 percent oxygen.

The blood in the capillaries of your lungs has very little oxygen.

The blood has a higher concentration of carbon dioxide than air.

1. Carbon dioxide diffuses into the alveoli. From there it is exhaled.
2. Fresh oxygen diffuses from the alveoli to the blood.

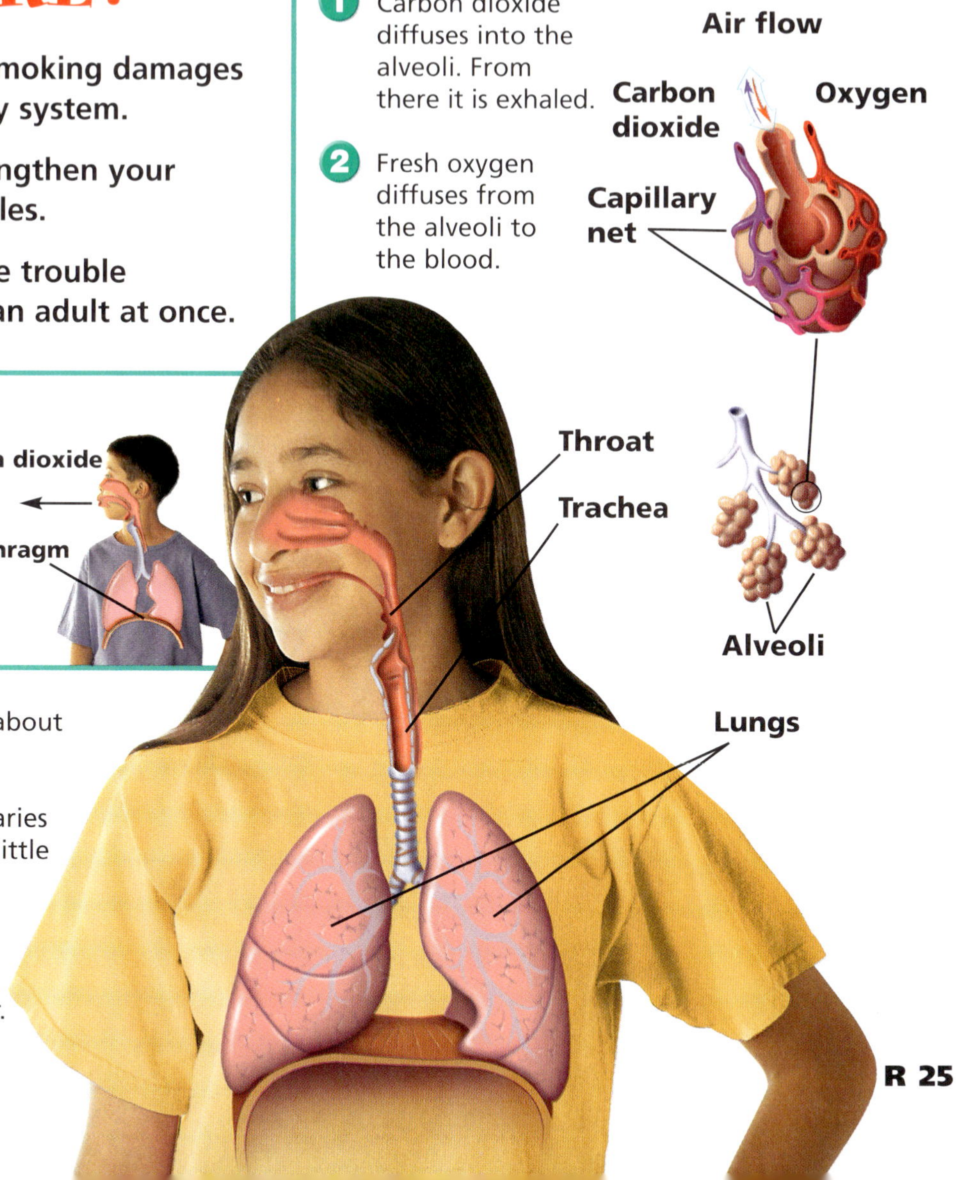

Activity Pyramid

Physical fitness is the condition in which the body is healthy and works the best it can. It involves working the skeletal muscles, bones, joints, heart, and respiratory system.

Occasionally Inactive pastimes such as watching TV, playing board games, talking on the phone

2–3 times a week Leisure activities such as gardening, golf, softball

3–5 times a week Aerobic activities such as swimming, biking, climbing; sports activities such as basketball, handball

Daily Substitute activity for inactivity—take the stairs, walk instead of riding, bike instead of taking the bus

CARE!

- Stay active every day.
- Eat a balanced diet.
- Drink plenty of water—6 to 8 large glasses a day.

The activity pyramid shows you the kinds of exercises and other activities you should be doing to make your body more physically fit.

Food Guide Pyramid

Fats, oils, and sweets
Use sparingly

Milk, yogurt, and cheese group
2–3 servings

Meat, poultry, fish, dry beans, eggs, and nuts group
2–3 servings

Vegetable group
3–5 servings

Fruit group
2–4 servings

Bread, cereal, rice, and pasta group
6–11 servings

The Digestive System

Digestion is the process of breaking down food into simple substances the body can use. Digestion begins when a person chews food. Chewing breaks the food down into smaller pieces and moistens it with saliva. Saliva is produced by the salivary glands.

Digested food is absorbed in the small intestine. The walls of the small intestine are lined with villi. Villi are tiny fingerlike projections that absorb digested food. From the villi the blood transports nutrients to every part of the body.

CARE!

- Chew your food well.
- Drink plenty of water to help move food through your digestive system.

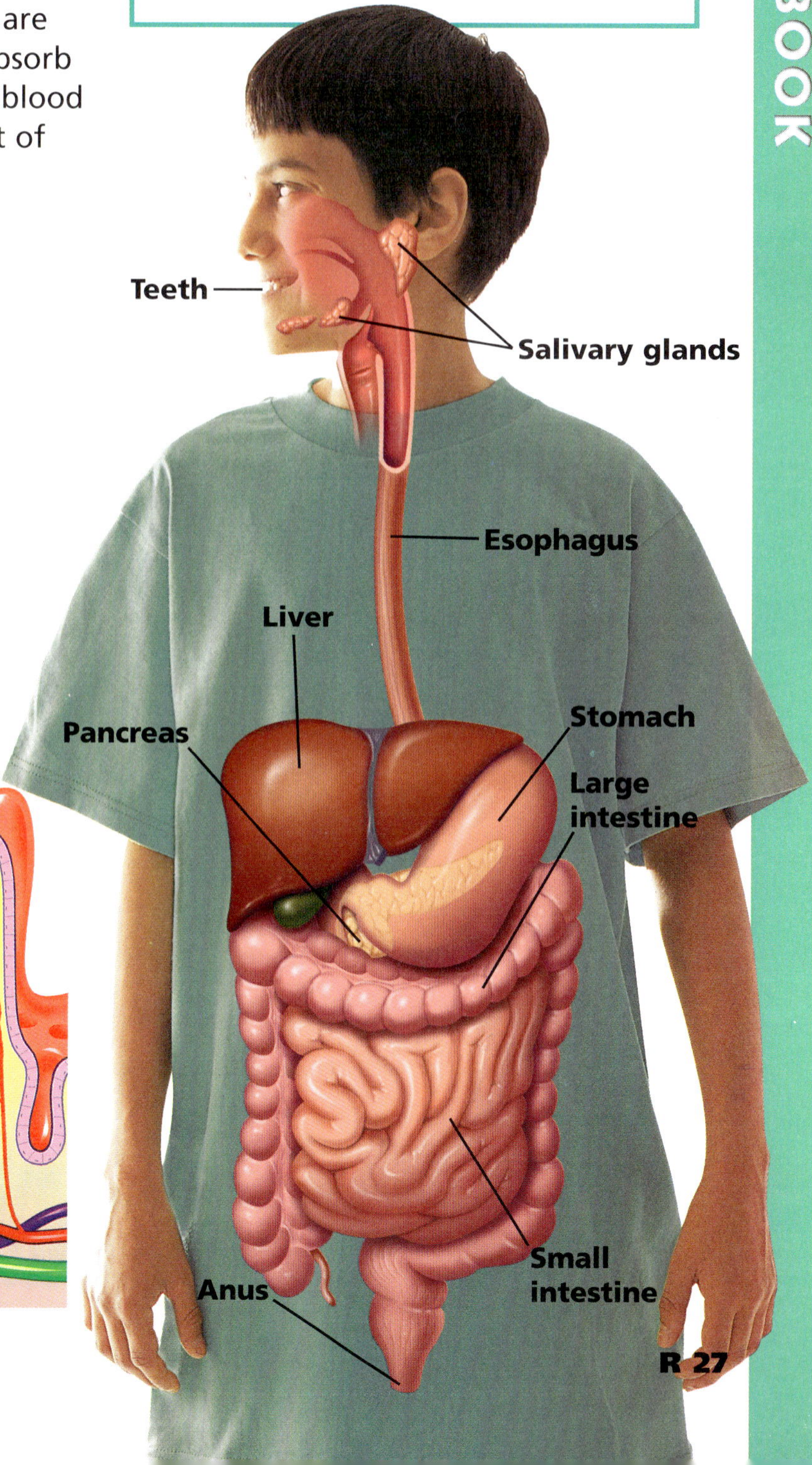

The shape of the small intestine's villi increases the amount of nutrients that can be absorbed from the food.

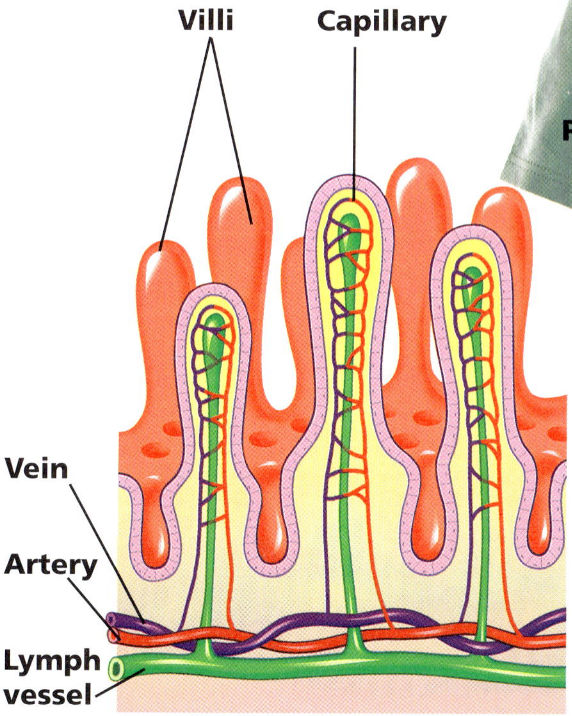

The Excretory System

Excretion is the process of removing waste products from the body. The liver filters wastes from the blood and converts them into urea. Urea is then carried to the kidneys for excretion. Each kidney contains more than a million nephrons. Nephrons are structures in the kidneys that filter blood.

The skin takes part in excretion when a person sweats. Glands in the inner layer of the skin produce sweat. Sweat is mostly water. Sweat tastes salty because it contains mineral salts the body doesn't need. There is also a tiny amount of urea in sweat.

Sweat is excreted by the sweat glands onto the outer layer of the skin. There it evaporates into the air. Evaporation takes place in part because of body heat. When sweat evaporates, a person feels cooler. On hot days or when exercising, a person sweats more to keep the body from overheating.

How You Sweat

Glands under your skin push sweat up to the surface, where it collects.

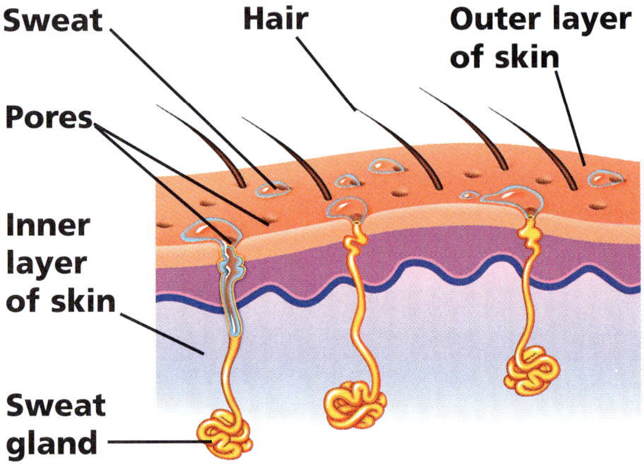

CARE!

- **Drink plenty of water to help the kidneys do their job and to replace water loss from sweating.**
- **Wash regularly to avoid body odor, clogged pores, and skin irritation.**

How Your Kidneys Work

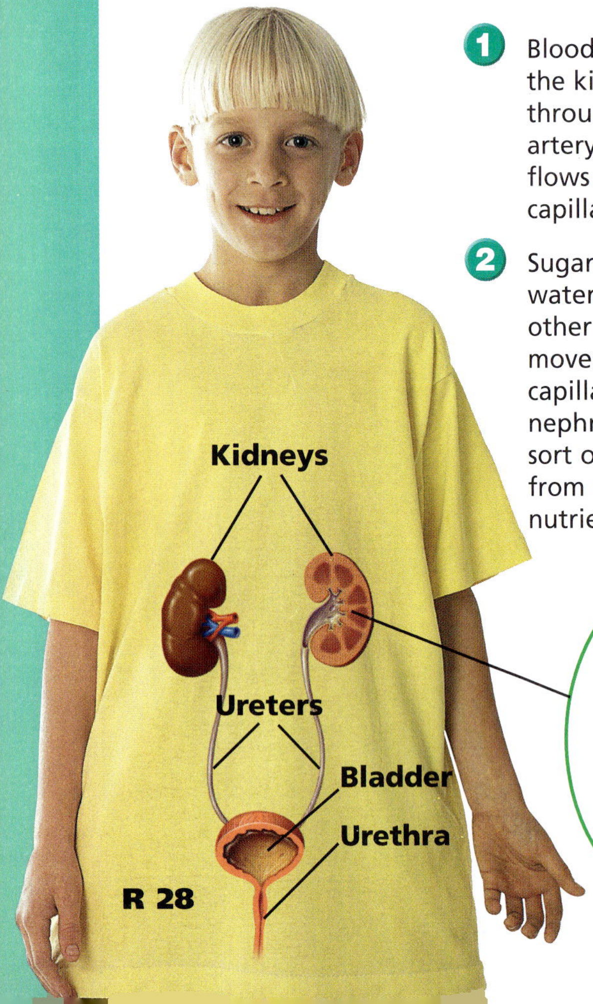

1. Blood enters the kidney through an artery and flows into capillaries.
2. Sugars, salts, water, urea, and other wastes move from the capillaries to tiny nephrons, which sort out wastes from the useful nutrients.
3. The nutrients return to the blood and flow back out through veins.
4. Urea and other wastes become urine, which flows down the ureters.
5. Urine is stored in the bladder and excreted through the urethra.

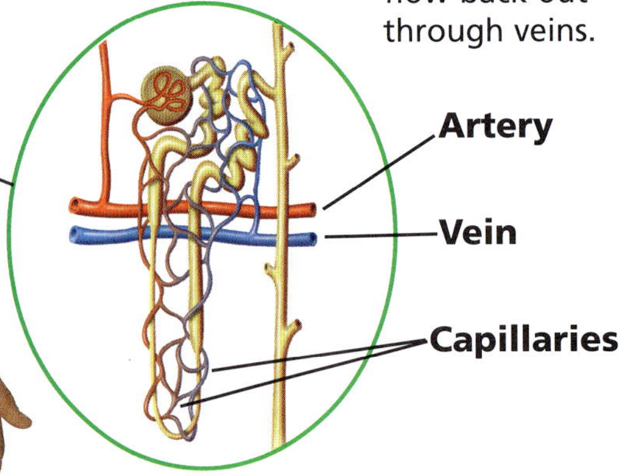

The Nervous System

The nervous system has two parts. The brain and the spinal cord are the central nervous system. All other nerves are the outer, or peripheral, nervous system.

The largest part of the brain is the cerebrum. A deep groove separates the right half, or hemisphere, of the cerebrum from the left half. Both the right and left hemispheres of the cerebrum contain control centers for the senses.

The cerebellum lies below the cerebrum. It coordinates the skeletal muscles so they work smoothly together. It also helps in keeping balance.

The brain stem connects to the spinal cord. The lowest part of the brain stem is the medulla. It controls heartbeat, breathing, blood pressure, and the muscles in the digestive system.

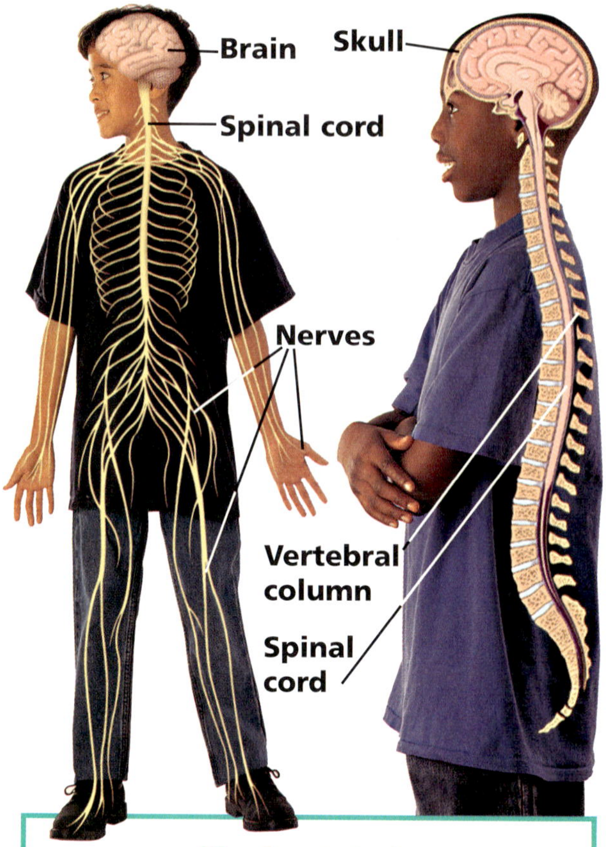

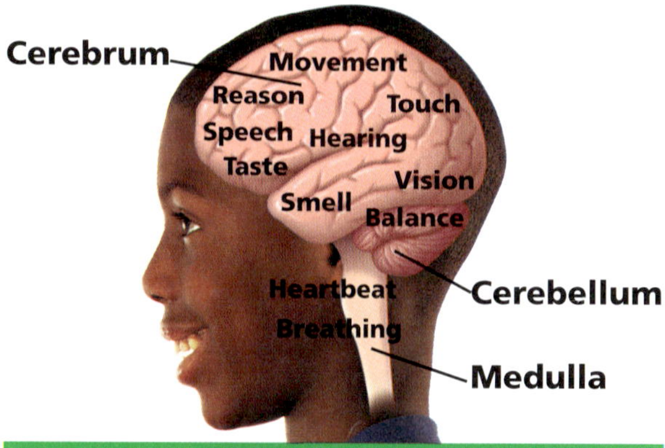

CARE!

- Wear protective headgear when you play sports or exercise.
- Stay away from drugs, such as stimulants, which can speed up the nervous system.
- Stay away from alcohol, which is a depressant and slows down the nervous system.

Parts of a Neuron

The nerves in the nervous system are made up of nerve cells called neurons. Each neuron has three main parts—a cell body, dendrites, and an axon. Dendrites are branching nerve fibers that carry impulses, or electrical signals, toward the cell body. An axon is a nerve fiber that carries impulses away from the cell body.

When an impulse reaches the tip of an axon, it must cross a tiny gap to reach the next neuron. This gap between neurons is called a synapse.

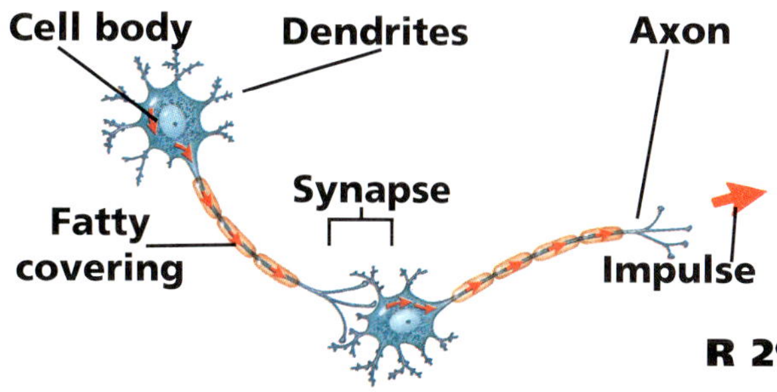

The Senses

Seeing

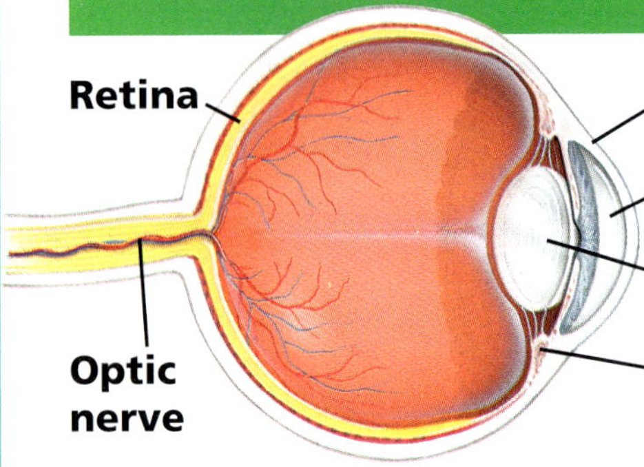

Light reflected from an object enters the eye and falls on the retina. Receptor cells change the light into electrical signals, or impulses. These impulses travel along the optic nerve to the vision center of the brain.

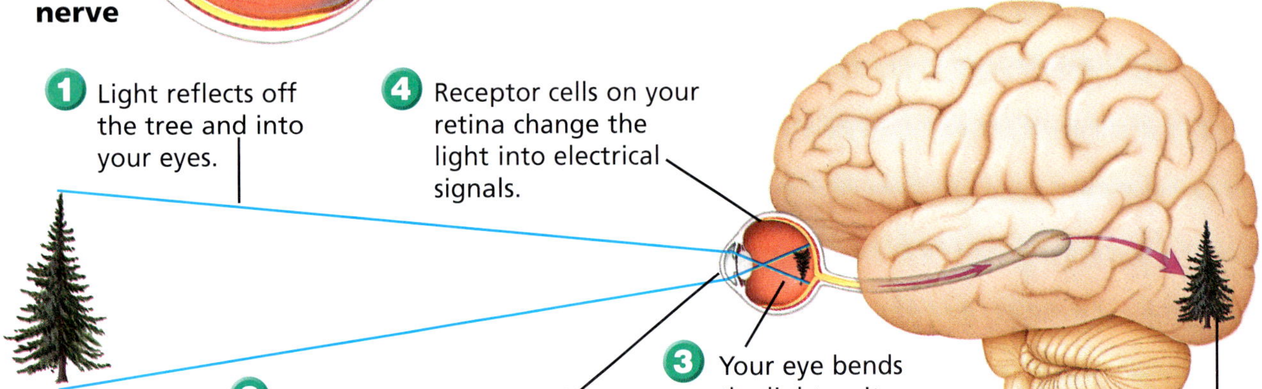

1. Light reflects off the tree and into your eyes.
2. The light passes through your cornea and the pupil in your iris.
3. Your eye bends the light so it hits your retina.
4. Receptor cells on your retina change the light into electrical signals.
5. The impulses travel along neurons in your optic nerve to the seeing center of your brain.

Hearing

Sound waves enter the ear and cause the eardrum to vibrate. Receptor cells in the ear change the sound waves into impulses that travel along the auditory nerve to the hearing center of the brain.

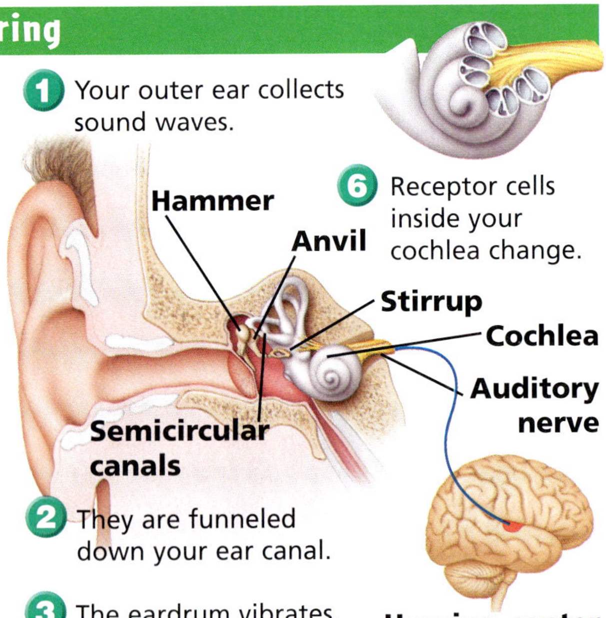

1. Your outer ear collects sound waves.
2. They are funneled down your ear canal.
3. The eardrum vibrates.
4. Three tiny ear bones vibrate.
5. The cochlea vibrates.
6. Receptor cells inside your cochlea change.
7. The impulses travel along your auditory nerve to the brain's hearing center.

CARE!

- **To avoid straining your eye muscles, don't sit too close to the TV screen or computer monitor.**
- **Avoid loud music. Turn down the volume when wearing headphones.**

The Senses

Smelling

The sense of smell is really the ability to detect chemicals in the air. When a person breathes, chemicals dissolve in mucus in the upper part of the nose. When the chemicals come in contact with receptor cells, the cells send impulses along the olfactory nerve to the smelling center of the brain.

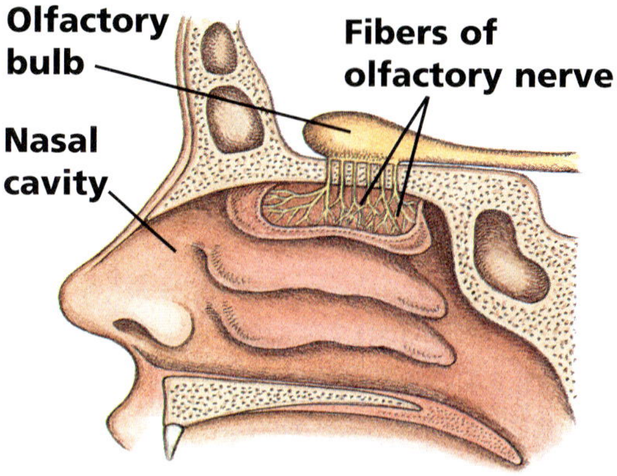

Tasting

When a person eats, chemicals in food dissolve in saliva. Saliva carries the chemicals to taste buds on the tongue. Inside each taste bud are receptors that can sense the four main tastes—sweet, sour, salty, and bitter. The receptors send impulses along a nerve to the taste center of the brain. The brain identifies the taste of the food, which is usually a combination of the four main tastes.

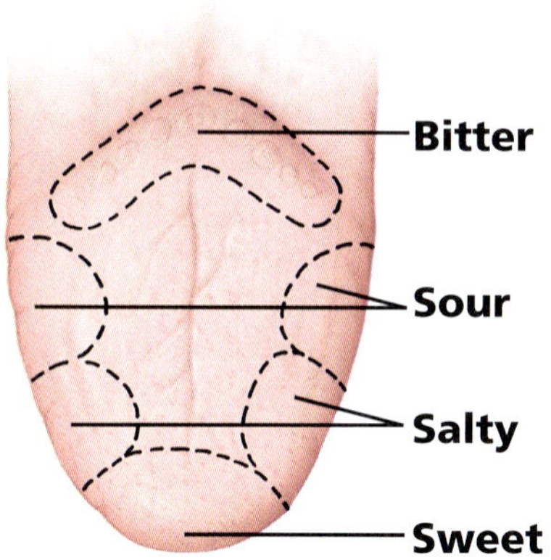

Touching

Receptor cells in the skin help a person tell hot from cold, wet from dry, and the light touch of a feather from the pressure of stepping on a stone. Each receptor cell sends impulses along sensory nerves to the spinal cord. The spinal cord then sends the impulses to the touch center of the brain.

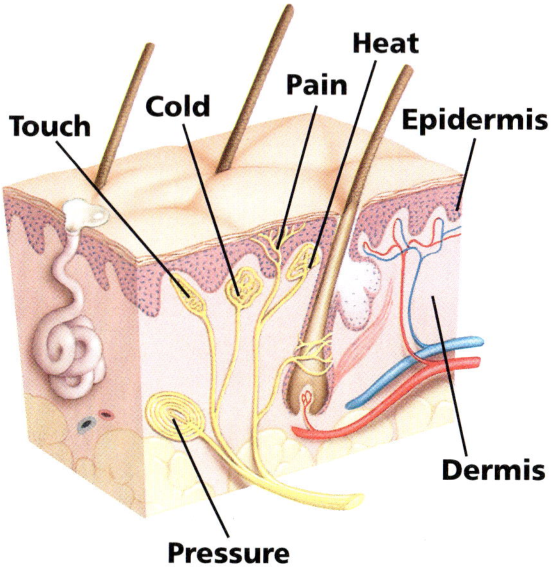

CARE!

- **To prevent the spread of germs, always cover your mouth and nose when you cough or sneeze.**

The Immune System

The immune system helps the body fight disease. Inside some bones is a soft tissue known as red marrow that fills the spaces in spongy bone. Red marrow makes new red blood cells, platelets that stop a cut from bleeding, and germ-fighting white blood cells.

There are white blood cells in the blood vessels and in the lymph vessels. Lymph vessels are similar to blood vessels. Instead of blood, they carry lymph. Lymph is a straw-colored fluid surrounding body cells.

Lymph nodes filter out harmful materials in lymph. Like red marrow, they also produce white blood cells to fight infections. Swollen lymph nodes in the neck are a clue that the body is fighting germs.

CARE!

- **Be sure to get immunized against common diseases.**
- **Keep cuts clean to prevent infection.**

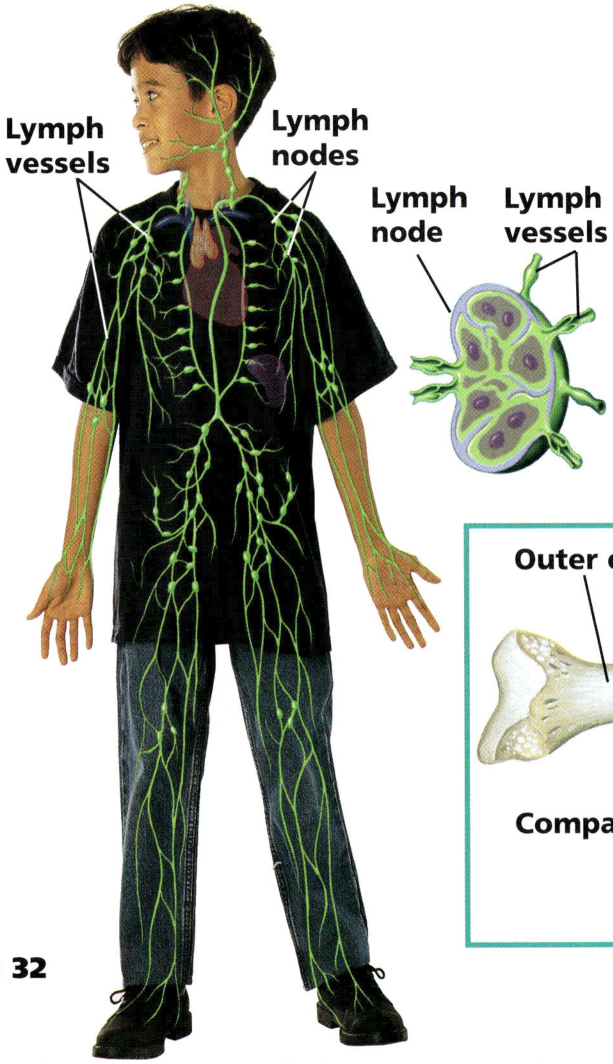

1. A bone is covered with a tough but thin membrane that has many small blood vessels. The blood vessels bring nutrients and oxygen to the living parts of the bone and remove wastes.

2. Inside some bones is a soft tissue known as marrow. Yellow marrow is made mostly of fat cells and is one of the body's energy reserves. It is usually found in the long, hollow spaces of long bones.

3. Part of the bone is compact, or solid. It is made up of living bone cells and nonliving materials. The nonliving part is made up of layers of hardened minerals such as calcium and phosphorus. In between the mineral layers are living bone cells.

4. Red marrow fills the spaces in spongy bone. Red marrow makes new red blood cells, germ-fighting white blood cells, and cell fragments that stop a cut from bleeding.

5. Part of the bone is made of bone tissue that looks like a dry sponge. It is made of strong, hard tubes. It is also found in the middle of short, flat bones.

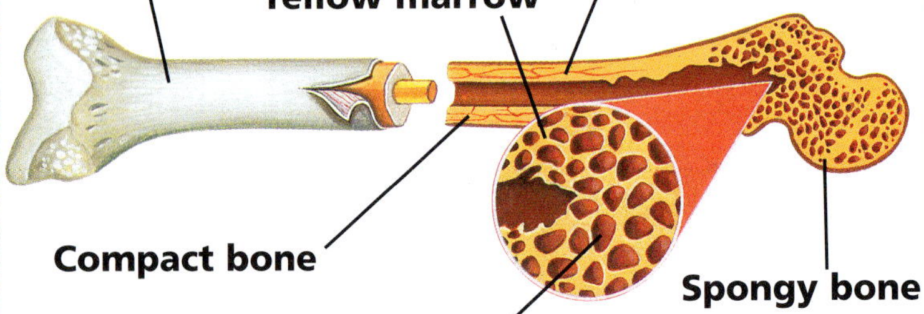

The Endocrine System

Hormones are chemicals that control body functions. A gland that produces hormones is called an endocrine gland. Sweat from sweat glands flows out of tubes called ducts. Endocrine glands have no ducts.

The endocrine glands are scattered around the body. Each gland makes one or more hormones. Every hormone seeks out a target organ, the place in the body where the hormone acts.

CARE!

- Doctors can treat many diseases, such as diabetes, caused by endocrine glands that produce too little or too much of a hormone.

Some Glands in the Endocrine System

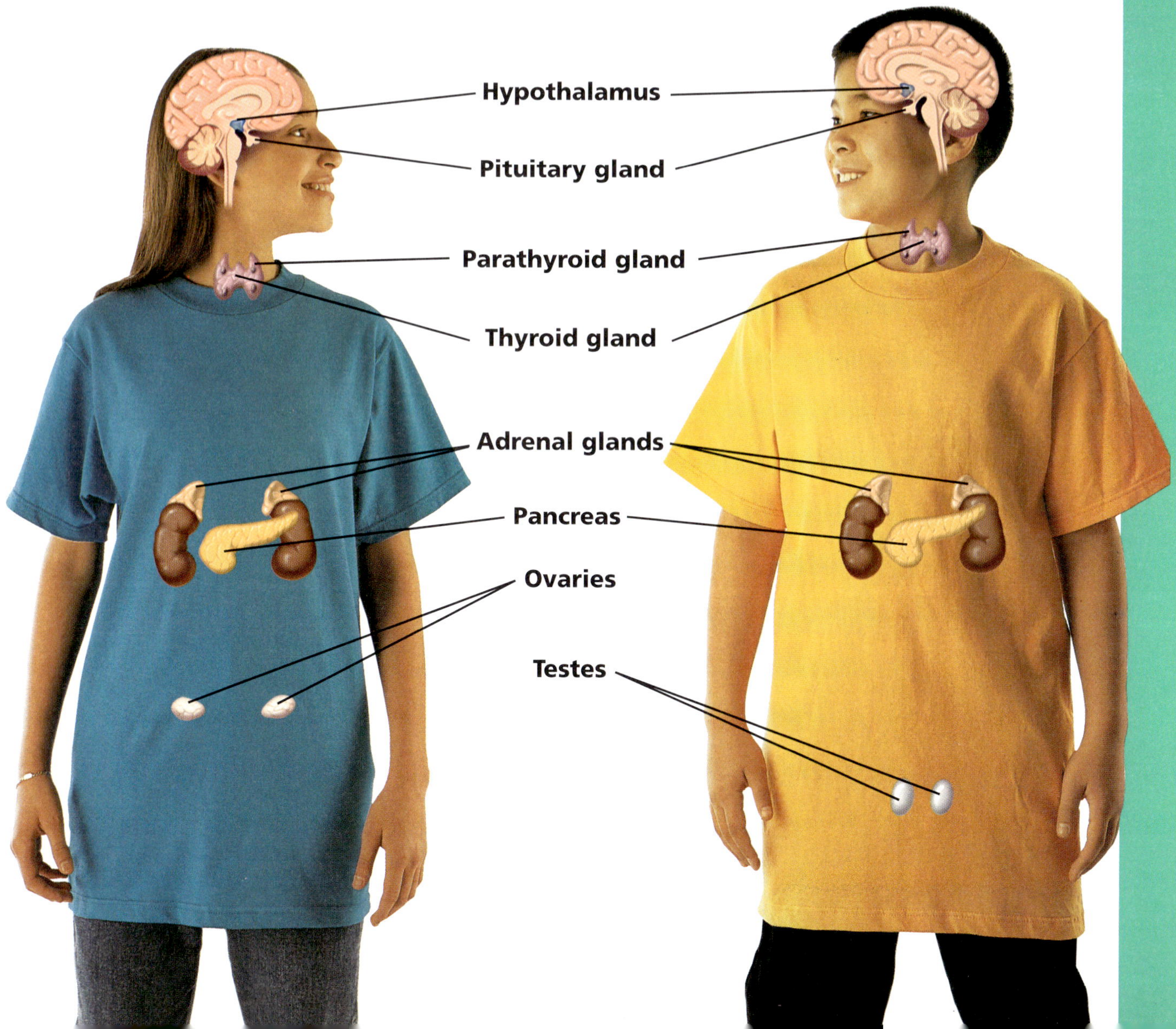

The Reproductive System

The testes are the male reproductive organs. At puberty the testes begin to produce sperm. Sperm move through sperm ducts, where they mix with fluid from endocrine glands.

The ovaries are the female reproductive organs, which contain eggs. After puberty one mature egg is released about once every 28 days. The egg moves to the oviduct, a narrow tube leading from the ovary.

CARE!

- **Abstinence is the only sure way to avoid sexually transmitted diseases.**

The Male Reproductive System

Sperm move from the testes through sperm ducts, where they mix with fluid from the glands. The sperm and fluid move through the urethra, a tube that leads out through the penis.

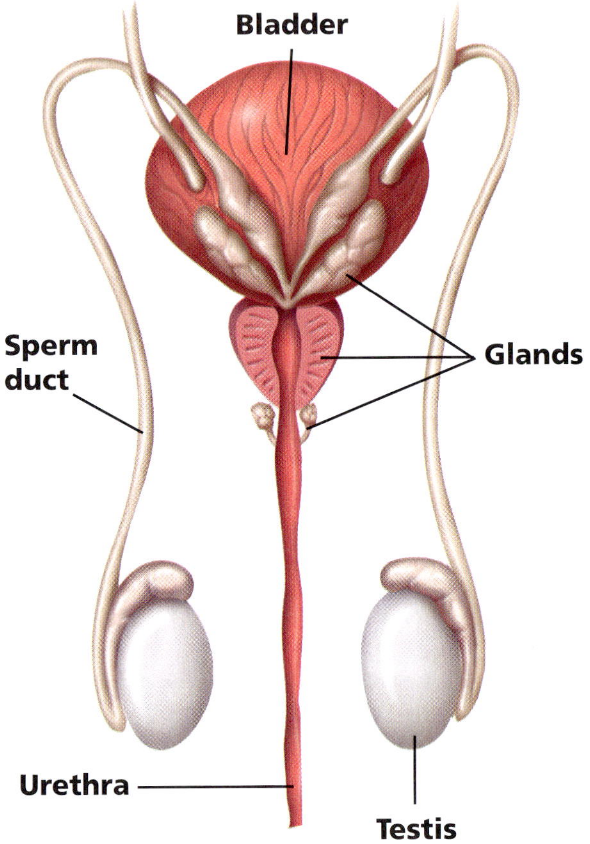

The Female Reproductive System

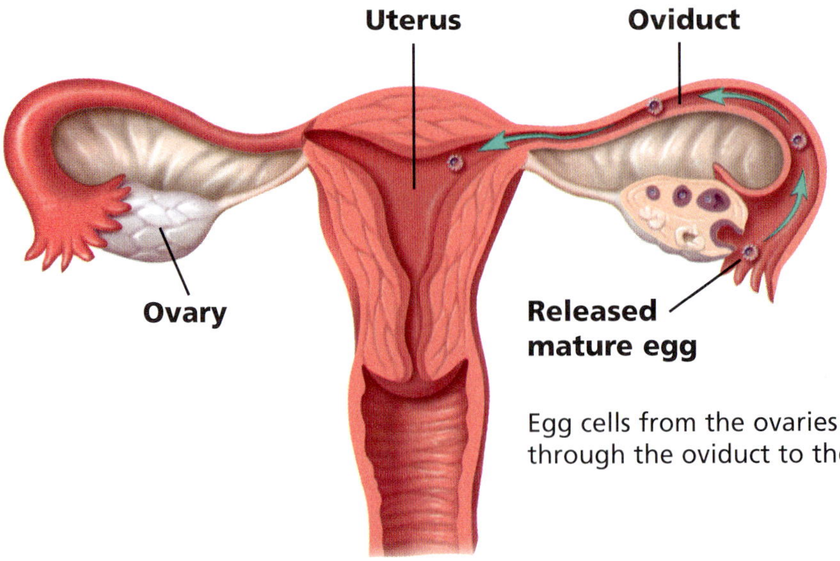

Egg cells from the ovaries move through the oviduct to the uterus.

Glossary

This Glossary will help you to pronounce and understand the meanings of the Science Words introduced in this book. The page number at the end of the definition tells where the word appears.

A

abiotic factor (ā'bī ot'ik fak'tər) A nonliving part of an ecosystem. (p. B6)

absorption (əb sôrp'shən) The disappearance of a sound wave into a surface. (p. F66)

abyssal plain (ə bis'əl plān) The vast flat lands beyond the continental shelf that cover almost half of the deep ocean floor. (p. C90)

acceleration (ak sel'ə rā'shən) Change in velocity with respect to time. (pp. F13, F22)

acid (as'id) A substance that tastes sour and turns blue litmus paper red. (p. E82)

acid rain (as'id rān) Moisture that falls to Earth after being mixed with wastes from burned fossil fuels. (p. C65)

acidity (ə sid'ə tē) The strength of an acid. (p. E86)

action (ak'shən) The force one object applies to a second, as in Newton's third law of motion, which states, "For every action, there is an equal but opposite reaction." *See* **reaction**. (p. F24)

adaptation (ad'əp tā'shən) A characteristic that enables a living thing to survive in its environment. (pp. A82, A106, B52)

aerial root (âr'ē əl rüt) A root that never touches the ground but can take in moisture from the air. (p. A21)

aerosol (âr'ə sōl') A type of colloid in which liquid drops or solid particles are spread throughout a gas. (p. E60)

air mass (âr mas) A large region of the atmosphere where the air has similar properties throughout. (p. D54)

air pressure (âr presh'ər) The force put on a given area by the weight of the air above it. (p. D11)

alkalinity (al'kə lin'i tē) The strength of a base. (p. E86)

alternation of generations (ôl'tər nā'shən uv jen'ə rā'shənz) The process in which offspring are reproduced sexually, their offspring are reproduced asexually, and so on. (p. A53)

alternative energy source (ōl tûr'nə tiv en'ər jē sôrs) A source of energy other than the burning of a fossil fuel. (p. C104)

PRONUNCIATION KEY

The following symbols are used throughout the McGraw-Hill Science 2002 Glossaries.

a	at	e	end	o	hot	u	**up**	hw	**white**	ə	about
ā	ape	ē	me	ō	old	ū	use	ng	song		taken
ä	far	i	it	ôr	fork	ü	rule	th	thin		pencil
âr	care	ī	ice	oi	**oil**	ù	pull	th	**this**		lemon
ô	law	îr	pierce	ou	**out**	ûr	turn	zh	measure		circus

' = primary accent; shows which syllable takes the main stress, such as **kil** in **kilogram** (kil'ə gram').
' = secondary accent; shows which syllables take lighter stresses, such as **gram** in **kilogram.**

ammonia (ə mōn′yə) A compound that contains the element nitrogen and is used as a fertilizer. (p. B34)

anemometer (an′ə mom′i tər) A device that measures wind speed. (p. D44)

aneroid barometer (an′ə roid bə rom′i tər) A spring enclosed in a pleated metal can that expands or contracts to indicate changes in air pressure. (p. D12)

angiosperm (an′jē ə spûrm′) A seed plant that produces flowers. *See* **gymnosperm.** (p. A58)

aquifer (ak′wə fər) An underground layer of rock or soil filled with water. (p. C75)

asexual reproduction (a sek′shü əl rē′prō duk′shən) The production of a new organism from only one cell. (p. A52)

atmosphere (at′məs fîr′) The blanket of gases that surrounds Earth. (pp. C12, D10)

atom (at′əm) The smallest unit of an element that retains the properties of that element. *See* **molecule**. (p. E26)

aurora (ə rôr′ə) The northern or southern lights that appear in the night sky, especially in polar regions. (p. D10)

aurum (ôr′əm) The Latin word for *gold*. (p. E23)

B

bacterium (bak tîr′ē əm) *sing., n. pl.* **bacteria** (-ē ə) A member of either of two kingdoms of one-celled living things that have no nucleus, or center, in their cell body. (p. A15)

balanced forces (bal′ənst fôrs′əz) Forces that cancel each other out when acting together on a single object. (p. F21)

barometer (bə rom′i tər) A device for measuring air pressure. (p. D12)

base (bās) A substance that tastes bitter and turns red litmus paper blue. (p. E82)

basin (bās′in) The floor of an ocean, containing mountains, valleys, and plains. (p. C84)

Beaufort scale (bō′fərt skāl) A system for measuring wind speed by observing its effect on the surface of the sea, using a scale of 0 (low) to 12 (high) for each effect. (p. D44)

bench mark (bench′märk′) A plaque left by surveyors to tell the exact location and elevation of a place. (p. C18)

benthos (ben′thos) Organisms that live on the bottom in aquatic ecosystems. (p. B72)

biomass (bī′ō mas′) Energy from plant matter or animal waste. (p. C106)

biome (bī′ōm) One of Earth's large ecosystems, with its own kind of climate, soil, plants, and animals. (p. B64)

biotic factor (bī ot′ik fak′tər) A living part of an ecosystem. (p. B7)

boiling point (boil′ing point) The particular temperature for each substance at which it changes state from a liquid to a gas. (p. E37)

buoyancy (boi′ən sē) The upward push of a liquid on an object placed in it. (p. E12)

C

cambium (kam′bē əm) The layer in plants that separates the xylem from the phloem. (p. A21)

camouflage (kam′ə fläzh′) An adaptation in which an animal protects itself against predators by blending in with the environment. (p. A108)

carbon cycle (kär′bən sī′kəl) The continuous exchange of carbon dioxide and oxygen among living things. (p. B37)

carnivore (kär′nə vôr′) An animal that eats another animal. (p. B20)

chemical change (kem′i kəl chānj) A change of matter that occurs when atoms link together in a new way, creating a new substance different from the original substances. (p. E71)

chemical formula (kəm′i kəl fôr′myə lə) A way to write a compound's name using symbols. The letters tell what elements are in the compound, and the subscripts tell the number of particles in the compound. (p. E25)

chemical reaction (kem′i kəl rē ak′shən) Another name for chemical change. (p. E71)

chemosynthesis (kē′mō sin′thə sis) In tube worms the process by which bacteria create nutrients from hydrogen sulfide and oxygen, using chemical reactions rather than light. (p. C93)

chlorophyll (klôr′ə fil′) A green chemical in plant cells that allows plants to use the Sun's energy for making food. (pp. A6, A32)

chloroplast (klôr′ə plast′) The part of a plant cell containing chlorophyll, the green substance that enables the plant to produce food. (p. A24)

cirrus cloud (sir′əs kloud) A high-altitude cloud with a featherlike shape, made of ice crystals. (p. D24)

classification (klas′ə fi kā′shən) The science of finding patterns among living things. (p. A8)

classification key (klas′ə fi kā′shən kē) A series of paired choices describing organisms that is arranged in a way that leads to the identity of a given organism. (p. A100)

classify (klas′ə fī) To place things that share properties together in groups. (p. S7)

cleavage (klē′vij) The tendency of a mineral to break along flat surfaces. (p. C34)

climate (klī′mit) The average weather pattern of a region. (p. D82)

climate zone (klī mat′ zōn) A region that has similar weather patterns based on temperature, precipitation, wind, distance from a coast, mountain ranges, ocean currents, and vegetation. (p. D82)

climax community (klī′maks kə mū′ni tē) The final stage of succession in an area, unless a major change happens. (p. B84)

cold front (kōld frunt) A front where cold air moves in under a warm air mass. (p. D56)

colloid (kol′oid) A special type of mixture in which the particles of one material are scattered through another and block the passage of light without settling out. (pp. E54, E60)

commensalism (kə men′sə liz′əm) A relationship between two kinds of organisms that benefits one without harming the other. (p. B57)

communicate (kə mü′ni kāt′) To share information. (p. S7)

community (kə mū′ni tē) All the living things in an ecosystem. (p. B10)

complete flower (kəm plēt′ flou′ər) A flower that has sepals, petals, stamens, and pistils. (p. A70)

compound (kom′pound) Any substance that is formed by the chemical combination of two or more elements and acts like a single substance. (p. E24)

compression (kəm presh′ən) **1.** The part of a sound wave where molecules are crowded together. (p. F51) **2.** A movement of plates that presses together or squeezes Earth's crust. (p. C20)

concave lens (kon kāv′ lenz) A lens that is thicker at the edges than at the middle. As it curves inward, it spreads light rays apart, making images appear smaller. (p. F100)

PRONUNCIATION KEY

a at; ā ape; ä far; âr care; ô law; e end; ē me; i it; ī ice; îr pierce; o hot; ō old; ôr fork; oi oil; ou out; u up; ū use; ü rule; ů pull; ûr turn; hw white; ng song; th thin; th this; zh measure; ə about, taken, pencil, lemon, circus

concave mirror (kon kāv′ mir′ər) A mirror that curves in on the shiny side. (p. F88)

condensation (kon′den sā′shən) *n.* The changing of a gas into a liquid. (pp. B32, D17) —**condense** (kən dens′) *v.* (p. E37)

conduction (kən duk′shən) *n.* The passing of heat through a material while the material itself stays in place. (p. E97) —**conduct** (kən dukt′) *v.* (p. E14)

conifer (kon′ə fər) Any of a group of gymnosperms that produce seeds in cones and have needlelike leaves. (p. A59)

conserve (kən′sûrv′) To save, protect, or use resources wisely. (p. C39)

constellation (kon′stə lā′shən) Any of the patterns formed by groups of stars in the night sky. To people in the past, these patterns looked like pictures of animals or people. (p. C14)

consumer (kən sü′mər) Any animal that eats plants or eats other plant-eating animals. (pp. B7, B20)

continental rise (kon′tə nen′təl rīz) A buildup of sediment on the sea floor at the bottom of the continental slope. It is a zone of sand and mud that stretches from the slope down to the deep-sea floor. (p. C90)

continental shelf (kon′tə nen′təl shelf) The underwater edge of a continent. (p. C90)

continental slope (kon′tə nen′təl slōp) The steep slope leading down from the continental shelf toward the sea floor. (p. C90)

contour plowing (kon′tür plou′ing) Preventing erosion by plowing across rather than up and down a slope. (p. C51)

contract (*v.*, kən trakt′) To shrink, as when a material gets colder. (p. E41)

convection (kən vek′shən) The flow of heat through a liquid or a gas, causing hot parts to rise and cooler parts to sink. (p. E97)

convection cell (kən vek′shən sel) A circular pattern of air rising, air sinking, and wind. (p. D38)

convex lens (kon veks′ lenz) A lens that is thicker at the middle than at the edges. As it curves outward, it brings light together, making images appear larger. (p. F100)

convex mirror (kon veks′ mir′ər) A mirror that curves out on the shiny side. (p. F88)

coquina (kō kē′nə) A sedimentary rock formed from seashell fragments. (p. C44)

Coriolis effect (kôr′ē ō′lis i fekt′) The curving of the path of a moving object caused by Earth's rotation. (p. D40)

cortex (kôr′teks) The layer of tissue just inside the epidermis of a plant's roots and stems. (p. A20)

cotyledon (ko′tə lē′dən) A tiny leaflike structure, also called a seedleaf, inside the seed of an angiosperm. (p. A62)

crop rotation (krop rō tā′shən) Growing different crops each year so that the soil does not use up the same kinds of minerals year after year. (p. C51)

crossbreeding (krôs′brēd′ing) Producing offspring by mating individuals from two distinct breeds or varieties of the same species. (p. A112)

cross-pollination (krôs′pol′ə nā′shən) The transfer of pollen from one flower to another. (p. A72)

crust (krust) The rocky surface that makes up the top of the lithosphere and includes the continents and the ocean floor. (p. C12)

crystal (kris′təl) The geometric shape a mineral forms when its atoms and molecules get into fixed patterns. (p. C32)

cumulus cloud (kū′myə ləs kloud) A puffy cloud that appears to rise up from a flat bottom. (p. D24)

current (kûr′ənt) An ocean movement; a large stream of water that flows in the ocean. (p. C86)

cycad (sī′kad) One of the evergreen gymnosperms that resemble palms and have seed-bearing cones. (p. A59)

D

decibel (dB) (des′ə bel′) A unit that measures loudness. (p. F58)

deciduous (di sij′ü əs) Said of a plant that loses its leaves each fall. *See* **evergreen.** (pp. A59, B70)

deciduous forest (di si′jə wəs fôr′ist) A forest biome with many kinds of trees that lose their leaves each autumn. (p. B70)

decomposer (dē′kəm pōz′ər) Any of the fungi or bacteria that break down dead plants and animals into useful things like minerals and rich soil. (pp. B7, B21, B34)

define based on observations (di fīn′ bāst ôn ob′zər vā′shənz) To put together a description that relies on examination and experience. (p. S7)

density (den′si tē) A measure of how tightly packed the matter in an object is. (pp. C35, E8)

deposition (dep′ə zish′ən) The dropping off of bits of eroded rock. (p. C25)

desalination (dē sal′ə nā′shən) Getting fresh water from seawater. (p. C73)

desert (dez′ərt) A sandy or rocky biome, with little precipitation and little plant life. (p. B69)

dicot (dī′kot′) An angiosperm with two cotyledons in each seed. *See* **monocot.** (p. A62)

dinoflagellate (din′ə flaj′ə lāt′) A protist containing chlorophyll that has two flagella for motion. When they overreproduce, they can cause "red tides." (p. A14)

distillation (dis′tə lā′shən) The process of separating the parts of a mixture by evaporation and condensation. (p. E64)

diversity (di vûr′si tē) A wide variety of traits in individuals from the same population. (p. A114)

Doppler effect (dop′lər i fekt′) The change in frequency (and pitch) as a source of sound moves toward or away from you. (p. F71)

downdraft (doun′draft′) A downward rush of air caused by the falling of rain during a thunderstorm. (pp. D38, D67)

E

echo (e′kō) A reflected sound wave. (p. F68)

echolocation (ek′ō lō kā′shən) Finding an object by using reflected sound. (p. F70)

ecological succession (ek′ə loj′i kəl sək sesh′ən) The gradual replacement of one community by another. (p. B82)

ecology (ē kol′ə jē) The study of how living and nonliving things interact. (p. B6)

ecosystem (ek′ō sis′təm) All the living and nonliving things in an environment, including their interactions with each other. (p. B6)

electromagnetic spectrum (i lek′trō mag net′ik spek′trəm) All the wavelengths of visible and invisible light in order, from short (gamma rays) to long (radio). (p. F119)

electromagnetism (i lek′trō mag′ni tiz′əm) The production of magnetism by electricity (and the production of electricity by magnets). (p. F118)

electron (i lek′tron) A particle in the space outside the nucleus of an atom that carries one unit of negative electric charge. (p. E27)

element (el′ə mənt) A pure substance that cannot be broken down into any simpler substances. (p. E22)

PRONUNCIATION KEY

a **a**t; ā **a**pe; ä f**a**r; âr c**are**; ô l**aw**; e **e**nd; ē m**e**; i **i**t; ī **i**ce; îr p**ier**ce; o h**o**t; ō **o**ld; ôr f**or**k; oi **oi**l; ou **ou**t; u **u**p; ū **u**se; ü r**u**le; ů p**u**ll; ûr t**ur**n; hw **wh**ite; ng so**ng**; th **th**in; th **th**is; zh mea**s**ure; ə **a**bout, tak**e**n, pen**c**il, lem**o**n, circ**u**s

elevation (el′ə vā′shən) The height of a place above sea level. (p. C18)

embryo (em′brē ō′) The immature plant inside a seed. (p. A74)

emulsion (i mul′shən) A type of colloid in which one liquid is spread throughout another. (p. E60)

epidermis (ep′i dûr′mis) An outermost layer of such plant parts as roots and leaves. (p. A20)

erosion (i rō′zhən) The picking up and carrying away of pieces of rocks. (p. C22)

evaporation (i vap′ə rā′shən) The slow changing of a liquid into a gas. (pp. B32, D16, E38)

evergreen (ev′ər grēn′) Said of a gymnosperm that keeps its leaves for at least a few years. *See* **deciduous.** (p. A59)

expand (ek spand′) To spread out, as when a material gets hotter. (p. E41)

experiment (ek sper′ə ment′) To perform a test to support or disprove a hypothesis. (p. S7)

F

fault (fôlt) A crack in Earth's crust whose sides show evidence of motion. (p. C18)

fault-block mountain (fôlt blok moun′tən) A mountain formed by blocks of Earth's crust moving along a fault. (p. C21)

fertilization (fûr′tə lə zā′shən) The joining of a sperm cell with an egg cell to make one new cell, a fertilized egg. (pp. A52, A73)

fertilizer (fûr′tə lī′zər) A substance used to add minerals to the soil. (p. B34)

fibrous root (fī′brəs rüt) One of the many hairy branching roots that some plants have. (p. A21)

filament (fil′ə mənt) The wire in a light bulb that gives off light and heat. (p. E92)

foam (fōm) A type of colloid in which a gas is spread throughout a liquid. (p. E60)

fog (fôg) A cloud that forms at ground level. (p. D24)

fold mountain (fōld moun′tən) A mountain made up mostly of rock layers folded by being squeezed together. (p. C20)

food chain (füd chān) The path of the energy in food from one organism to another. (p. B18)

food web (füd web) The overlapping food chains in an ecosystem. (p. B20)

force (fôrs) A push or pull exerted by one object on another, causing a change in motion. (p. F6)

form a hypothesis (fôrm ə hī poth′ə sis) To make a statement that can be tested to answer a question. (p. S7)

fossil (fos′əl) Any remains or imprint of living things of the past. (p. C45)

fossil fuel (fos′əl fū′əl) A fuel formed from the decay of ancient forms of life. (p. C64)

fracture (frak′chər) The characteristic way some minerals break in uneven patterns. (p. C35)

freezing point (frēz′ing point) Another name for *melting point,* that temperature at which a substance changes state, either from a liquid to a solid or from solid to liquid. (p. E37)

frequency (frē′kwən sē) The number of times an object vibrates per second. (p. F57)

friction (frik′ shen′) A force that opposes the motion of one object moving past another. (p. F8)

frond (frond) The leaf of a fern. (p. A51)

front (frunt) A boundary between air masses with different temperatures. (p. D55)

fruit (früt) The ripened ovary of a flowering seed plant. (p. A75)

fundamental frequency (fun′də men′təl frē′kwən sē) The lowest frequency at which an object vibrates. (p. F72)

fungus (fung′gəs) *n.,* **fungi** (fun′jī) *pl.* Members of a kingdom that contains one-celled and many-celled living things that absorb food from their environment. (p. A13)

G

gas (gas) A form of matter that does not take up a definite amount of space and has no definite shape. (p. E36)

gel (jel) A type of colloid in which a solid is spread throughout a liquid. (p. E60)

gem (jem) A mineral valued for being rare and beautiful. (p. C38)

geologist (jē olʹə jist) A scientist who studies rocks to tell how they formed and to predict when an earthquake may occur. (p. C18)

geothermal energy (jēʹō thûrʹməl enʹər jē) Earth's internal energy. (p. C104)

germination (jûrʹmə nāʹshən) The sprouting of a seed into a new plant. (p. A75)

ginkgo (gingʹkō) *n., pl.* **ginkgoes** A large gymnosperm with fan-shaped leaves. (p. A59)

gnetophyte (neʹtō fītʹ) One of the gymnosperms that are closely related to flowering plants and live in both deserts and the tropics. (p. A59)

grassland (grasʹlandʹ) A biome where grasses, not trees, are the main plant life. Prairies are one kind of grassland region. (p. B66)

gravitropism (gravʹī trōʹpiʹzəm) The response of a plant to gravity. (p. A80)

gravity (gravʹi tē) A force of attraction, or pull, between any object and any other objects around it. Gravity is a property of all matter. (pp. C8, F35)

greenhouse effect (grēnʹhousʹ i fektʹ) The ability of the atmosphere to let in sunlight but not to let heat escape. (p. D87)

groundwater (ground wôʹtər) Precipitation that seeps into the ground and is stored in tiny holes, or pores, in soil and rocks. (pp. B33, C74, D28)

gymnosperm (jimʹnə spûrmʹ) A seed plant that does not produce flowers. *See* **angiosperm**. (p. A58)

H

habitat (habʹi tat) The place where a plant or animal naturally lives and grows. (p. B11)

hail (hāl) Pellets made of ice and snow. (p. D27)

hardness (härdʹnis) How well a mineral resists scratching. (p. C34)

herbivore (hûrʹbə vôrʹ) An animal that eats plants, algae, and other producers. (p. B20)

heredity (hə redʹi tē) The passing down of inherited traits from parents to offspring. (p. A110)

hertz (Hz) (hûrts) A unit for measuring frequency. One hertz equals a frequency of one vibration per second. (p. F57)

heterogeneous (hetʹər ə jēʹnē əs) Differing in kind or nature; dissimilar; not homogeneous. (p. E54)

high-pressure system (hīʹpreshʹər sisʹtəm) A pattern surrounding a high pressure center, from which winds blow outward. In the Northern Hemisphere these winds curve to the right in a clockwise pattern. (p. D42)

host (hōst) The organism a parasite lives in or on and is harmed by. (p. B56)

humidity (hū midʹi tē) The amount of water vapor in the air. (p. D16)

humus (hüʹməs) Decayed plant or animal material in soil. (pp. B14, C49)

hurricane (hûrʹi kānʹ) A very large, swirling storm with very low pressure at the center. (p. D70)

PRONUNCIATION KEY

a **a**t; ā **a**pe; ä f**a**r; âr c**ar**e; ô l**aw**; e **e**nd; ē m**e**; i **i**t; ī **i**ce; îr p**ier**ce; o h**o**t; ō **o**ld; ôr f**or**k; oi **oi**l; ou **ou**t; u **u**p; ū **u**se; ü r**u**le; ù p**u**ll; ûr t**ur**n; hw **wh**ite; ng so**ng**; th **th**in; th **th**is; zh mea**s**ure; ə **a**bout, tak**e**n, penc**i**l, lem**o**n, circ**u**s

hybrid (hī′brid) An organism produced by the crossing of parents that have different forms of the same trait. (p. A112)

hydrocarbon (hī′drə kär′bən) Any of the large group of compounds made solely from hydrogen and carbon atoms. (p. E32)

hydroelectric plant (hī′drō i lek′trik plant) A factory where running or falling water spins a generator to make electricity. (p. C104)

hydrosphere (hī′drə sfîr′) Earth's water, found in continents and oceans, including the fresh water in ice, lakes, rivers, and underground water. (p. C12)

hydrotropism (hī drot′rə piz′əm) The response of a plant to a nearby source of water. (p. A81)

hyperthermia (hī′pər thûr′mē ə) The overheating of the body that can be caused by overexposure in a hot, dry climate. (p. D90)

hypothesis (hī poth′ə sis) A guess or *if . . . then* statement that can be answered clearly in an experiment. (p. A35)

I

ice age (īs āj) Any period when glaciers and ice sheets covered much of Earth's surface. (p. B58)

igneous rock (ig′nē əs rok) A rock formed when melted rock material cools and hardens (p. C43)

image (im′ij) A "picture" of the light source that light rays make in bouncing off a polished, shiny surface. (p. F89)

imperfect flower (im pûr′fikt flou′ər) A flower with either a stamen or a pistil, but not both. (p. A70)

incomplete flower (in′kəm plēt′ flou′ər) A flower that lacks sepals, petals, stamens or pistils. (p. A70)

indicator (in′di kā′tər) A substance such as litmus paper whose color changes when it is mixed with an acid or a base. (p. E84)

inertia (i nûr′shə) The tendency of a moving object to keep moving in a straight line or of any object to resist a change in motion. (pp. C9, F7)

inexhaustible resource (in′eg zôs′tə bəl rē′sôrs′) A resource that cannot be depleted or used up easily. (p. B40)

infer (in fûr′) To form an idea from facts or observations. (p. S7)

inherited trait (in her′i təd trāt) A characteristic that is passed from parents to offspring. (p. A110)

insolation (in′sə lā′shən) The amount of the Sun's energy that reaches Earth at a given time and place. *Insolation* is short for *in*coming *sol*ar radi*ation*. (p. D6)

instinct (in′stingkt′) An inherited behavior, one that is not learned but is done automatically. (p. A110)

insulate (in′sə lāt′) To prevent heat from passing through. (p. E14)

interpret data (in tûr′prit dā′tə) To use the information that has been gathered to answer questions or solve a problem. (p. S7)

intertidal zone (in′tər tī′dəl zōn) The shallowest section of the marine, or ocean, ecosystem, where the ocean floor is covered and uncovered as the tide goes in and out. (p. B73)

invertebrate (in vûr′tə brit) An animal that does not have a backbone. (p. A95)

ionized (ī′ə nīzd′) Electrically charged by radiation, as gas particles of auroras in the night sky. (p. D10)

isobar (ī′sə bär′) A line on a weather map connecting places with equal air pressure. (p. D42)

K

kinetic energy (ki net′ik en′ər jē) The energy of any moving object. (p. E95)

L

land breeze (land brēz) Wind that blows from land to sea. (p. D39)

laser (lā′zər) A device that produces a thin stream of light of just a few close wavelengths. (p. F122)

lava (lä′və) Magma that reaches Earth's surface. (pp. C21, C43)

law of reflection (lô uv ri flek′shən) The angle between an incoming light ray and a surface equals the angle between the reflected light ray and the surface. (p. F87)

light ray (līt rā) A straight-line beam of light as it travels outward from its source. (p. F85)

lightning (līt′ning) One of the huge electric sparks that leap from clouds to the ground in thunderstorms. (p. D66)

limiting factor (lim′ə ting fak′tər) Anything that controls the growth or survival of a population. (p. B50)

liquid (lik′wid) A form of matter that takes up a definite amount of space and has no definite shape. (p. E36)

lithosphere (lith′ə sfîr′) The hard outer layer of Earth, about 100 km thick. (p. C12)

long-day plant (lông′dā plant) A plant that blooms when there is much more daylight than darkness. (p. A82)

low-pressure system (lō′presh′ər sis′təm) A pattern surrounding a low-pressure center, in which winds blow in toward the center. In the Northern Hemisphere, these winds blow to the right in a counterclockwise pattern. (p. D42)

luster (lus′tər) The way light bounces off a mineral's surface. (p. C33)

M

magma (mag′mə) Hot, molten rock deep below Earth's surface. (p. C21)

magnetic (mag net′ik) The property of a material like iron in which the particles line up pole to pole, causing it to be attracted or repelled by a magnet. (p. E15)

make a model (māk ə mod′əl) To make something to represent an object or event. (p. S7)

mare (mär′ā) *n., pl.* **maria** (mär′ē ə) Dark-colored land on the Moon that is dry and flat and is surrounded by mountains and ridges. (p. C13)

mass (mas) A measure of the amount of matter in an object. (p. E6)

matter (ma′tər) Anything that has mass and takes up space. (pp. E6, F51)

measure (mezh′ər) To find the size, volume, area, mass, weight, or temperature of an object, or how long an event occurs. (p. S7)

melting point (melt′ing point) The particular temperature for each substance at which it changes state from a solid to a liquid. (p. E37)

membrane (mem′brān) A thin envelope surrounding the nucleus of a cell. (p. A14)

metal (met′əl) Any of a group of elements found in the ground that conducts heat and electricity. (p. C38)

metamorphic rock (met′ə môr′fik rok) A rock formed under heat and pressure from another kind of rock. (p. C46)

meteorite (mē′tē ə rīt′) A chunk of rock from space that strikes the surface of Earth or the Moon. (p. C26)

mid-ocean ridge (mid ō′shun rij) Chain of mountains that wind along all the world's major oceans. (p. C91)

PRONUNCIATION KEY

a at; ā ape; ä far; âr care; ô law; e end; ē me; i it; ī ice; îr pierce; o hot; ō old; ôr fork; oi oil; ou out; u up; ū use; ü rule; ů pull; ûr turn; hw white; ng song; th thin; th this; zh measure; ə about, taken, pencil, lemon, circus

mimicry (mim′i krē) An adaptation in which an animal is protected against predators by its resemblance to another, unpleasant animal. (p. A106)

mineral (min′ə rəl) A solid material of Earth's crust with a definite composition. (p. C32)

mixture (miks′chər) A physical combination of two or more substances that are blended together without forming new substances. (p. E52)

molecule (mol′ə kūl′) A particle that contains more than one atom joined together. (p. E30) *See* **atom**. (p. E26)

monocot (mon′ə kot′) An angiosperm with one cotyledon in each seed. *See* **dicot.** (p. A62)

mountain breeze (moun′tən brēz) A cool night wind that blows down a mountain slope to replace the warmer air in the valley. (p. D39)

mutualism (mū′chü ə liz′əm) A relationship between two kinds of organisms that benefits both. (p. B54)

N

neap tide (nēp tīd) The slightest changes from high to low tide that occur when the Sun, the Moon, and Earth form a right angle or are perpendicular to each other. (p. C89)

nekton (nek′tən) Organisms that swim through the water in aquatic ecosystems. (p. B72)

neutral (nü′trəl) Neither acid nor base. (p. E82)

neutron (nü′tron) A particle in the nucleus of an atom that has no net electric charge. (p. E27)

newton (nü′tən) A basic unit measuring the amount of pull or push a force such as gravity produces between two masses. (pp. E7, F20)

NEXRAD (neks′rad′) A new form of Doppler radar that is used to track storms. The word stands for *NEXt generation of weather RADar.* (p. D77)

niche (nich) The role of an organism in a community. (p. B11)

nitrogen cycle (nī′trə jən sī′kəl) The continuous trapping of nitrogen gas into compounds in the soil and its return to the air. (p. B38)

nonrenewable resource (non′ri nü′ə bəl rē′sôrs′) A resource that cannot be replaced within a short period of time or at all. (pp. B40, C64)

nonvascular (non vas′kyə lər) Containing no plant tissue through which water and food move. (p. A9)

nucleus (nü′klē əs) **1.** A dense structure inside the cell. (p. A14) **2.** One of the airborne dust particles around which water condenses as droplets or ice crystals before falling as precipitation. (p. D26) **3.** An atom's dense center, where most of its mass is. (p. E27)

O

observe (əb sûrv′) To use one or more of the senses to identify or learn about an object or event. (p. S7)

occluded front (ə klüd′id frunt) A front formed where a warm front and a cold front meet. (p. D56)

omnivore (om′nə vôr′) An animal that eats both plants and animals. (p. B21)

opaque (ō pāk′) Completely blocking light from passing through it. (p. F96)

orbit (ôr′bit) The path of a planet traveling around a star. (p. C6)

ore (ôr) A mineral containing a useful substance. (p. C38)

organ (ôr′gən) A group of tissues that work together to do a certain job. (p. A94)

organism (ôr′gə niz′əm) Any living thing that can carry out its life on its own. (p. B6)

ovary (ō′və rē) A structure containing egg cells; the base of a pistil in a flower. (p. A70)

overtone (ō′vər tōn′) One of a series of pitches that blend to give a sound its quality. (p. F72)

ozone layer (ō′zōn lā′ər) A layer of ozone gas in the atmosphere that screens out much of the Sun's UV (ultraviolet) rays. (p. C63)

P

parasitism (par′ə sī tiz′əm) A relationship in which one organism lives in or on another organism and benefits from that relationship while the other organism may be harmed by it. (p. B56) —**parasite** (par′ə sīt′) (p. A61)

perfect flower (pûr′fikt flou′ər) A flower with both male and female parts, that is, both a stamen and a pistil. (p. A70)

permafrost (pûr′mə frôst′) A layer of permanently frozen soil found in arctic and antarctic regions. (p. B68)

pH (pē′aitch′) The scale that tells how acidic or basic a solution is. (p. E86)

phloem (flō′em) The tissue through which food from the leaves moves down through the rest of a plant. (p. A21)

photon (fō′ton) The tiny bundles of energy by means of which light travels. (p. F119)

photoperiodism (fō′tō pîr′ē ə diz′əm) The flowering response of a plant to changing periods of daylight and darkness. (p. A82)

photosynthesis (fō′tə sin′thə sis) The food-making process in green plants that uses sunlight. (p. A32)

phototropism (fō tot′rə piz′əm) The response of a plant to changes in light. (p. A80)

phylum (fī′ləm) *n., pl.* **phyla** (-lə) One of the large groups in the animal kingdom. (p. A12)

physical change (fiz′i kəl chānj) A change of matter in size, shape, or state without any change in identity. (p. E70)

pioneer community (pī′ə nîr′ kə mū′ni tē) The first community thriving in a once lifeless area. (p. B83)

pioneer species (pī′ə nîr′ spē′shēz) The first species living in an otherwise lifeless area. (p. B83)

pitch (pich) How high or low a sound is. (p. F56)

planet (plan′it) Any of the nine objects that travel around the Sun and shine by reflecting its light. (p. C6)

plankton (plangk′tən) Organisms that float on the water in aquatic ecosystems. (p. B72)

plate (plāt) One of the moving pieces of Earth's crust that has been broken by upward pressure from the mantle. (p. C19)

plate tectonics (plāt tek ton′iks) A scientific theory that Earth's crust is made of moving plates. (p. C19)

polarization (pō′lər ə zā′shən) Allowing light vibrations to pass through in only one direction. (p. F97)

pollen (pol′ən) Dustlike grains in the flower of a plant that contain its male sex cells. (p. A64)

pollination (pol′ə nā′shən) The transfer of a pollen grain to the egg-producing part of a plant. (p. A72)

pollute (pə lüt′) *v.* To add unnatural substances to Earth's land, water, or air. (p. C50) —**pollutant** (pə lü′tənt) *n.* Something that pollutes. (p. C50) —**pollution** (pə lü′shən) *n.* A polluted condition. (p. C50)

PRONUNCIATION KEY

a **a**t; ā **a**pe; ä f**a**r; âr c**ar**e; ô l**aw**; e **e**nd; ē m**e**; i **i**t; ī **i**ce; îr p**ier**ce; o h**o**t; ō **o**ld; ôr f**or**k; oi **oi**l; ou **ou**t; u **u**p; ū **u**se; ü r**u**le; u̇ p**u**ll; ûr t**ur**n; hw **wh**ite; ng so**ng**; th **th**in; th **th**is; zh mea**s**ure; ə **a**bout, tak**e**n, penc**i**l, lem**o**n, circ**u**s

population (pop′yə lā′shən) All the members of one species in an area. (p. B10)

potential energy (pə ten′shəl en′ər jē) Stored energy. (p. E95)

precipitation (pri sip′i tā′shən) Any form of water particles that falls from the atmosphere and reaches the ground. (pp. B33, D26)

predator (pred′ə tər) An animal that hunts other anmals for food. (pp. A106, B21)

predict (pri dikt′) To state possible results of an event or experiment. (p. S7)

prey (prā) A living thing that is hunted for food. (p. B21)

primary color (prī′mer′ē kul′ər) Red, green, or blue. Mixing these colors can produce all the colors of the spectrum. (p. F110)

primary pigment (prī′mer′ē pig′mənt) Magenta, cyan, or yellow. Materials with any of these colors absorb one primary color of light and reflect the other two. (p. F112)

primary succession (prī′mer′ē sək sesh′ən) The beginning of a community where few, if any, living things exist, or where earlier communities were wiped out. (p. B82)

prism (priz′əm) A cut piece of clear glass (or plastic) with two opposite sides in the shape of a triangle or other geometric shape. (p. F108)

producer (prə dü′sər) Any of the plants and algae that produce oxygen and food that animals need. (p. B7)

product (prod′ukt) A new substance produced by a chemical change. (p. E71)

prop root (prop rüt) One of the roots that grow out of a plant's stemlike main roots and help prop up the plant. (p. A21)

property (prop′ər tē) A characteristic of matter that can be observed, such as mass, volume, weight, or density. (pp. E6, E24)

protective coloration (prə tek′tiv kul′ə rā′shən) A type of camouflage in which the color of an animal blends in with its background, protecting it against predators. (p. A109)

protein (prō′tēn) A substance rich in nitrogen that the body uses for growth and the repair of cells. (p. B38)

protist (prō′tist) A member of a kingdom that contains one-celled and many-celled living things, some that make food and some that hunt for food. (p. A14)

proton (prō′ton) A particle in the nucleus of an atom that carries one unit of positive electric charge. (p. E27)

Q

quality (kwol′i tē) The difference you hear between two sounds of the same loudness and pitch. (p. F72)

R

radar (rā′där) A device for tracking the position and path of a distant moving object. It works by sending out radio waves and recording their echoes. The word stands for *RAdio Detecting And Ranging.* (p. D76)

radiation (rā′dē a′shən) The transfer of heat through electromagnetic rays. (p. E97)

radiative balance (rā′dē a′tiv bal′əns) A balance between energy lost and energy gained. (p. D86)

rarefaction (râr′ə fak′shən) The part of a sound wave where molecules are spread apart. (p. F51)

raw material (rô mə tîr′ē əl) Material not yet refined, manufactured, or processed. (p. B40)

reactant (rē ak′tənt) An original substance at the beginning of a chemical reaction. (p. E71)

reaction (rē ak′shən) The force with which an object responds to an action, as in Newton's third law of motion, which states, "For every action, there is an equal but opposite reaction." *See* **action**. (p. F24)

reflection (ri flek′shən) The bouncing of a sound wave off a surface. (p. F66)

refraction (ri frak′shən) The bending of light rays as they pass from one substance into another. (p. F98)

relative humidity (rel′ə tiv hū mid′i tē) A comparison between how much water vapor is in the air and how much the air could hold at a given temperature if it were full, or saturated. (p. D18)

renewable resource (ri nü′ə bəl rē′sôrs′) A resource that can be replaced in a short period of time. (pp. B40, C62)

reservoir (rez′ər vwär′) A storage area for fresh water supplies. (p. C75)

resonance (rez′ə nəns) In an instrument or object, a unique blend of the fundamental frequency and its overtones. When an external force vibrates at the same frequency, a buildup of that resonance can occur. (p. F72)

resource (rē′sôrs′) Any material that helps support life on Earth. (p. C12)

respiration (res′pə rā′shən) The release of energy in plants and animals from food (sugar). (p. A33)

response (ri spons′) What a living thing does as a result of a stimulus. (p. A80)

rhizoid (rī′zoid) One of the hairlike fibers that anchor a moss to the soil and take in water from the soil. (p. A48)

rhizome (rī′zōm) The underground stem of a fern. (p. A51)

rock (rok) A naturally formed solid in the crust made up of one or more minerals. (p. C42)

rock cycle (rok sī′kəl) Rocks changing from one into another in a never-ending series of processes. (p. C52)

root cap (rüt kap) A thin covering made up of cells that protect the root tip of a plant as it grows into the soil. (p. A20)

root hair (rüt hâr) Any of the threadlike projections from a plant root that absorb water and dissolved minerals from the soil. (p. A20)

rotate (rō′tāt) To make a complete spin on an axis, causing one day on a planet. A day differs in length from planet to planet. (p. C10)

runoff (run′ôf) Precipitation that flows across the land's surface or falls into rivers and streams. (pp. B33, D28)

S

savanna (sə van′ə) A tropical grassland with some trees and shrubs. (p. B66)

scanning tunneling microscope (scan′ing tun′əl ing mī′krə skōp′) A device that uses electric current flowing through a needle to trace the contours of atoms and magnify them as much as 30 million times. (p. E26)

scavenger (skav′ən jər) A meat-eating animal that feeds on the remains of dead animals. (p. B21)

sea breeze (sē brēz) Wind that blows from sea to land. (p. D39)

sea-floor vent (sē′flôr′ vent) An opening in a mid-ocean ridge where mineral-saturated water boils up from the seafloor crust. (p. C93)

seamount (sē′mount′) A huge underwater volcanic mountain that may emerge from the ocean surface as an island. (p. C90)

secondary succession (sek′ən der′ē sək sesh′ən) The beginning of a new community where an earlier community already exists. (p. B82)

sedimentary rock (sed′ə men′tə rē rok) A rock made of bits of matter joined together. (p. C44)

PRONUNCIATION KEY

a **at**; ā **ape**; ä **far**; âr **care**; ô **law**; e **end**; ē **me**; i **it**; ī **ice**; îr **pierce**; o **hot**; ō **old**; ôr **fork**; oi **oil**; ou **out**; u **up**; ū **use**; ü **rule**; u̇ **pull**; ûr **turn**; hw **white**; ng **song**; th **thin**; <u>th</u> **this**; zh **measure**; ə **about**, **taken**, **pencil**, **lemon**, **circus**

seed (sēd) An undeveloped plant with stored food sealed in a protective covering. (p. A58)

seed coat (sēd kōt) The outer covering of a seed. (p. A74)

seed dispersal (sēd di spûr′səl) The movement of a seed from the flower to a place where it can sprout. (p. A75)

self-pollination (self′pol′ə nā′shən) The transfer of pollen from an anther to a stigma in the same plant. (p. A72)

sexual reproduction (sek′shü əl rē′prō duk′shən) The production of a new organism from a female sex cell and a male sex cell. (p. A52)

shear (shîr) A movement of plates that twists, tears, or pushes one part of Earth's crust past another. (p. C20)

short-day plant (shôrt′dā plant) A plant that blooms when there is more darkness and less daylight. (p. A82)

smog (smog) A mixture of smoke and fog. (p. C64)

solar system (sō′lər sis′təm) The Sun and the objects that are traveling around it. (p. C6)

solid (sol′id) A form of matter that has a definite shape and takes up a definite amount of space. (p. E36)

solubility (sol′yə bil′i tē) The ability of a substance to be dissolved by another substance. (p. E58)

solute (sol′ūt) A substance that is dissolved by another substance to form a solution. (p. E57)

solution (sə lü′shən) A mixture of substances that are blended so completely that the mixture looks the same everywhere. (p. E54)

solvent (sol′vənt) A substance that dissolves one or more other substances to form a solution. (p. E57)

sound wave (sound wāv) A vibration that spreads away from a vibrating object. (p. F51)

spectrum (spek′trəm) A band of colors produced when light goes through a prism. (p. F108)

speed (spēd) How fast an object's position changes with time at any given moment. (p. F11)

spore (spôr) Cells in seedless plants that grow into new organisms. (p. A48)

spring (spring) A place where groundwater seeps out of the ground. (p. C75)

spring tide (spring tīd) The greatest changes from high to low tide that occur when the Sun, the Moon, and Earth are lined up. (p. C89)

state of matter (stāt uv mat′ər) One of the three forms that matter can take—solid, liquid, or gas. (p. E36)

stationary front (stā′shə ner ē frunt) An unmoving front where a cold air mass and a warm air mass meet. (p. D57)

statistical forecasting (stə tis′ti kəl fôr′kas′ting) Predicting weather by using past weather records, based on the chances of a pattern repeating itself. (p. D60)

stimulus (stim′yə ləs), *n., pl.* **stimuli (-lī)** Something in the environment that causes a living thing to react. (p. A80)

stomata (stō′mə tə) *pl. n., sing.* **stoma** Pores in the bottom of leaves that open and close to let in air or give off water vapor. (p. A24)

storm surge (stôrm sûrj) A great rise of the sea along a shore caused by low pressure clouds. (p. D72)

stratus cloud (strā′təs kloud) A cloud that forms in a blanketlike layer. (p. D24)

streak (strēk) The color of the powder left when a mineral is rubbed against a hard, rough surface. (p. C34)

strip farming (strip fär′ming) Trapping runoff by alternating tightly growing grasses with more widely spaced plants. (p. C51)

subscript (sub′skript′) A number in a chemical formula that tells the number of atoms in the compound. (p. E25)

surveyor (sər vā′ər) A specialist who makes accurate measurements of Earth's crust. (p. C18)

suspension (sə spen′shən) A mixture in which suspended particles can easily be seen. (p. E59)

symbiosis (sim′bē ō′sis) A relationship between two kinds of organisms that lasts over time. (p. B54)

synoptic weather map (si nop′tik weth′ər map) A type of map showing a summary of the weather using station models. (p. D60)

system (sis′təm) A group of organs that work together to carry on life functions. (p. A94)

T

taiga (tī′gə) A cool forest biome of conifers in the upper Northern Hemisphere. (p. B67)

taproot (tap′rüt′) A root that has few hairy branches and grows deep into the ground. (p. A21)

temperate (tem′pər it) Free from extremes of temperature. (p. B66)

tension (ten′shən) A movement of plates that stretches or pulls apart Earth's crust. (p. C20)

terracing (ter′is ing) Shaping hillsides into steps so that runoff and eroded soil get trapped on the steps. (p. C51)

texture (teks′chər) An identifying quality of a rock based on how coarse, fine, or glassy it is and on how angular or rounded it is. (p. C42)

thunder (thun′dər) The noise caused by lightning-heated air during a thunderstorm. (p. D66)

thunderhead (thun′dər hed′) A cumulonimbus cloud in which a thunderstorm forms. (p. D66)

thunderstorm (thun′dər stôrm′) The most common severe storm, formed in cumulonimbus clouds. (p. D66)

tissue (tish′ü) A group of similar cells that work together at the same job. (pp. A7, A94)

topsoil (top′soil′) The dark, top layer of soil, rich in humus and minerals, in which many tiny organisms live and most plants grow. (p. B14)

tornado (tôr nā′dō) A violent whirling wind that moves across the ground in a narrow path. (p. D68)

trade wind (trād wind) A belt of winds around Earth moving from high pressure zones toward the low pressure at the equator. (p. D41)

translucent (trans lü′sənt) Letting only some light through, so that objects on the other side appear blurry. (p. F96)

transparent (trans pâr′ənt) Letting all light through, so that objects on the other side can be seen clearly. (p. F96)

transpiration (tran′spə rā′shən) The loss of water through a plant's leaves, which draws water up through the plant to replace it. (pp. A25, D17)

trench (trench) A deep valley in the sea floor. (p. C91)

tropical rain forest (trop′i kəl rān fôr′ist) A hot, humid biome near the equator, with much rainfall and a wide variety of life. (p. B71)

tropism (trō′piz′əm) A growth response of a plant toward or away from a stimulus. (p. A80)

troposphere (trop′ə sfîr′) The layer of the atmosphere closest to Earth's surface. (p. D10)

PRONUNCIATION KEY

a **a**t; ā **a**pe; ä f**a**r; âr c**ar**e; ô l**aw**; e **e**nd; ē m**e**; i **i**t; ī **i**ce; îr p**ier**ce; o h**o**t; ō **o**ld; ôr f**or**k; oi **oi**l; ou **ou**t; u **u**p; ū **u**se; ü r**u**le; u̇ p**u**ll; ûr t**ur**n; hw **wh**ite; ng so**ng**; th **th**in; th **th**is; zh mea**s**ure; ə **a**bout, tak**e**n, penc**i**l, lem**o**n, circ**u**s

tube worm (tüb wûrm) Large wormlike animals that live near sea floor vents and obtain their food through bacterial chemosynthesis. (p. C93)

tundra (tun′drə) Large, treeless plain in the arctic regions, where the ground is frozen all year. (p. B68)

U

ultrasonic (ul′trə son′ik) Said of a sound with a frequency too high to be heard by humans. (p. F57)

unbalanced forces (un bal′ənst fôrs′əz) Forces that do not cancel each other out when acting together on a single object. (p. F21)

updraft (up′draft′) An upward rush of heated air during a thunderstorm. (pp. D38, D66)

use numbers (ūz num′bərz) To order, count, add, subtract, multiply, and divide to explain data. (p. S7)

use variables (ūz vâr′ē ə bəlz) To identify and separate things in an experiment that can be changed or controlled. (p. S7)

V

vacuum (vak′ū əm) A space through which sound waves cannot travel because it contains no matter. (p. F116)

valley breeze (val′ē brēz) A cool wind that blows up a mountain slope and replaces the slope's rising Sun-warmed air. (p. D39)

variable (vâr′ē ə bəl) One of the changes in a situation that may affect the outcome of an experiment. (p. A35)

vascular (vas′kyə lər) Containing plant tissue through which water moves up and food moves down. (p. A9)

velocity (və los′i tē) The speed and direction of a moving object. (p. F12)

vertebrate (vûr′tə brit) An animal that has a backbone. (p. A95)

vibration (vī brā′shən) A back-and-forth motion. (p. F50)

volume (vol′ūm) **1.** A measure of how much space an object takes up. (p. E6) **2.** The loudness or softness of a sound. (p. F58)

W

warm front (wôrm frunt) A front where warm air moves in over a cold air mass. (p. D56)

water cycle (wô′tər sī′kəl) The continuous movement of water between Earth's surface and the air, changing from liquid to gas to liquid. (pp. B33, C74, D29)

water table (wô′tər tā′bəl) The top of the water-filled spaces in the ground. (p. C75)

water vapor (wô′tər vā′pər) Water in the form of a gas. (pp. B32, D16)

waterspout (wô′tər spout′) A tornado that forms over water. (p. D69)

weather (weth′ər) What the lower atmosphere is like at any given place and time. (p. D12)

weather vane (weth′ər vān) A device that indicates wind direction. (p. D44)

weathering (weth′ər ing) Breaking down rocks into smaller pieces. (p. C22)

weight (wāt) The force of gravity between Earth and an object. (pp. E7, F36)

well (wel) A hole dug below the water table that water seeps into. (p. C75)

wind (wind) Air that moves horizontally. (p. D38)

X

xylem (zī′ləm) The tissue through which water and minerals move up through a plant. (p. A20)

Y

year (yîr) The time it takes a planet to orbit the Sun. A *year* is different from planet to planet. (p. C7)

Index

A

* Indicates an activity related to this topic.

B

C

*Indicates an activity related to this topic.

D

E

F

*Indicates an activity related to this topic.

I

J

K

L

M

*Indicates an activity related to this topic.

N

*Indicates an activity related to this topic.

Q

R

*Indicates an activity related to this topic.

T

*Indicates an activity related to this topic.

X

Y

Credits

Page placement key: (t) top, (tr) top right, (tl) top left, (tc) top center, (m) middle, (l) left, (r) right, (b) bottom, (br) bottom right,(bl) bottom left, (bc) bottom center, (bg) background, (i) inset

Cover Design and Illustration: Robert Brook Allen

Cover Photos: ©Tim Flach/Stone; (bg) ©Darrell Gulin/Natural Selection; (i) ©PhotoSpin 2000.

Illustrations: Kenneth Batelman: pp. C9, C89, F24, F35, F37, F39; Tom Bean: p. S2; Denny Bond: p. B36; Ka Botzis: pp. B20, B21; Drew-Brook-Cormack: p. D20; Susan Carlson: p. A12; Andrea Champlin: pp. F31, C10, C11, D6, D42, D70, D82, D84, E12, E62, E63, E64; Barbara Cousins: pp. R24, R26, R27, R28; Marie Dauenheimer: pp. A6, A7; John Edwards: pp. C6, E7, E10, E12, F70, F84, F85, F89, F90, F100; Peter Fasolino: pp. E43, E60; Robert Frank: p. B38; Function Thru Form: pp. A32, A62, A117, B18, B20, B21, B24, B25, B27, B40, B51, C8, C31, C33, C37, C39, C46, C50, C65, C72, C76, C103, D6, D7, D8, D10, D11, D16, D17, D25, D26, D30, D35, D39, D41, D43, D51, D53, D81, D85, D86, D89, D93, E15, E26, E27, E29, E30, E31, E32, E36, E37, E39, E46, E69, E82, ,E86, E92, E97, F6, F7, F10, F11, F12, F18, F19, F20, F21, F22, F23, F36, F38, F51, F55, F57, F59, F60, F61, F66, F69, F71, F76, F108, F112, F117, F119, F124, F125; Thomas Gagliano: pp. D36, D37, D39; Peter Gunther: p. F30; Greg Harris: pp. B73, D55; Carlyn Iverson: pp. B32, B80, B81; Sidney Jablonski: p. C86; John Karapelou: pp. R29, R30, R31; Virge Kask: pp. A12, A70, A72, A73, A74, A76, B18, B24, B25; George Kelvin: pp. A24, A32, A35, A52, A53, A54, A79, A81, A82, A88, C12, C14, C19, C20, C25, C47, C49, C62, C63, C74, C75, C88, C90, C91, C102, C103, F27, F85, F101, F118; Katie Lee: pp. B6, B7, B84; Tom Leonard: pp. F102, R20, R21, R22, R32; Rebecca Merrilees: pp. A20, A21, A22, A37, A38, A51; Dave Merrill: pp. B9, B52, B54, C21, D85; Mowry Graphics: pp. D28, D54, D89; Steve Oh: pp. A95, F3, F14, F22, F25, F26, F27, F34, R27, R28, R29, R32, R33, R34,; Chris Porter: pp. B6, C14; Saul Rosenbaum: pp. D8, D9, D27, D38, D56, D57, D66, D67, D87, F99, F116, F117; Wendy Smith: pp. A8, A10, A11, A60, A62, F112; Steve Stankiewicz: pp. B64, B89, C32, C52, C73, C78, C100, D18, D40, D53, D60, D69, D89, E38, E42, E92, E94, F74, F86, F93, F101, F104, F105, F110, F122, R8, R9, R13; Patricia Wynne: pp. R23, R31.

Photography Credits: All photographs are by the Macmillan/McGraw-Hill School Division (MMSD) and Dan Howell for MMSD except as noted below.

Contents: iv: ©Norbert Wu. v: ©Tim Flach/Stone. vi: l ©Jules Cowan/Index Stock Imagery; b ©Joyce Photographics/Photo Researchers, Inc; r ©A.J. Copley/VU. vii: l ©NOAA, colored by John Wells/Science Photo Library/Photo Researchers, Inc; r ©Runk/Schoenberger/Grant Heilman. viii: l ©Roger Ressmeyer/Corbis; b ©Science/VU; ix: ©Duomo/Corbis.

National Geographic Invitation to Science: S1: ©Gianni Tortoli/Photo Researchers, Inc. S2: ©Tom Bean/Tom & Susan Bean Photography Inc. S3: ©Chris Hondros/Liaison Agency Inc. S4: ©Carlos Munoz-Yague/ Eurelios/Science Photo Library/Photo Researchers, Inc. S5: ©Mark Pilkington/Geological Survey of Canada/Science Photo Library/Photo Researchers, Inc. S7: ©Richard Hutchings.

National Geographic Unit Opener A: A0 ©Kelvin Aitken/Peter Arnold,Inc;A1 ©Norbert Wu; A1 ©Kelvin Aitken/Peter Arnold,Inc. **Unit A:** A2: ©William Waterfall/The Stock Market. A4: ©Ted Levin/Animals Animals/Earth Scenes. A5: ©Richard Hutchings. A6: ©Peter Miller/Photo Researchers, Inc. A7: ©Dick Thomas/VU. A9: ©Rob Hadlow/Bruce Coleman, Inc. A13: (tr) ©Doug Sokell/VU; (br) ©R.M. Meadows/Peter Arnold, Inc.; (bl) ©Veronika Burmeister/VU. A14: (br) ©Cabisco/VU; (bl) ©Gilbert S. Grant/Photo Researchers, Inc.; (bl) ©Patrick W. Grace/Science Source/Photo Researchers, Inc.; (br) ©R. Kessel-G. Shih/VU; (bl) ©Veronika Burmeister/VU. A15: (br) ©A. & F. Michler/Peter Arnold, Inc.; (bl) ©Telegraph Colour Library/FPG. A16: (b) ©Adam Jones/Dembinsky Photo Associates; (br) ©Arthur R. Hill/VU. A17: ©Manfred Kage/Peter Arnold, Inc. A18: ©Dominique Braud/Dembinsky Photo Associates. A19: ©Richard Hutchings. A23: (tl) ©George Bernard/Animals Animals/Earth Scenes; (tr) ©Robert Maier/Animals Animals/Earth Scenes; (tr) ©Willard Clay/Dembinsky Photo Associates. A25: ©G.Buttner/OKAPIA/Photo Researchers, Inc. A26: (tr) ©David S. Addison/VU; (m) ©Tim Hauf/VU. A27: ©James R. Holland/National Geographic Society. A 28: (bl) ©Michael J. Balick/Peter Arnold, Inc.; (br) ©Ray Pfortner/Peter Arnold, Inc. A29: ©J.C. Teyssier/Publiphoto/Photo Researchers, Inc. A30: ©Robert Maier/Animals Animals/Earth Scenes. A31: ©Richard Hutchings. A32: ©PHOTODISC/Gettyone. A34: ©Willard Clay/Dembinsky Photo Associates. A36: (t) ©Gerry Ellis/ENP Images; (bl, br) ©Jack M. Bostrack/VU. A37: ©Phil Degginger/Color-Pic. A40: ©Jim Olive/Pictor/Uniphoto. A41: (tl) ©courtesy of Katherine Banks/Prof. K. Banks; (tr) ©Hans Reinhard/Bruce Coleman, Inc.; (r) ©WHM Bildarchiv/Peter Arnold, Inc. A42: ©1998 PhotoDisc, Inc. A43: ©Hans Reinhard/Bruce Coleman, Inc. A44: ©Bob Krist/Corbis. A46: ©Michael Fogden/Bruce Coleman, Inc. A47: ©Richard Hutchings. A48: (br) ©David Sieren/VU; (bl) ©Doug Sokell/VU; (bl) ©John Trager/VU. A49: (bc) ©E.F.Anderson/VU; (bl) ©Ed Reschke/Peter Arnold, Inc.; (bl) ©Mike Perry/Pictor/Uniphoto. A50: (tl) ©Dan Suzio/Photo Researchers, Inc.; (br, tr) ©Richard Hutchings. A51: ©David Dennis/Animals Animals/Earth Scenes. A54: ©Dick Keen/VU. A55: ©Ed Degginger/Color-Pic, Inc. A56: ©Michael Gadomski/Animals Animals/Earth Scenes. A57: ©Richard Hutchings. A58: (bl) ©Jim Hughes/VU; (br) ©V.P. Weinland/Photo Researchers, Inc.; (br) ©W. Ormerod/VU. A59: (m) ©Ed Degginger/Bruce Coleman, Inc.; (br) ©E. Webber/VU; (bl) ©Gerald & Buff Corsi/VU;(bl) ©Jan Taylor/Bruce Coleman, Inc.; (bl) ©John N. Trager/VU. A60: (b) ©Dick Keen/VU; (tr) ©V. McMillan/VU. A61: (br) ©Bud Nielsen/VU; (t) ©E.F. Anderson/VU. A63: (br) ©Arthur R. Hill/VU; (br) ©Mark S. Skalny/VU. A64: (tr) ©Jerome Wexler/Photo Researchers, Inc.; (tl) ©John Gerlach/VU. A66: (tl) ©Jeff Greenberg/VU; (tr) ©Larry Lefever/Grant Heilman Photography, Inc. A67: ©Jim Sugar Photography/Bettmann/CORBIS. A68: ©Robert P. Carr/Bruce Coleman, Inc. A69: ©Richard Hutchings. A71: (b) ©Adam Jones/Photo Researchers, Inc.; (tl) ©Derrick Ditchburn/VU; (m) ©Doug Sokell/VU. A74: ©Henry T. Kaiser/Pictor/Uniphoto. A75: (tl) ©Inga Spence/VU; (m) ©Ken Wagner/VU; (tr) ©Stephen J. Lang/VU. A76: ©Scott T. Smith. A78: ©Mack Henley/VU. A80: ©David Newman/VU. A81: ©R. Calentine/VU. A83: (m) ©Dick Keen/VU; (br) ©Richard Hutchings. A84: (b) ©Bill Beatty/VU; (tr) ©Parke H. John, Jr./VU. A85: ©Runk/Schoenberger/Grant Heilman Photography, Inc. A86: (bg) ©Brock May/Photo Researchers, Inc.; (tr) ©Joel Sartore/Grant Heilman Photography, Inc. A87: ©Catherine Karnow/CORBIS. A88: (bl) ©Hans Reinhard/Bruce Coleman, Inc.; (bl) ©John McAnulty/CORBIS. A90: ©R&V Taylor/Bruce Coleman, Inc. A92: ©Frank Krahmer/Bruce Coleman, Inc. A95: (bl) ©BIOS Klein/Hubert/Peter Arnold, Inc.; (m) ©Joe McDonald/Bruce Coleman, Inc.; (tr) ©John Hyde/Bruce Coleman, Inc. A96: (m) ©Ed Degginger/Bruce Coleman, Inc.; (br) ©Ed Degginger/Color-Pic; (tr) ©Jeff Mondragon/Mondragon Photography; (bl) ©Scott Johnson/Animals Animals/Earth Scenes; (tl) ©Susan Blanchet/Dembinsky Photo Associates; (tl) ©Tom E. Adams/Peter Arnold, Inc. A97: (bl) © Breck P. Kent/Animals Animals/Earth Scenes; (tr, br) ©Fred Bavendam/Peter Arnold, Inc.; (tl) ©Hans Pfletschinger/Peter Arnold, Inc.; (bl) ©Jeff J. Daly/Stock Boston; (br) ©Pictor/Uniphoto; (m) ©Robert Lubeck/Animals Animals/Earth Scenes. A98: (br) ©Gary Meszaroa/Bruce Coleman, Inc.; (m) ©Marilyn Kazmers/Dembinsky Photo Associates; (bl) ©Norbert Wu/Peter Arnold, Inc.; (bl) ©Skip Moody/Dembinsky Photo Associates; (m) ©Pictor/Uniphoto; (tl) ©Zig Leszczynski/Animals Animals/Earth Scenes. A99: (br) ©Bob Cranston/Animals Animals/Earth Scenes; (tl) ©Darrell Gulin/CORBIS; (m) ©Des & Jen Bartlett/Bruce Coleman, Inc.; (m) ©Ed Degginger/Color-Pic; (tl) ©Michael Newman/PhotoEdit; (tl) ©Rob Simpson/Pictor/Uniphoto; (tl) ©Pictor/Uniphoto. A100: (m) ©Ed Degginger/Color-Pic; (br) ©Jim Roetzel/Dembinsky Photo Associates; (m) ©John Cancalosi/Peter Arnold, Inc.; (br) ©John Shaw/Bruce Coleman, Inc.; (bc) ©Skip Moody/Dembinsky Photo Associates. A101: ©Graham Pizzey/Bruce Coleman, Inc. A104: (bg) ©John Gerlach/Dembinsky Photo Associates; (m) ©Rolf Kopfle/Bruce Coleman, Inc. A106; (bl) ©L. West/Bruce Coleman, Inc.; (br) ©Stan W. Elems/VU. A107: (bl) ©Ed Degginger/Color-Pic; (m) ©Rod Planck/Dembinsky Photo Associates; (tl, br) ©Stan W. Elems/VU. A108: ©Steve Kaufman/Peter Arnold, Inc. A109: ©Kim Taylor/Bruce Coleman, Inc. A110: ©Ed Degginger/Color-Pic. A111: (b) ©D. Robert Franz/Bruce Coleman, Inc.; (br) ©Erwin & Peggy Bauer/Bruce Coleman, Inc.; (m) ©John Shaw/Bruce Coleman, Inc.; (tl) ©John Snyder/Bruce Coleman, Inc.; (tr) ©Skip Moody/Dembinsky Photo Associates. A112: (tl, tr) ©Ed Degginger/Color-Pic; (tl) ©Randa Bishop/Pictor/Uniphoto. A113: (br) ©Fritz Prenzel/Animals Animals/Earth Scenes; (br, m) ©Hans Reinhard/Bruce Coleman, Inc. A114: ©Stan Osolinski/Dembinsky Photo Associates. A115: ©Gerard Lacz/Animals Animals/Earth Scenes. A118: ©Courtesy of HSWRI. A119: ©Courtesy of HSWRI.

National Geographic Unit Opener B: B0 ©Tim Flach/Stone; B1 ©Art Wolfe/Stone; B1 ©Tim Flach/Stone. **Unit B:** B2: ©Lee Rentz/Bruce Coleman, Inc. B4: ©Zig Leszczynski/Animals Animals/Earth Scenes. B5: ©Richard Hutchings. B8: (t) ©John Shaw/Bruce Coleman, Inc.; (br) ©John Shaw/Bruce Coleman, Inc. B9: (tc) ©David J. Sams/Stock, Boston; (tr) ©Joe McDonald/CORBIS; (tl) ©John Giustina/Bruce Coleman, Inc. B10: ©Lee Rentz/Bruce Coleman, Inc. B11: (tr) ©Laura Riley/Bruce Coleman, Inc.; (br) ©Robert M. Balou/Animals Animals/Earth Scenes. B12: (br) ©Bruce Coleman, Inc.; (tr) ©N.E. Swedberg/Bruce Coleman, Inc. B13: ©Joe McDonald/Animals Animals/Earth Scenes.B14: ©John Shaw/Bruce Coleman, Inc. B16: ©Beverly Joubert/National Geographic Collection/GettyOne Images. B19: ©1998 PhotoDisc, Inc. B22: (m) ©Gary Braasch/Tony Stone Images; (b) ©Joe McDonald/Bruce Coleman, Inc.; (m) ©Larry West/Bruce Coleman Inc. B23: (tr) ©Doug Wechsler/Animals Animals;

(bl) ©Scott Smith/Animals Animals. B26: (tr) ©Jeff Foote/Bruce Coleman, Inc.; (m) ©John Pontier/Animals Animals. B27: ©Zig Leszczynski/Animals Animals. B28: (bl) ©Artville/PictureQuest, Burke/Triolo PictureQuest. B29: (bl) ©Artville/PictureQuest, Burke/Triolo PictureQuest; (tl) ©B. Daemmrich/Stock Boston. B30: ©John Shaw/Bruce Coleman, Inc. B31: ©Richard Hutchings. B34: ©Ed Degginger/Earth Scenes. B35: ©Cesar Llacuna.B41: ©Peter Beck/The Stock Market. B42: (bg) ©Joe Sroka/Dembinsky Photo Associates; (t) ©Lynn Funkhouser/Peter Arnold, Inc. B43: (br) ©Fred Bavendam/Peter Arnold, Inc.; (bl) ©Kelvin Aitken/Peter Arnold, Inc. B45: ©N.E. Swedberg/Bruce Coleman, Inc. B46: ©Kennan Ward/The Stock Market. B48: ©James Randklev/Tony Stone Images. B49: ©Richard Hutchings. B50: (br) ©B&C Calhoun/Bruce Coleman, Inc.; (bl) ©John Shaw/Bruce Coleman, Inc. B51: (b) ©Jeff Foott/Bruce Coleman, Inc. B52: ©Patti Murray/Earth Scenes. B53: ©Linda Bailery/Earth Scenes. B56: (tr) ©David Overcash/Bruce Coleman, Inc.; (br) ©John Shaw/Bruce Coleman, Inc. B57: (t) ©Gregory Brown/Animals Animals; (bl) ©Patty Murray/Earth Scenes. B58: (b) ©Bob Burch/Bruce Coleman, Inc.; (tr) ©Tom Bean/CORBIS. B60: (bl) ©Kevin Schafer/Bettmann/CORBIS; (tr) ©Rod Williams/Bruce Coleman, Inc. B61: ©David Burder/Tony Stone Images. B62: ©Pictor/Uniphoto. B63: ©Richard Hutchings. B64: (tr) ©Breck P. Kent/Earth Scenes; (m) ©Lee Rentz/Rentl/Bruce Coleman, Inc.; (m) ©Nigel J.H. Smith/Earth Scenes. B65: (tr) ©Eastcott/Momatiuk/Earth Scenes; (tl) ©J.C. Carton/Bruce Coleman, Inc.; (m) ©M. Timothy O'Keefe/Bruce Coleman, Inc. B66: ©A.&M. Shah/Animals Animals. B67: ©Eastcott/Momatiuk/Earth Scenes. B68: ©Joe McDonald/Bruce Coleman, Inc. B69: (bl) ©Jen & Des Bartlett/Bruce Coleman, Inc.; (m) ©Joy Spurr/Bruce Coleman, Inc. B70: (bl) ©Jeff Foott/Bruce Coleman, Inc.; (m) ©John Shaw/Bruce Coleman, Inc. B71: (br) ©E&P Bauer/Bruce Coleman, Inc.; (tr) ©Joe McDonald/CORBIS. B72: (m) ©1998 PhotoDisc, Inc. B74: ©M. Newman/Bruce Coleman, Inc. B75: ©N. Devore III/Bruce Coleman, Inc. B76: (bg) ©Danny Lehman/CORBIS; (l) ©John D. Cunningham/Visuals Unlimited. B78: ©Gary Braasch/CORBIS. B79: ©John Shaw/Bruce Coleman, Inc. B80: ©John Elk III/Bruce Coleman, Inc. B82: (r) ©David Falconer/Bruce Coleman, Inc.; (bl) ©Patti Murray/Earth Scenes. B83: ©John Lemker/Earth Scenes. B85: (bl) ©Ed Degginger/Earth Scenes; (m) images copyright ©1998 PhotoDisc, Inc. B86: (m) ©Ed Degginger/Earth Scenes; (tr) ©S. Jonasson/Bruce Coleman, Inc. B87: ©Richard Hutchings. B88: ©1998 PhotoDisc, Inc. B90: ©John H. Hoffman/Bruce Coleman, Inc. B91: ©John Elk III/Bruce Coleman, Inc. B94: ©Craig Dickson/Woods Hole Oceanographic Institute. B94: (bg) ©Jeffrey L. Rotman/Peter Arnold, Inc. B95: (r) ©Ralph White/CORBIS.

National Geographic Unit Opener C: C0, C1 ©Jules Cowan/Index Stock Imagery. **Unit C:** C2: ©Peter French/Bruce Coleman, Inc. C5: ©Richard Hutchings. C7: ©Richard Hutchings. C8: (t) ©Blocker CollectionsUT Medical Bank. C13: (bl, br) ©NASA; (bg) ©Science/VU; (t) ©World Perspectives/Explorer/Photo Researchers, Inc. C14: ©Pekka Parviainen/Dembinsky Photo Associates. C15: ©E.Karkoschka/UA/NASA. C16: ©AFB/CORBIS. C17: ©Richard Hutchings. C18: (r) ©John D. Cunningham/VU; (l) ©Sinclair Stammers/Science Photo Library/Photo Researchers, Inc. C21: ©Dr. Ed Degginger/Color-Pic. C21: (r) ©Stella Snead/Bruce Coleman, Inc. C22: (l) ©Jerry Schad/Photo Researchers, Inc.; (r) ©Jim Steinberg/Photo Researchers, Inc.; (m) ©Robert Godwin/National Audubon Society/Photo Researchers, Inc. C23: (tr) ©David Austin/Stock Boston; (bl) ©Gilbert Grant/Photo Researchers, Inc. C24: ©Renee Lynn/Photo Researchers, Inc. C25: ©Terranova International/Photo Researchers, Inc. C26: (tr) ©Bruce Coleman, Inc.; (tr) ©David Scharf/Peter Arnold, Inc.; (t) ©NASA/PhotoTake. C28: (bg) ©Dave Bartruff/Stock Boston; (b) ©Mark Mellett//Stock Boston. C29: (l) ©Annie Griffiths Belt/Bettmann/CORBIS; (bg) ©Dave Bartruff/Stock Boston; (r) ©Morton Beebe,S.F./Bettman/CORBIS. C30: ©George Lepp/CORBIS. C32: (bl) ©Cesar Llacuna; (bc) ©Charles D. Winters/Timeframe Photography, Inc./Photo Researchers, Inc.; (bl) ©E. R. Degginger/Photo Researchers, Inc.; (br) ©George Whiteley/Photo Researchers, Inc.; (bc) ©Joyce Photographics/Photo Researchers, Inc. C33: (bc, br) ©Cesar Llacuna; (bl) ©David Lees/CORBIS; (br) ©J.H. Robinson/Photo Researchers, Inc.; (bc) ©Kaj R. Svensson/Science Photo Library/Photo Researchers, Inc.; (bl) ©Roberto De Gugliemo/Science Photo Library/Photo Researchers, Inc. C34: (tl) ©John D. Cunningham/VU; (tc) ©Mark A. Schneider/VU; (tr) ©Tom Pantages/PhotoTake. C35: (tc) ©A.J. Cunningham/VU. C36: (tr) ©A.J.Copley/VU; (m) ©Joyce Photographics/Photo Researchers, Inc.; (bl) ©Ross Frid/Korner Gems, Traverse City, MI/VU. C37: ©Peter Aitken/Photo Researchers, Inc. C38: (bl) ©A.J. Copley/VU; (bl) ©David Young-Wolf PhotoEdit/PictureQuest; (tr) ©Richard T. Nowitz/Photo Researchers, Inc.; (tr) ©Zale Corporation/Zales. C40: ©Lee Rentz/Bruce Coleman, Inc. C41: (bc) ©Doug Sokell/VU; (br) ©Richard Hutchings. C42: (br) ©Andrew J. Martinez/Photo Researchers, Inc.; (bl) ©Andrew J. Martinez/Photo Researchers, Inc. C43: (br) ©Biophoto Associates/Photo Researchers, Inc. C44: (bl) ©A.J. Copley/VU; (bl) ©Andrew J. Martinez/Photo Researchers, Inc.; (bl) ©Joyce Photographics/Photo Researchers, Inc.; (bl) ©Martin G. Miller/VU. C45: (b) ©John D. Cunningham/VU; (bl) Joyce Photographics/Photo Researchers, Inc.; (bl) ©Kjell B. Sandved/Photo Researchers, Inc. C46: (m) ©Arthur R. Hill/VU; (br) ©Charles R. Belinky /Photo Researchers, Inc.; (bl) ©Ed Degginger/Photo Researchers, Inc.; (m) ©L.S. Stepanowicz/VU. C47: ©Michael P. Gadomski/Photo Researchers, Inc. C48: ©Joyce Photographics/Photo Researchers, Inc. C50: ©G. Büttner/Naturbild/OKAPIA/Photo Researchers, Inc. C51: (tr) ©Christian Grzimek/OKAPIA/Photo Researchers, Inc.; (t) ©Ron Spomer/VU. C53: (m) ©John Elk III/Stock Boston. C54: (br) ©G. I. Bernard/Animals Animals/Earth Scenes; (m) ©Michael Newman/PhotoEdit. C55: ©W. Geiersperger/Stock Boston. C57: (tr) ©NASA/JPL/Caltech/NASA. C58: ©Paul Steel/THE STOCK MARKET. C60: ©NASA. C61: ©Richard Hutchings. C64: (t) ©Gary Withey/Bruce Coleman, Inc.; (tr) ©Hattie Young/Science Photo Library/Photo Researchers, Inc.; (tl) ©Phil Degginger/Color-Pic. C65: ©Simon Fraser/Science Photo Library/Photo Researchers, Inc. C67: (b) ©Chase Swift/CORBIS; (bl) ©Tom McHugh/Photo Researchers, Inc. C68: ©JPL/NASA. C69: (tr) ©Photo Researchers, Inc.; (tl) ©NASA. C70: ©IFA/Peter Arnold, Inc. C71: ©Richard Hutchings. C73: ©Calvin Larsen/Photo Researchers, Inc. C76: ©Simon Fraser/Science Photo Library/Photo Researchers, Inc.; C77: ©Richard Hutchings. C80: ©Victoria McCormick/Animals Animals/Earth Scenes. C81: ©Kevin Schafer/Peter Arnold, Inc. C82: ©Dave G. Houser/Pictor/Uniphoto. C84: (tr) ©L.Lipsky/Bruce Coleman, Inc.; (m) ©VCG/FPG. C85: ©Jan Stromme/Bruce Coleman, Inc. C86: ©NASA/Tom Pantages. C87: ©Ira Rubin/Dembinsky Photo Associates. C88: ©Jeff Greenberg/Stock Boston/PhotoEdit. C92: (br) ©Emory Kristof/National Geographic/Gettyone; (tr) ©R&V Taylor/Bruce Coleman, Inc. C93: ©Norbert Wu/Norbert Wu Productions. C94: (t) ©Chinch Gryniewicz/Ecoscene/CORBIS; (br) ©Fulvio Eccardi/Bruce Coleman, Inc. C95: ©L.Lipsky/Bruce Coleman, Inc. C96: ©Rod Catanach/Woods Hole Oceanographic Institute. C97: ©Woods Hole Oceanographic Institute. C98: ©Ron Sherman/Stock Boston. C99: ©Richard Hutchings. C100: (br) ©Joseph Nettis/Photo Researchers, Inc.; (bl) ©Phil Degginger/Color-Pic. C101: ©Ted Speigel/Bettmann CORBIS. C104: (bl) ©Phil Degginger/Color-Pic; (b) ©Russell D. Curtis/Photo Researchers, Inc.; (m) ©Simon Fraser/Science Photo Library/Photo Researchers, Inc. C105: (tl) ©John Keating/Photo Researchers, Inc.; (br) ©Kevin Schafer/Peter Arnold, Inc. C106: ©Patrick Grace/Photo Researchers, Inc. C107: ©Matt Meadows/Peter Arnold, Inc. C109: ©John Keating/Photo Researchers, Inc. C110: (r) ©Randy White/USGS; (bg) ©Roger Ressmeyer/CORBIS. C111: ©Doug Wechsler/Animals Animals/Earth Scenes.

National Geographic Unit Opener D: D0 ©NOAA, colored by John Wells/Science Photo Library/Photo Researchers, Inc; D1 ©World Perspectives/Stone. **Unit D:** D2: ©Steve Terrill/The Stock Market. D4: ©G.L. Kooyman/Earth Scenes; (br) ©Price, R. -Surv. OSF/Animals Animals/Earth Scenes. D5: ©Richard Hutchings. D12: (tr) ©Runk/Schoenberger/Grant Heilman/Grant Heilman Photography, Inc.; (r) ©Yoav Levy/PhotoTake. D13: ©Ed Degginger/Color-Pic. D14: ©Wolfgang Kaehler/CORBIS. D15: ©Richard Hutchings. D16: ©Amy C. Etra/PhotoEdit. D17: ©Richard Hutchings. D18: ©Ed Degginger/Color-Pic. D22: ©Bonnie Kamin/PhotoEdit. D23: ©Richard Hutchings. D24: (tr) ©A.J. Copley/VU; (m) ©Henry W. Robison/VU; (m) ©Mark A. Schneider/VU. D26: (br) ©Bettmann/CORBIS; (bl) ©D. Cavagnaro/VU; (br) ©Mark E. Gibson/VU; (bl) ©W. Banaszewski/VU. D27: (br) ©Jeff J. Daly/Fundamental Photographs; (m) ©Michael P. Gadomski/Dembinsky Photo Associates. D30: ©Runk/Schoenberger/Grant Heilman Photography, Inc. D33: ©Digital Stock. D34: ©Vince Streano/CORBIS. D35: ©Richard Hutchings. D38: ©Superstock. D41: ©NASA. D43: ©Richard Hutchings. D44: (tr) ©Ed Degginger/Bruce Coleman, Inc.; (tr) ©Science/VU. D45: (r) ©McGraw-Hill School Division (m) ©Paul A. Souders/CORBIS. D46: ©John H. Clark/CORBIS. D47: (br) ©DRA/Still Pictures/Peter Arnold, Inc.; (t) ©Susan Blanchet/Dembinsky Photo Associates. D50: ©Stephen Ingram/Animals Animals/Earth Scenes. D52: ©Bertram G. Murray/JR Animals Animals/Earth Scenes. D58: ©NASA/Accuweather. D61: ©Charles Palek/Animals Animals/Earth Scenes. D62: ©CORBIS-Bettmann/CORBIS. D63: (br) ©NASA/National Weather Service/AP/Wide World. D64: ©Peter Beck Pictor/Uniphoto. D68: ©Richard Hutchings. D69: ©Joyce & Frank Burek/Animals Animals/Earth Scenes. D71: ©Science/VU. D72: ©Carlos Guerrero. D73: ©Annie Griffiths Belt/CORBIS. D74: ©Joan Iaconetti/Bruce Coleman, Inc. D78: ©Richard Huthings. D80: ©Arthur Gloor/Animals Animals/Earth Scenes. D83: ©Richard Hutchings. D88: (bl) ©Science/VU (br) ©VU. D89: ©Jim Sugar Photography/CORBIS. D90: (tr) ©Don Smetzer/Stone; (br) ©Jeff Greenberg/PhotoEdit D91: ©Frost Fair on the Thames, Abraham Hondius, Museum of London, UK/The Bridgeman Art Library International Ltd. D93: ©Mark A. Schneider/Dembinsky Photo Associates. D94: (r) ©CORBIS; (tl) ©courtesy of Dr. Henry Diaz/Climate Diagnostics Ctr, NOAA. D95: ©Jim Sugar/CORBIS.

National Geographic Unit Opener E: E0, E1 ©Roger Ressmeyer/Corbis. **Unit E:** E2: ©Christine Osborne/CORBIS. E4: ©Michael T.

Sedam/CORBIS. E5: ©Richard Hutchings. E6: ©Ken Karp/McGraw-Hill School Division. E8: (b,bl,br) ©Ken Karp/McGraw-Hill School Division. E9: ©Richard Hutchings. E11: (bl) ©Buddy Mays/Bettmann/CORBIS; (m) ©The Purcell Team/Bettmann/CORBIS; (m) ©Vaughan Fleming/ Science Photo Library/Photo Researchers, Inc.; (bc) ©Wolfgang Kaehler/Bettmann/CORBIS. E13: ©Walter Meayers Edwards. E14: ©Kim Sayer/CORBIS. E14: (tr) ©Phil Degginger/Color-Pic; (br) ©Phil Degginger/Color-Pic. E16: (m) ©IBM Research/Peter Arnold, Inc.; (tr) ©Lawrence Livermore National Laboratory/Science Photo Library/Photo Researchers, Inc.; (b) ©National Railway of Japan/PhotoTake. E18: ©Rod Plack/Photo Researchers, Inc. E20: ©NASA/Science Photo Library/Photo Researchers, Inc. E21: ©Richard Hutchings. E22: (m) ©Lowell Georgia/Photo Researchers, Inc.; (b) ©Rich Treptow/Photo Researchers, Inc. E23: (br, m, tr) ©Charles D. Winters/Photo Researchers, Inc.; (m) ©Russ Lappa/ Science Source/Photo Researchers, Inc.; (tc) ©Science/VU/Visuals Unlimited. E24: (bl) ©Bill Beatty/VU/Visuals Unlimited.; (m) ©Charles D. Winters/Photo Researchers, Inc.; (br) ©1998 PhotoDisc, Inc.; (bc) ©Yoav Levy/PhotoTake. E25: (tl) ©David Taylor/Photo Researchers, Inc.; (tc) ©David Taylor/Photo Researchers, Inc.; (tr) ©David Taylor/Photo Researchers, Inc. E28: (br) ©Charles D. Winters/Photo Researchers, Inc.; (tr) ©Dr. E. R. Degginger/Color-Pic; (br) ©Dr. E. R. Degginger/Color-Pic; (m) ©George Bernard/Photo Researchers, Inc.; (m) ©Klaus Guldbrandsen/Science Photo Library/Photo Researchers, Inc.; (br) ©Russ Lappa/Photo Researchers, Inc. E32: (bl, m) ©Christine Coscioni/CO2, Inc.; (tr) ©Leonard Lessin/Peter Arnold, Inc. E33: (m) ©The Image Bank/GETTYONE. E34: ©W.Wisniewski/Okapia/Photo Researchers, Inc. E35: (br) ©Richard Hutchings. E36: (bc) ©Clyde H. Smith/Peter Arnold, Inc.; (bl) ©Gordon Wiltsie/Peter Arnold, Inc.; (br) ©Jeff & Alexa Henry/Peter Arnold, Inc. E37: ©Cesar Llacuna. E40: (tr) ©Carolina Biological Supply/PhotoTake.; (tr) ©Cesar Llacuna; (br) ©Charles D. Winters/Photo Researchers, Inc.; (m) ©Christine L. Coscioni/CO2, Inc. E41: (b) ©Richard Hutchings. E42: (m) ©Jack Plekan/Fundamental Photographs; (tr) ©Richard Choy/Peter Arnold, Inc.; (b) ©Chris Rogers/The Stock Market. E44: (tr) ©Vic Bider/PhotoEdit. E45: (m) ©Charles Pefley/Stock Boston; (b) ©Deborah Davis/PhotoEdit; (tr) ©Hal Charms/PhotoEdit. E48: ©Paul A. Souders/CORBIS. E50: ©Nathan Benn/CORBIS. E51: (br) ©Richard Hutchings. E52: (bl) ©Charles D. Winters/Photo Researchers, Inc.; (br) ©Jacana/Photo Researchers, Inc. E53: (m) ©Becky Luigart-Stayner/CORBIS; (tl) ©Dr. Ed Degginger/Color-Pic; (m, tc) ©Phil Degginger/Color-Pic. E54: (bl, br) ©Phil Degginger/Color-Pic; (m) ©Richard Hutchings. E55: (br) ©Adam Jones/Photo Researchers, Inc.; (m) ©Artville; (br) ©EyeWire/GETTYONE; (tr) ©Phil Degginger/Color-Pic. E56: (tr) ©Charles D. Winters/Photo Researchers, Inc.; (b) ©Phil Degginger/Color-Pic. E57: ©Richard Hutchings; (tl) ©Richard Megna/Fundamental Photographs. E59: (m) ©Joyce Photographics/Photo Researchers, Inc.; (bl, br) ©Richard Hutchings. E60: (t) ©S. Strickland/Naturescapes/VU. E61: (m) ©M.I. Walker/Photo Researchers, Inc.; (br, bl) ©Richard Hutchings. E64: (b) ©Mark E. Gibson/VU. E65: (m) ©PhotoDisc. E66: ©Larry Lefever/Grant Heilman Photography, Inc. E67: (l) ©David R. Frazier/Photo Researchers, Inc.; (tr) ©David S. Addison/VU. E68: ©Nik Wheeler/CORBIS. E70: ©Richard Hutchings. E71: ©Richard Hutchings. E72: (bl) ©Ed Degginger/Color-Pic; (br) ©Richard Hutchings. E73: (br) ©Lee Snyder/Photo Researchers, Inc.; (tr, tl) ©Richard Hutchings; (bl) ©Richard Megna/Fundamental Photographs. E74: (tr) ©Christine L. Coscioni/CO2, Inc.; (tr) ©Leonard Lessin/Peter Arnold, Inc.; (br) ©NASA; (br) ©Richard Hutchings. E76: (tr) ©Cesar Llacuna; (bl) ©Christine Coscioni/CO2, Inc. E78: (br) ©Henry Horenstein/Stock Boston; (bg) ©LSF OSF/Animals Animals/Earth Scenes. E79: ©Michael Newman/PhotoEdit. E80: ©Michael P. Gadomski/Photo Researchers, Inc. E82: (br) ©PhotoDisc; (br) ©Ed Degginger/Color-Pic; (bl) ©Ken Karp; (bl) ©Richard Megna/Fundamental Photographs. E83: ©Kristen Brochmann/Fundamental Photographs. E84: ©Ken Karp. E85: ©Renee Lynn/Photo Researchers, Inc. E87: (b, m) ©Dan Howell; (tr) ©Ed Degginger/Color-Pic. E88: ©Paul Silverman/Fundamental Photographs. E89: ©Tony Freeman/PhotoEdit. E90: ©Denise Mattia/Denise Mattia Underwater Photography. E91: ©Richard Hutchings. E96: (bl) ©Andrew McClenaghan/Photo Researchers, Inc.; (r) ©Science/VU. E97: ©Michael Dalton/Fundamental Photographs. E98: ©Richard Hutchings. E99: ©Sheila Terry/Photo Researcher, Inc. E101: ©Craig Lovell/Bettmann/CORBIS. E102: (tr) ©Courtesy of Dr Mario Molina/MIT; (m) ©NASA/Science Photo Library/Photo Researchers, Inc. E103: (m) ©NASA/Photo Researchers, Inc.

National Geographic Unit Opener F: F0 ©Comstock; F1 ©Duomo/Corbis. **Unit F:** F2: ©Photri/Tom Sanders/The Stock Market. F4: ©Annie Griffiths Belt/CORBIS. F7: ©Paul Silverman/Fundamental Photographs. F8: (m) ©NASA/Ed Degginger/Color-Pic; (b) ©Neil Rabinowitz/CORBIS. F9: (br) ©Duomo/Chris Trotman/Duomo Photography Inc.; (bl) ©Joe McDonald/CORBIS; (tl) 'Museum of Flight'/CORBIS. F10: ©Bill Aron/Photo Researchers, Inc. F11: ©Jerry Wachter/Photo Researchers, Inc. F12: ©Peter Turnley/CORBIS. F13: (b) ©George Lepp/CORBIS; (tr) ©Robert Mathena/Fundamental Photographs. F15: ©TSM/Photri/The Stock Market. F16: ©Ed Kashi/CORBIS. F20: (tr) ©Ed Degginger/Color-Pic; (tr) ©Tony Freeman/PhotoEdit. F21: (tr) ©Ed Degginger/Color-Pic; (m) ©Phil Degginger/Color-Pic. F22: ©LBJ Space Center/Nasa NASA. F28: (bc) ©Kevin R. Morris/CORBIS; (tr) ©Paul A. Souders/CORBIS; (m) ©Peter Turnley/CORBIS (m) ©Russ Schleipman/CORBIS. F30: (bg) ©Barney McGrath/Science Photo Library/Photo Researchers, Inc.; (m) ©JPL/NASA; (b) ©MSSS/JPL/NASA/ Science Photo Library/Photo Researchers, Inc. F32: ©Bettmann/CORBIS. F35: ©G.Sauvage/Vandystadt/Photo Researchers, Inc. F36: ©J-L Charmet/Science/Photo Library/Photo Researchers, Inc. F40: (tl) ©Davis Barber/PhotoEdit; (bl) ©Kevin R. Morris/CORBIS; (tl) ©The Image Bank/Gettyone. F41: ©NASA/Media Dallas. F42: (bg) ©JSC/NASA; (bl) ©Zero/JSC/NASA. F45: ©NASA. F46: ©Miro/Vintoniv/Stock Boston F48: ©NASA/Galaxy Contact/Oxford Scientific Film and Photo Library. F49: ©Richard Hutchings. F52: ©Ken Fisher/Stone. F54: ©Ulrike Welsch. F55: ©Richard Hutchings. F56: ©Artville LLC 1997. F57: ©Tim Davis/Photo Researchers, Inc. F58: (bl) ©Courtesy Alexander Graham Bell/National Historic Park; (tr) ©William James Warren/CORBIS. F59: ©George Hall/CORBIS. F60: ©1998 PhotoDisc, Inc. F61: ©Dr. Jeremy Burgess/Photo Researchers, Inc. F63: ©Brenda Tharp/Photo Researchers, Inc. F64: ©Kevin Fleming/CORBIS. F65: ©Richard Hutchings. F66: (br) Allsport/Brian Bahr; (bl) ©Duomo/CORBIS. F67: (tr) ©Marty Loken/Stone; (br) ©Museum der Stadt, Vienna/Austria Superstock. F68: ©TSM/John M. Roberts/The Stock Market. F69: ©Wolfgang Kaehler/CORBIS. F72: ©Joseph Schuyler/Stock Boston. F73: ©Luc Novovitch/Gamma Liaison Agency. F78: ©VCG/FPG. F80: ©Richard Cummins/CORBIS. F81: ©Richard Hutchings. F82: (tr) ©Arthur Morris/VU; (b) ©Robert Holmgren/Peter Arnold, Inc. F83: (t) ©Barb Gerlach/VU; (tr) ©C.P. George/VU; (m) ©Rich Treptow/VU. F84: ©Richard Hutchings. F85: ©Image courtesy of Barry Luokkala, Department of Physics/Carnegie Mellon University. F86: ©Richard Hutchings. F87: (tr) ©Paul Silverman/Fundamental Photographs; (bl, m) ©Richard Hutchings. F88: (tr) ©Richard Hutchings; (bc, bl) ©Roger Ressmeyer/CORBIS. F90: ©Cesar Llacuna. F91: ©Dr. EdDegginger/Color-Pic. F92: (bc) ©North Wind Picture Archive/North Wind Pictures; (bl) ©Science Photo Library/Photo Researchers, Inc.; (r) ©Wolfgang Kaehler/CORBIS. F93: (bl) ©The Queens Borough Public Library, Long Island Division, Latimer Family Papers/The Queens Borough Library; (bc) ©The Schenectady Museum. F94: ©Jack Plekan/Fundamental Photographs. F95: ©Richard Hutchings. F96: (br) ©Alfred Pasieka/Science Photo Library/Photo Researchers, Inc.; (b) ©Richard Hutchings; (tr) ©Science/VU. F97: (tr) ©Jeff Greenberg/VU; (bl, br) ©Richard Hutchings. F98: (tr) ©Bill Beatty/VU; (bl, br) ©Richard Hutchings. F100: (tl) ©PhotoDisc, 2000; (m, bc) ©Richard Hutchings. F103: ©James Webb/PhotoTake. F106: ©Jeremy Walker/Stone Gettyone. F107: ©Richard Hutchings. F109: ©Richard Hutchings. F113: ©Ed Degginger/Color-Pic. F114: ©NASA/Media Dallas. F116: ©Richard Hutchings. F118: ©Bettmann/CORBIS. F119: ©Hewlitt Packard Fundamental Photographs. F120: (br) ©1998 PhotoDisc, Inc.; (br) ©Science/VU. F121: ©Carolyn A. McKeone/Photo Researchers, Inc. F122: ©Science/VU. F126: ©Gary Gold/Rennsslaer Polytechnical Institute. F127: ©courtesy of Dr. Shirley Jackson/Rennsslaer Polytechnical Institute.

Science and Health Handbook: All photos ©Richard Hutchings with the following exceptions: R10: (m) ©Jim Harrison/Stock Boston/PNI. R14: (m) ©G.R. Roberts/Photo Researchers, Inc.